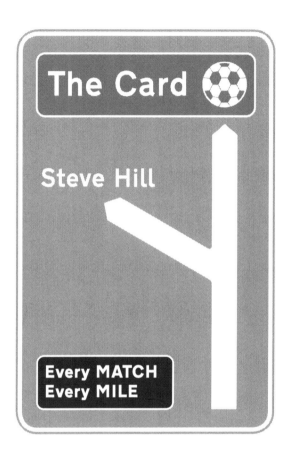

The Card

Steve Hill

Every MATCH
Every MILE

OCKLEY BOOKS
.com

ABOUT THE AUTHOR

Steve Hill has written for numerous publications including
FourFourTwo, loaded, Maxim, Esquire, Vive Le Rock,
PokerPlayer, PC Zone, The Independent and The Non-League
Paper. He lives in North West London and can see Wembley
Stadium from his bedroom window. To date, Chester
have never played there.

TWITTER: @HillyTheFish

"Hilarious, heroic and utterly futile, this is *Withnail & I* for non-league football."

Dan Davies, author, *In Plain Sight*

"Steve Hill's everyman deconstruction of the full time football fan is heartbreaking and hilarious. Yes, we've all been there... but not 50 times in the same season."

Steve McKevitt, author, *Playing With The Boys*

"Admirable blind faith in finding the end of a blue and white rainbow."

Jonathan Legard, BBC

"Non-league ground-hoppers take note: there's a new sheriff in town. A very funny read."

Alex Narey, editor, *The Non-League Paper*

The Card →

Published by Ockley Books Limited, Huddersfield, England

First published June 2018

ISBN - 978-1-910906-132

Layout & design by Michael Kinlan, edited by Richard Foster

Printed & bound by:

Biddles Printing, King's Lynn

For Her Indoors and The Boy

the card (kɑːd)
noun

Every first team fixture of a football club's season.
usage. 1. *doing the card*. To attend every fixture of a season.
2. *on the card*. To be in the process of attempting to complete
one's card. eg, "I hear Hill is on the card. What a tit."

Gateshead (A)

Saturday
6th August
2016

3pm K.O.

Game 1 of 50 →

Fuck this life. 6:16am. Toothbrush in hand, I peer out of the bathroom window. In the distance, the Wembley Arch cruelly mocks my plight. A different international stadium is the destination today, as the so-called fixture computer has deemed that Chester FC will begin their season at Gateshead, a mere 242 miles north as the crow, or indeed British Airways, flies. The first trip is the longest: the first cut is the deepest.

The Uber driver to Paddington wonders why I have no baggage. He doesn't see the 32 years of emotional baggage accrued from following this shower of shit, season after season, game after game, all over this land. I absolutely love it. Today is something of a first, however. After years of idly talking about it, we've actually booked a flight to the match, with the 8:30am from Heathrow to Newcastle offering ample time for a tear-up, the game, and then a flight back the same evening. I'm not sure if it counts, but technically I did fly to a game once before, taking a plane from San Francisco to Heathrow, from where The Driver took me directly to Mansfield. Won 3-1.

Four days before the start of this season, The Driver sent me a text saying, "We have decided to move to France."

"Got to be my last chance for the card," I replied hilariously.

The Heathrow Express delivers me to Terminal 5, where The Driver and The Hack are already waiting, having travelled from Newbury and Brighton respectively, more or less. Each resplendent in replica shirts, I'm letting the side down, and The Hack is disappointed, keen that three pricks in Chester tops should be something of a talking point. In the event, nobody gives the tiniest shit, and we're not even the only football fans on the flight, with a lone Newcastle supporter licking his wounds after a Friday night defeat at Fulham.

Following a failed attempt to get into the BA lounge, I take advantage of a shop giving out free vodka, and assume a window seat on the big bird. It's with giddy excitement — and obligatory terror — that we take off, actually flying to a game like a triumvirate of massive overgrown show-offs. That said, it's considerably cheaper than the train, and you are at least guaranteed a seat.

The blind optimism of the opening match of the season is a universal trait, whatever the predicament. We have a rookie manager at the helm, with former assistant Jon McCarthy having been appointed in the summer after winning three of his four games as caretaker. Furthermore, our three best players have left for pastures new, and we haven't got a pot to piss in. But as it stands we're equal top of The National League, and it really is a national league, stretching from Torquay to Gateshead and all points in between.

Literally anything could happen today, by which I mean a win, a draw or a defeat. Or a postponement, highly unlikely given the sweltering weather. The Metro takes us straight into the heart of Newcastle city centre, and it feels odd to be so far away without the pain of a five-hour motorway slog. Bowling around the Bigg Market before the pubs are even open, the streets are largely deserted, but there is a strong sense that something happened here a few short hours earlier, a feral combination of drinking, fighting and rutting. In other words, the very stuff of life itself.

Piling into a pub at the crack of 11am, The Hack studiously surveys the pumps and finally orders an entirely random Real Ale, declaring — not for the first time — that he can really taste the hops. Meanwhile, The Driver is still operating on British Lager Time and joins me in a fruity pint of fizzy piss. It's early August and such is the overlap of the sporting seasons that England are still embroiled in a Test Match with Pakistan. Watching it on the big screen, they are already a couple of wickets down when a familiar face strolls past the pub window. It is Howie, a CAMRA Man of some repute who stands back and to my left on The Harry McNally Terrace. Tempting him in, he joins us for a swift half of swill, and explains that he saw The Damned in Carlisle the night before, a fortuitous piece of scheduling that sees him hit the Toon in plenty of time for supping, or drinking as it's more commonly known. Mildly impressed to learn that we have flown here, he sups up and fucks off.

Claiming some local knowledge due to a stint at Durham University, The Driver leads us in concentric circles until we find somewhere that serves a full English breakfast, replete with craft beer, whatever that is. Somehow, The Hack has never been to Newcastle before, and while shovelling a burger into his maw he expresses his horror at the amount of fat people in evidence, something that may be related to the astonishing number of Greggs, which has its headquarters in Newcastle. Apparently, at night they have bouncers on the doors, presumably lest a scuffle should break out over the last steak slice.

With still hours until kickoff we watch half a Scottish match in another pub, and then head for the river, basking in the heat outside a rammed Pitcher & Piano. It's next to the Gateshead Millennium Bridge, on the other side of which lies our destiny. The match suddenly appears in jeopardy when the bridge is cleared and proceeds to slowly tilt on its axis to let a pleasure craft through. The boat then has to immediately turn round and come back, as the next bridge is impassable, rendering the entire exercise a massive waste of effort and money that, more importantly, has cost us valuable drinking time.

Speed-walking over the newly intact bridge, The Driver, who has been here before, leads us on a tetchy, sweaty route past interminable lock-ups, warehouses and potential murder venues towards an alleged pub. This apparently is Gateshead, distinct from Newcastle by virtue of being the other side of a river, much like North and South London.

With tempers fraying, we finally stumble upon The Schooner, hidden among the trees. All the major faces are present and correct, appearing as if by magic like an annual version of Brigadoon. In the same way that racehorses all have their birthdays on the first day of the year, the fans are all one season older, sporting new shirts, old scars, and years of disappointment etched on their faces. There's barely time to pour a lager into my face, and we're on the march again, taking our seats in Gateshead International Stadium in time to see the players come out. That's living all right...

Essentially an athletics venue, it's an absolutely shocking place to watch football, and any new players are rendered almost indistinguishable by virtue of being so far away. Intimate it is not, and you have to feel sorry for the poor pricks that turn up here every other week. The first half is goalless, and I reward myself with what is described by the vendor as a "mince pie", the hard shell concealing a blob of indeterminate meat. I wash it down with a Diet Coke, as the diet bit cancels out the pie. The second half is a dismal affair, and our only effort of note is a free kick from new boy Elliott Durrell that sails out of the stadium and quite possibly into the Tyne. Gateshead leather in three goals without reply, and we end the game equal bottom of the league, only above Southport on alphabetical order. At least I've ticked off a new ground...

Enraged by beer and despair, I hold my arms outstretched like a pair of wings and bellow, "One hour on a plane for this, McCarthy!" I don't quite have the wingspan of the nearby Angel of the North, and he doesn't hear me anyway — he's about half a mile away. I didn't see, I only heard, but apparently some Chester Youth left early and went back to The Schooner for what has been described as "a stand-off" that at some stage involved a banger being thrown into the pub. Hopefully Dennis The Menace turned up with his catapult to sort things out.

Back in Toon, more meat and beer is consumed, the latter at a Wetherspoons, the default pub for the non-league fan — it's cheap, crap, and full of weirdoes. The party continues at Newcastle Airport, which, presumably to the chagrin of the locals, is home to a pop-up Sunderland AFC shop. Back on the plane, the steward sympathises with our plight as he's a Brentford fan, and they've also lost their first game. As such he plies us with gin and tonic for the duration of the short flight. Back at Heathrow, The Driver — for once unleashed from his vehicle — insists that we drink even more as he waits for his lift. Unless I'm mistaken, I appear to be spending Saturday night drinking a can of gin and tonic at an airport. A Tube and a bus eventually deliver me to within walking distance of home, and I thread across a sports field listening to Happy Mondays in a state of near delirium. Strong day, shame about the score.

Attendance: 991 Position: 23rd ↓

Dagenham
& Redbridge (H)

Tuesday
August 9th
2016

7.45pm K.O.

Game 2 of 50 →

During the opening months of the season, The National League is relentless. You get Sunday to nurse your hangover and recover your voice, Monday to silently digest the result and study league tables, and then you're back on the road on Tuesday. This particular road is the M40, about an hour to Junction 10 and the nondescript village of Ardley, where you can park your car for free. It's only a few football pitch lengths from Cherwell Valley Services, where you can't. Although if you arrive early, there is ample opportunity to have an overpriced coffee and browse the leather goods.

As usual, The Woman With The Dogs is in her garden, still seemingly baffled as to why grown men in polyester shirts get in and out of a series of German cars on Saturday mornings and Tuesday afternoons. As usual, I'm early, sitting in my car like a plum, stealing Wi-Fi from an unsuspecting villager. The Driver's never early, he's always late, proffering an assortment of excuses ranging from going back to switch the gas off, re-hoovering the car, or watching *Ben Hur*.

Thankfully, he makes up the time on the road. As has become something of a tradition prior to home matches, we have to meet The Driver's aging father for lunch. The Sandstone pub in Cheshire is our default destination, handily placed for The Sandstone Trail, whatever that is. On this occasion the routine is thrown into chaos with the revelation that there's no chef. There's an awkward standoff, and the offer of sandwiches and soup is dismissed as derisory. As a rule of thumb, I like to order things in restaurants that I couldn't or wouldn't make myself. I could and I would and I have made sandwiches and soup. Drinks are cancelled, they are politely told to shove it, and while we don't exactly storm out, there is a definite undertone of indignation.

Some other wanky place is eventually located, The Pheasant Inn near The Candle Factory. It's absolutely rammed, and we have to wait for a table, mid-afternoon on a Tuesday. Apparently, in the height of summer, people go for walks, visit candle factories and have expensive glorified pub lunches. I am astonished to learn that attendances are down at The Candle Factory. Who wouldn't want to know how candles are made? Not TV's Adrian Chiles; the West Brom man is apparently a self-professed candle fan.

As The Driver discusses his intended move to France with his dad, I silently sink pints of pissy lager and entertain elaborate fantasies involving the waiting staff, who are incongruously dressed as French prostitutes. The match is still hours away, so we head to The Driver's dad's house to drink tea. My plan was to sit in the garden and read a book, but we are driven inside by an icy wind, only three days after the Gateshead heatwave. The Rio Olympics offers a tantalising choice between dressage and rugby sevens. We choose the latter on the basis that it is actually a recognisable sport, and pleasingly one that only lasts seven minutes per half. Someone somewhere is penning a tiresome piece about what football could learn from the Olympics, namely that if you're really rich you can take a horse to South America and make it dance to The Bee Gees.

We eventually get to Telford's Warehouse well before kickoff. Within minutes of sitting down, a train driver lectures me about how I choose to imbibe the national drug. He assures me that I am not enjoying my cold, crisp lager, and that I would much prefer room temperature slops with a silly name. The Real Ale war has been raging for years, although unofficially the campaign is over. What is there to campaign about? It's everywhere, gallons of Nutty Slack poured down the drip tray and then resold to hapless CAMRA Men armed with moleskine notepads and bulging guidebooks. In this phoney war, The Driver is a rare neutral. He's Switzerland. In the summer he operates on British Lager Time, then switches to Slack once the clocks go back. This infuriates the Real Alers no end — if there's one thing they hate more than a lager drinker, it's a lager drinker who enjoys Real Ale.

Finally arriving at the ground, there is the traditional beginning-of-season buzz about the place. It's the Deva Stadium's 26th season yet it still feels like the new ground, despite visible signs of decay. Assuming position on the patch of terrace that has been my home for the bulk of this tenure, greetings are proffered to the various faces. In my mind, I am one of the faces. As ever, Big Al is in before us, and after a couple of decades it's probably too late to ask his surname. The home end left corner flag steward is in buoyant form. Previously dubbed "Nice Pie" due to his repeated questioning of everybody who walked past him with a pastry item, he has changed tack for the home opener and is now inquiring, "Missed it, have you? Missed it? Have you missed it?" to anyone who makes eye contact, and anyone who doesn't. While employing people from all parts of the educational spectrum is to be commended, one can't help wondering what would happen if the main stand was on fire or there were 200 Wrexham on the pitch. Pissed it, have you?

I'm not sure when the tradition started, but before the match the stadium announcer, Cleggy, reads out a list of fans who have died during the closed season. It's a chilling reminder that we are all on a relentless conveyor belt from one damp hole to another and so should probably make the most of it. At least the fallen made it to the end of a season, simply for the sake of closure. It would be extremely annoying to drop dead in the middle of a cup run.

It's good to see everyone, although we clearly haven't got a chance against newly relegated Dagenham, one of the title favourites. Bang! Durrell with a 25-yard volley. Twat! Tom Shaw drills one into the top corner. At 2-0 up, The Driver is still incredibly twitchy, but when James Alabi bullets in a header from a late corner, the game is won. Alabi later thanks God. If there is a god, I would like to think she has more pressing concerns than Chester making it safe against The Daggers on a Tuesday night. Whatever the result, it's still a twat of a journey back, and while we don't exactly glide home on a fluffy cushion of three points, the mood is jubilant. Even an M6 closure can't dampen our spirits, despite an unscheduled diversion through Walsall. Fuck Walsall.

The obligatory £20 diesel money is handed to The Driver in Ardley after midnight — Christ knows what an unsuspecting witness would make of it. He in turn gives me his season ticket for next Saturday as he's going on holiday. Back in my own vehicle, it's at this point in my life that I find myself roaring down the M40 at 100 miles per hour in short trousers shouting along to the Sex Pistols with a foam hand on the parcel shelf. And all because I once went to a football match on a whim in 1984.

Attendance: 1,841   Position: 10th ↑

Game 3 of 50 →

After taking in the first two games of the season, The Driver has gone to France, an annual ritual that he stringently embarks upon in order to sabotage any possibility of doing another Card. He did the full Card in 1989-90 — before I knew him — a season in which the team somehow managed to go six months between away wins. An experience like that can change a man. Nevertheless, he knows that if he gets to Christmas with his attendance intact he'll feel obliged to push through and attempt another one. He can't take the pressure.

It's also an early opportunity to spend time with his other team, Bordeaux, who play in France's top division in front of tens of thousands. He randomly went to a match while on holiday several years ago, and has supported them ever since, frequently flying or driving across the channel to take in a game. If Chester is his stoic wife, then Bordeaux is his exotic French mistress. He's an absolute disgrace.

More importantly, his French connection has inconvenienced me, as it means that I have to find my own way to the Deva Stadium. As such, I have convinced Her Indoors that she, The Boy and I all stay at her late parents' house near Milton Keynes on the Friday night, squatting in the House of Doom in order to get a notional head start on the Saturday morning. Technically, this is our summer holiday. Having bombarded me with photos of ghastly Greek hotels for weeks, I have to break the news that we will instead be heading to the historic walled city of Chester so I can take in the home game against The Stones. Following this, we will hit the North and hole up in The Lakes for three days before the assault on Barrow, returning home triumphantly with six points in the bag. Greece...

It's a stressful drive, largely because I'm driving instead of staring out of the window, reading the paper, or lapsing into unconsciousness. Boldly defying The Driver's sage advice to avoid the M6 at all costs, the traffic predictably grinds to a halt. Like a great man once said, after Stoke it starts to crawl. In a state of minor panic I get off the motorway and find myself stuck behind a series of farm vehicles for the next couple of hours. Are we nearly there yet? Are we nearly there yet? No we're not.

As well as the massive game at The Deva, there's also the trifling matter of the first day of the Premier League season to contend with. As such, my family are thrilled to listen to full live radio commentary of Leicester beginning their title defence with a surprise defeat at Hull, a team that we used to frequently play and even occasionally beat. I only went to Boothferry Park once — it rained non-stop for the entire day, and we conceded the only goal of the game in the first minute. Good times.

Thanks to the necessarily cautious early start, we are safely at the top of Bumper's Lane a good hour before kickoff. In a state of mutual hunger-induced rage, we head to Pizza Hut, a long goal kick from the site of the old stadium, which is now home to a B&M, whatever that is. Furious to discover that Pizza Hut doesn't do the all-you-can-eat buffet on weekends, I compensate by abusing the unlimited drink refills to the point of caffeine-induced palpitations, throwing in a dose of nausea by wolfing down a rubbery disc of cheese and meat. It's not exactly fast food, and I have to leave the family to pick up the bill as I make the long walk down Bumper's Lane to The Deva, and destiny. But not before I've nipped into the Blues Bar and poured lager into my head — for my nerves.

Taking my usual place amidst the bustling crowd on The Harry McNally Terrace, I've rarely felt so alone, although I have done entire seasons on my own. The Driver is lost in France, and as I later learn, Big Al is on a cruise with his wife, whose name I do not know. What is wrong with these people? If you want a holiday, have it in the closed season. I do manage a cursory chat with Howie, who stands a few feet away from his brother, yet according to The Driver, they haven't spoken in years due to some unresolved historic dispute.

Following the thrilling 3-0 win in midweek, we are of course going to thrash Maidstone. But football doesn't work that way, and we are all over the place from the start. We go behind early, briefly equalise, before succumbing to a desultory 3-1 defeat, very much a case of After The Lord Mayor's Show. To add insult to injury, scorer Alabi is sent off for an ill-advised lunge on the keeper late on, earning himself a three-match ban. If it were up to God, it would probably have been a yellow card.

Trudging back up Bumper's Lane in a trough of despond, I find myself behind three buoyant Maidstone fans who are making the long walk to the railway station. Essentially middle-aged thugs, they resemble hand drawn characters from *Viz*, like Sid The Sexist's gormless mates. There's a short one, a nondescript all-rounder, and a lumbering tank with rolls of fat on the back of his head. The latter is bragging about having stolen some badges from the Chester club shop. The short one proclaims that, "This time in seven hours we'll be walking down Maidstone High Street," which doesn't even make temporal sense. He also claims that he'll be putting some rocks up his nose from a nice bit of marble, whatever that means.

The family are dutifully waiting in a supermarket car park, having spent the entire match milling around the out-of-town retail park that has stealthily infested the area over the last few decades, absorbing the sites of both the old football ground and the greyhound stadium. In retrospect, instead of worshipping at the altar of rampant consumerism, they may as well have come to the match, although it's debatable who has had the worst time. The Boy seems happy enough, however, having for some reason been bought a miniature *Teenage Mutant Ninja Turtles* pinball table, which makes for a relaxing drive.

Her Indoors takes the wheel while I sulk about the result and stare into middle distance, inadvertently taking in the majesty of the scenery, and I don't mean Wigan. Once you're past the urban sprawl of Merseyside and Lancashire, the northern part of the M6 takes on a rugged, almost magical quality. With shafts of light dramatically breaking through the clouds, it's like a scene from *Game Of Thrones*, six lanes of traffic notwithstanding. One almost expects a fire-breathing dragon to loom over the mountains and incinerate us. It'd be doing me a favour.

The satnav takes care of business, but it's a fairly straightforward route that essentially involves heading north then turning left at Penrith. Before the village of Penrith was immortalised in *Withnail & I* as the place where the titular characters go "on holiday by mistake" it was mainly know as the scene of one of Chester's more embarrassing FA Cup exits, when we were beaten 1-0 in 1980. This was before I had started supporting them and so automatically assumes a sepia-toned quality, like news that happened before I was born. I accept that the events occurred as described, but they don't carry the same resonance as if I was there or knew or cared at the time. Still, Penrith. What a disgrace.

Checking into our self-proclaimed luxury spa hotel in Cockermouth, despite costing hundreds of pounds per night, it's little more than a country pub with an indoor swimming pool and an outdoor hot tub. Due to my policy of leaving everything to the last minute, I left everything to the last minute, and was surprised and infuriated to discover that virtually all accommodation in the Lake District was sold out in the middle of a sweltering August. I only managed to secure this place by cashing in my lifetime collection of BA Air Miles, all 109,000 of them, with the minuscule amount earned by flying to Gateshead serendipitously giving me just enough to book three nights here, leaving me with ten miles in the bank.

I'm fairly certain we're the only ones here for the match, particularly as it's taking place some 50 miles south in about 72 hours. Until then, we simply wait, and eat. After enjoying some rudimentary fare in the ancient nearby pub, back in our split-level family apartment I settle in for *Match Of The Day*. It's the first one of the season, and Gary Lineker has honoured his promise to present the show in his underpants after Leicester's unlikely Premier League title success. As has been repeatedly pointed out, technically they're more like shorts, but it's still a genuinely absurd sight and I can't help but whoop with laughter. It's arguably the highlight of the entire day.

Attendance: 1,912 Position: 18th ↓

Barrow (A)

Tuesday
August 16th
2016

7.45pm K.O.

Game 4 of 50 →

This isn't even our first football-related visit to the Lake District. Back when Chester FC were bossing the Evo-Stik Northern Premier League in 2012, The Driver booked a cottage for a week in the remote village of Boot. While the women and children formed an advance party, he and I took in a perfunctory 2-0 victory over Whitby Town at The Deva before heading north. Three days later we put in a mint performance at Kendal Town, rolling them over 3-0 in a game so cold that I watched some of it out of the window of the social club, notable for its murals of seemingly arbitrary musicians, including a particularly disturbing rendition of Stewart Copeland, the drummer out of The Police. The following Saturday we packed up and headed to South Yorkshire for a 2-1 victory over Stocksbridge Park Steels — former home of Jamie Vardy — before wrapping up the title with a 1-1 draw at home to Northwich Victoria on the Bank Holiday Monday in front of a staggering crowd of 5,009.

Now that we have resumed our rightful place in The National League, attendances are barely a third of that, proof if proof were needed that whatever the opposition, people will turn up to watch a winning team. Back to this season, we awake on Sunday morning in the majesty of the mountains, the tranquillity only breached by the thunderous sound of low-flying RAF jets, much to the delight of The Boy, who cannot wait to tell Sid; a reference to his curly-haired school friend, not the 1980s advert that urged punters to buy shares in British Gas.

With the match due to take place on Tuesday evening, all we have to do is kill time. Fortunately we are staying in an area of outstanding natural beauty, some of which you can stare at for at least ten minutes. As the name of the national park suggests, there are a lot of lakes in the district, all of them broadly similar. Having dipped our toes in a few, both proverbially and literally, we head for civilisation in the shape of the nearby town of Keswick, despite Her Indoors' misguided protestations that nothing will be open, in the middle of August, in a heatwave.

Keswick is of course teeming with holidaymakers and people enjoying a 'nice day out'. In my experience, most holidays are little more than periods of anger between meals. They also provide an opportunity to endure unreliable Wi-Fi and miss the televised football that you would otherwise be watching if you'd stayed at home. Today is the first so-called *Super Sunday* of the season, and Sky are showing Arsenal versus Liverpool with the obligatory frenzied level of hype. Having left the radio commentary with the game 1-1 at half-time, I tentatively stick my head into a pub to discover that it is now 2-4, a scoreline that I exclaim out loud to the amusement of a nearby table. Pleading my case, I manage to negotiate a one-pint stay and watch Liverpool eventually win 4-3, a result no doubt celebrated long and hard in the pubs of Chester.

Monday morning brings the disturbing news that former Aston Villa striker Dalian Atkinson has died after being tasered by police in Telford. In the celebrity cull of 2016, it's a footnote, but a deeply unpleasant incident nevertheless. With one more full day to endure before sticking it up the Barrow, we head for the coast and an opportunity to look at a different type of water. A place called Maryport is the nearest resort of any size, a Roman remnant with both a lighthouse and an aquarium. We visit neither, instead heading for the beach, the route taking us past fishing boats bedecked in pro-Brexit flags, celebrating the recent referendum result. The archetypal coastal town that they forgot to close down, Armageddon appears to have already come to Maryport as the beach is deserted, with a crumbling pier the only evidence that man was ever here. In the distance, the mountains of Scotland accentuate the remoteness.

We have spent two full days looking at lakes, walking in and around lakes, throwing shit into lakes, and even drinking Real Ale next to lakes. It's a minor aberration, but drinking fizzy lager seems almost vulgar amidst such splendour, plus you get dirty looks from the hardcore walkers — CAMRA men, every last fucking one of them.

It's been a beautiful — and mercifully brief — time, but it's finally match day and it's all business, although there are still the daylight hours to fill before the evening kickoff. First stop is the picturesque town of Ambleside, for no other reason than it inspired the title of the 12th album by Half Man Half Biscuit, 2008's excellent *CSI: Ambleside*, which I listen to on repeat for the entire journey. The album cover features a photo of a pub in the town, The Priest Hole. We find it and have a drink outside, spotting the differences since the picture was taken. Astonishingly, there's no blue plaque or indeed any acknowledgment of its place in musical history. Instead, by way of tribute I manually superimpose the CD cover against the actual building and take my own photo.

The cultural tour continues apace, as due to her showbiz connections, Her Indoors has secured free tickets to the Peter Rabbit museum in nearby Bowness-on-Windermere. With full VIP honours, we are fast-tracked to the front of the baying hordes, although disappointingly they haven't emptied the museum for our visit, like Michael Jackson at Disneyland. The exhibition is reasonably faithful to the source mate-rial, there are some innovative interactive elements, but ultimately I'd rather be watching some men kick a ball round a field. The Boy seems to enjoy it however, retrospectively awarding it a solid 8/10.

Barrow-In-Furness draws ever nearer, and it must be time to start drinking. Newby Bridge provides a suitable pit stop, and I sink a cold lager while the family paddle, completing the full Card of lake, sea, and now river. The coastal road to Barrow brings destiny ever closer, although first we find ourselves at a place called Rampside. Overseen by a sinister tower, it's essentially a long stretch of land that sticks into the sea. At the bottom of it, a boat takes people to a small island then brings them back again, an option we choose not to take.

Throughout the entire trip, Her Indoors has had one job: find accom-modation in Barrow. What she comes up with is an apartment in a block of flats on a building site. It's the kind of place where they would have knocked down the door in an episode of *The Bill*, or made deliveries to in *The Wire*. It's as much as she can do not to burst into tears, but there's no time to find anywhere else so we check in and fuck off.

In need of sustenance, we head into town and catch the first thrilling glimpse of the ground, the distant floodlights hinting at the drama that will later unfold under their gaze. A nearby pub has no food, but a friendly barman in a string vest serves us three drinks and two packets of crisps for less than a fiver. He then resumes his game of pool, while the only other customer sits at the bar and watches the seemingly unending Rio Olympics.

The next pub is a Hungry Horse family affair; teeming with kids and their sweaty parents. The sight of British people in hot weather is reminiscent of the Shane Meadows film, *Dead Man's Shoes*, as pasty creatures attempt to entertain themselves in unfamiliar circumstances. One such individual is at the bar ranting loudly to no-one and everyone about how we all complain when it's too hot and also complain when it's too cold. Avoiding eye contact, I stare straight ahead and order the drinks. In the seated area outside, the same man pushes one of his offspring up and down in a buggy while maintaining an endless non-internal monologue. If you shared a cell with him you'd have to kill him in the night for your own safety. At one point he looks in my direction and requests "registration papers", before barking, "Should you be in this country?"

Another pub near the ground, still not eaten. I crack a bottle and drink it in the car. Her Indoors drops me off at the away turnstiles, returning briefly to give me a jumper. After all, this is England. And this is Chester: having survived the opening half hour, Elliott Durrell attempts an ill-advised back pass, which is pounced upon by Ross Hannah who calmly rounds the keeper and rolls it into the net. Last season he scored 24 goals for us, now he scores against us in front of 103 of the same fans that sang his name only a few short months ago. As is the modern way, he doesn't milk the celebrations, out of respect. Although if he really wanted to respect us he could have scuffed it wide. Another goal follows two minutes later, and we reach half-time 2-0 down.

Holker Street is another new ground, as in new to me, so I can at least claim some kind of achievement, although a dictionary definition might suggest otherwise. It's not the worst in the league, but is some distance from the best. Wandering around the away end, I discover a pile of twisted metal at the base of one of the floodlights, and take a picture of it on my phone. I also have a brief chat with Chas, Club Historian and Statistician, at the urinal, the only meaningful social intercourse of another solitary match, much of which I spend hurling invective at the Barrow goalkeeper for his blatant time wasting. At one point I start counting out loud the number of seconds he has the ball in his hands. Some of the away end join in and we get to about 14 before he finally releases it, the referee seemingly oblivious to the rarely enforced six-second rule.

Two goals soon become three, and it appears our race is run. However, a brace of Chester goals in the space of three minutes gives us hope of a famous comeback with 20 minutes still on the clock. Chances come and go, but sadly none are taken, and we trudge into the night with that familiar feeling.

An absurdly cheap cab takes me back to the grief hole, and I spend the rest of the evening watching a ludicrous Olympic cycling event where they all chase a moped, someone breaches the rules, and they all start again, and again, and again. It feels like a low point. The Boy is so upset that he pisses the bed. I can only apologise.

Getting straight out of Dodge in the morning, we leave the faded grandeur of Barrow in our wing mirrors and head north, then eventually south. Then west, to Blackpool, in an attempt to squeeze a last drop of joy from what has quite literally been a pointless excursion. Once a regular stop on the league fixture list, I have even seen us win here. Even more memorable was a home game at Sealand Road in 1985. Minutes after kickoff, what seemed like the entire Blackpool end invaded the pitch, ran the full length of it and started punching our fans about the head and face as the referee led the players off. The good old days.

Just as we drive past the monstrosity that is Pleasure Beach, The Boy wakes up and announces, "Awesome! Better than Star Wars!" High praise indeed, young Padawan (not his real name). Sadly, the parking is less than awesome, and it takes us an hour to find somewhere where we can park for an hour. This gives us time for little more than chippy on the beach and a paddle in the sea, which is now remarkably free of human excrement. It takes the whole of the rest of the day to get home. Six days, five nights, three goals, no points.

Attendance: 1,351 Position: 19th ↓

Game 5 of 50 →

After one of the longest trips of the season, it's one of the shortest, at least for me. Situated ten miles north, the place is called Boreham-wood, the train station is called Elstree & Borehamwood, and the film studios are called Elstree. Famous for such cultural touchstones as *Star Wars*, James Bond, *The Prisoner*, and the Hammer Horror films, they currently churn out the likes of *Strictly Come Dancing*, *EastEnders* and *Holby City*.

The football club is called Boreham Wood (spot the difference) and is famous for very little, other than being bankrolled by a movie mogul, and hosting the Arsenal women's team. It is however a place that I associate with deep pride as well as intense shame.

First, the pride. In the season before this one, the fixtures aligned to send The Mighty Chester to Boreham Wood on the same rainy November day that Her Indoors had *Strictly* business at Elstree. Having driven there *en famille*, following cheesy chips in The Alfred Arms with The Hack and Wife, Her Indoors departed to a world of glitter balls and chiffon, while The Boy and I made our way to Meadow Park for leather balls and shin pads. Due to the club's gross incompetence at the single away turnstile, we inadvertently made the cardinal sin of getting in after kickoff, thus missing the only incident of note in the entire game when Chester's Ross Hannah had the ball in the net, only for it to be ruled offside.

As the horizontal rain blew into our faces and a turgid 0-0 draw played out in front of us, The Boy bemoaned the lack of singing, finally taking matters into his own hands. Mustering all the energy his four-year-old lungs could manage, to the perennial tune of The Beach Boys' *Sloop John B*, he piped up, "Steve Burr had a dream/To build a football team/He had no money so he signed some players on loan".

By now necks were craning to find the source of this squeaky refrain, as he finished with a rousing salvo of "We play from the back!/Hobson in attack!/Chester FC/We're on our way back..." As one, the away section joined in appreciative applause for this stirring solo as his young cheeks glowed with pride.

Now the shame. Towards the end of that same season, Steve Burr's dream had turned into a nightmare. With the team sleepwalking towards relegation, the board pulled the trigger with four matches to go and replaced him with his assistant, Jon McCarthy. Still in peril with two games left, The Blues faced a difficult trip to high-flying Grimsby, as did I. Playing it safe on the Friday night, I decided to attend the filming of a friend's new video game-based TV show in Wembley, planning on having a couple of easy pints in the green room and being tucked up for midnight ahead of the early start. Inviting a neighbour to join me, a quick drink back at hers afterwards didn't seem too dangerous. Predictably, one drink became 5am, and I staggered home in some disrepair having listened to what seemed like the entire collected works of the recently deceased Prince, in whom I have almost no interest, now or then.

Following a couple of hours of fitful sleep, I frantically phoned The Hack and Wife, and was devastated to learn that they were already on the M1. Barely able to stand or see, there was no suggestion of driving myself, and I retired to bed sickened at this mindless act of self-sabotage. Rising some hours later, I attempted to salvage something from the day by attending Boreham Wood versus Guiseley, as a result for the away team would ensure Chester's safety. With no chance of us getting anything at Grimsby, this was arguably the bigger game (as I told myself while stood alone eating a bacon sandwich amidst an unfamiliar bunch of disparate desperadoes all barking into the wind).

In the event, Guiseley did us no favours, going down 1-0 while Chester pulled off an epic season-defining 2-1 victory at Blundell Park. Listening to the BBC commentary on my phone in the away end at Meadow Park, I silently punched the air while bemoaning my lifestyle choices. The Driver even made it, somehow getting from Berkshire to Cleethorpes in less than three hours despite earlier assertions. But not me. Having put in a solid eight-month shift, I shamefully missed the climax of the season. I had seen the gig, but missed the encore. Maybe it was at that moment that a seed was planted, suggesting that missing matches was not the correct course of action. Or perhaps I still have a subconscious fear of Grimsby, having once been shot in the arse there pre-match — chips in the air, and a glimpse of an air rifle disappearing into a speeding Mini. Or it's possible that I just got arseholed and missed a game of association football. As a random footnote, it's scant consolation but I ended up writing jokes for the second series of the TV show, *Dara Ó Briain's Go 8 Bit*, filmed at Elstree, in Borehamwood.

Which brings us back to this season. Having spent Friday night at ours, my younger brother drives us to Borehamwood where we prowl the high street in search of a pre-match meal. It's one of the few places in Britain to still boast a Wimpy, but for all the nostalgic value you wouldn't want to eat there. Instead we pile into a generic greasy spoon, all "hello darling", buckets of tea, rubbery eggs in a lake of beans, and well-thumbed tabloid newspapers. If the truth weren't so wildly different, we could almost convince ourselves that we were proper geezers.

Next we go to a bloody boozer, The Wishing Well, to watch Stoke versus Man City plus some Scottish game. With my younger brother on soft drinks and frowning at his phone, I sink pints at the bar and chat to the Irish landlord. He tells me that he has been pulled over eight times for drink-driving despite having never consumed alcohol. The pub gradually fills up with blokes who weirdly seem to have just come out for a drink, with no sporting occasion involved. A Bromley-based Chester fan called Rob pops in for a pint en route to The Alfred Arms, where we eventually end up.

The gang's all here and we head to the ground mob-handed, football's unlikeliest firm. The Driver risks a late one in Wetherspoons yet mysteriously appears at the ground in good time. It later transpires that he and Howie saw an open gate and took their chances, strolling in for free. Good for them. Fuck Boreham Wood. They charge for under-5's and they even charge for visiting press, an unprecedented move that has earned them contempt throughout The National League. Furthermore, judging from our prior visit, their stewards are over-aggressive arseholes. And it always rains.

And they're 1-0 up, an early goal compounding what is already turning into a shit start to the season. Chester huff and puff, but there appears no way back. As the referee turns down a second-half penalty appeal, we beseech the nearside linesman, who had a clear view of the incident but offers no help.

"You fat prick!" I bellow, just at the moment that everything goes quiet.

Spinning on his heel, the attendant steward barks, "Who said that?"

As he scans the crowd, I should just keep my head down, but I sheepishly own up, raising my hand, much to the amusement of the youngsters seated behind me. Beckoning me forward like a naughty schoolboy, I trot down the steps and get my retaliation in first, punching him to the ground in a frenzied attack. Not really. I apologise for my abhorrent behaviour and explain that I have Tourette's and got carried away in the heat of the moment.

"Do it again and I'll throw you out," he admonishes, relishing the power.

Thanking him for his lenience in the face of such a heinous crime, I retake my seat to gales of laughter. As I explain to the guffawing onlookers, I thought I was at a football match.

Minutes later, I'm extremely glad that I am. Picking up the ball in his own half, substitute Elliott Durrell shrugs off a couple of players and strides just over the halfway line. Then in what initially seems like an act of petulance, he simply leathers the ball high towards the Boreham Wood goal. But with the keeper stranded on the edge of his area, he scampers back in vain as it sails over his head and astonishingly into the top corner. It's a moment of rapture that we may never witness again. Losing any semblance of control, I shout non-words and sprint to the end of the row of seats, where I have to quickly turn round and run back again, embracing The Hack in sheer delirium.

We hold on for a 1-1 draw and I shake the steward's hand on the way out, thanking him again for his morality and understanding. Repairing to The Alfred Arms for extensive 'post match analysis', numbers are eventually whittled down to a triumvirate of myself, Pauline, the Cambridge-based chair of The Chester Exiles, and a bloke called Gaz who works at Airbus near Chester. He has a season ticket in the smaller stand at The Deva, but due to work commitments has to leave evening matches after 25 minutes. As such, when we beat

Aldershot 8-2 last season, he left with the match poised at 2-1, which doesn't seem like great value.

A lot more analysis takes place, pint after pint of it. We do actually attempt to leave, but due to a train malfunction are forced back in, albeit via a kebab shop called Divan, where I buy a doner the size of a pillow. I eventually crawl home for *Match Of The Day*.

"Where the fuck have you been?" asks Her Indoors.

Attendance: 335 Position: 19th ➡️⬅️

Game 6 of 50 →

Nobody had ever heard of Sutton United until they knocked Coventry out of the FA Cup in 1989, and nobody has ever heard of them since. Yet here they are, on their way to the Deva Stadium to play on the same hallowed turf trodden by some of the titans of the game. They're even travelling first class. With a hashtag. The game's gone...

The National League new boys are in rude form, having won three of their first five games. Prior to their Deva debut, manager Paul Doswell, who nobody in Chester had ever heard of, delivered a bizarre rant to the press, which went like this: "We will go up to Chester on Saturday morning by first class on Virgin trains with the hashtag #justapubteam. That's what most teams' supporters are calling us — just a pub team from Sutton — and we're laughing about it. They've said we have a shit ground, shit players, shit facilities and shit food — then we beat them and we're enjoying every minute. The bigger ex-League Two clubs don't give us enough respect when they come to Gander Green Lane. A lot of them are living in the past with their past glories."

The past, it is a foreign country. How can we go there? How can we go where we once went? We can't. We can only play what's put in front of us. So while the players and management of Sutton United are enjoying extended legroom, plus complimentary snacks, drinks and unreliable Wi-Fi, I'm embarking on a two-car shuffle commencing at the House of Doom. On my suggestion, we are staying there *en famille* for the August Bank Holiday weekend on the pretence of clearing out the house, with the added bonus of it being slightly nearer to Chester.

The Driver is running late due to unspecified trouble on the A34, which gives us time to visit a recycling centre and drop off various artefacts and boxes of old CD's. It's a thoroughly depressing place to spend a wet Saturday morning, and whatever happens in the match, it can only be an improvement.

Today's interim meeting point is Banbury, or at least a round-about near Banbury, just off the M40. Not any old roundabout, but one served by a Premier Inn, an Esso petrol station, and both a Costa Coffee Drive Thru and a Starbucks On The Go. And for the discerning diner, there's the choice of a Toby Carvery or a Frankie and Benny's, where I'm not ashamed to say I have drunk alone. There's even a cricket club. Essentially, there is everything required for human life, with easy access to the motorway system. As such, I have previously maintained that I could comfortably live there indefinitely. And I don't even like coffee.

The Driver eventually rocks up, impossibly cheery, Chester FC car-scarf stretched across his rear windscreen in time-honoured fashion, the tassels discoloured from countless hours of motorway filth. Otherwise, his vehicle is immaculate, vacuumed to within an inch of its life, everything fitted symmetrically into the boot like a live action game of *Tetris*. Conversely, I tend to treat our car as a combination of spare room and auxiliary dustbin. As such, at any stage of the season it will be filled with newspapers, books, football programmes, CD's in the wrong cases, clothes, toys, litter from several eras, and for an extended period, a watermelon.

On The Driver's arrival, Her Indoors immediately interrogates him as to his intended emigration to France, a conversation that I do not and will not entertain. The switch is made and Her Indoors and The Boy head northeast to her brother's house near Daventry, whereas The Driver and I head northwest, to the North West. First port of call is The Sandstone, where they appear to have resolved their chef issues, and where The Driver Senior meets us for obligatory familial interaction. The trademark Sandstone Pie is the default pre-match meal, a deep ramekin of meat with a flaky pastry top, accompanied by chips the size of staplers. It pretty much sets you up for the day, precluding the need for a "nice pie" at half-time.

There's still time for further fizzy lager in the Blues Bar in order to numb the pain of the inevitable defeat. It's hard to believe now, but there was a time when drinking wasn't such an integral part of the match day experience. As teenagers, we would get into Sealand Road an hour before kickoff and simply watch the players warming up while dissecting the Friday night's drinking (us, not the players).

But a few scoops definitely help. Following extensive research, I have concluded that three pints is the optimum pre-match amount, steadying your nerves while emboldening you enough to hurl abuse at strangers and perform repetitive chants. Any more than three and you find yourself watching through one eye while attempting to hold on until half-time for a piss. Apparently, there is also a law forbidding one to drink and drive, not something that The Driver ever appears to pay much heed to.

With the key elements of travel, eating, and drinking all taken care of, there is still a football match to attend. As ever, it takes up only a fraction of the day, but is of course the most important part, defining the success or otherwise of the entire venture. Sutton look decent, but we grab an early goal. And another! Despite being up against it for almost the entire match, we snag two more goals in the final six minutes for a freak 4-0 win. You couldn't make it up. Clearly, you could, but it's unlikely that many people did. As well as surprising everyone, the match also provided a pressing reminder as to why you should always get in for kickoff and stay until the final whistle. If you'd strolled in ten minutes late and then left ten minutes early to beat the proverbial traffic you'd have missed all of the relevant action.

Obviously there are occasions when tardiness can't be helped. Indeed, my younger brother and I once drove from Bournemouth to Chester for a game against Scunthorpe only to encounter bad traffic and arrive at half-time. Beating on the doors to be let in, thankfully the game was still goalless and we sneaked a 1-0 win, albeit against ten men, a minor detail that neither of us was aware of until the next day.

Regrettably, I have missed my fair share of goals through general ineptitude, including a belter from Big Cyrille Regis at Leyton Orient. As such, if at all possible I do insist on getting in for the start of the game. There are other sports where it is of little consequence if you miss the odd point or run or pot or dart, but goals can come at any time, and if you miss one, you've missed a huge part of the narrative. I once got stuck in the pub at Brighton and got in late to discover that the home team had already scored what turned out to be the only goal of the game, an embarrassing error that left me feeling deeply unsatisfied. If you're going to have your guts ripped out, you may as well witness it. Likewise, the rampant frenzy of seeing your team score can only be enjoyed in the moment; a deferred celebration is never as intense.

As for leaving early, walking out simply because your team isn't winning is not only defeatist, it's childish. I've never done it, even when it meant chasing my departed lift down the road. Losing is a key part of the experience of supporting a football club. Suck it up. Stay to the end, take your medicine, and then either commend the players on their thwarted efforts or if necessary give them dog's abuse. Don't melodramatically swan off because things aren't going your way. It's not about you. Embarrassingly, some Premier League grounds resemble a fire drill towards the latter stages of a match, whatever the score. Trust me, if your life revolves around 11 men kicking a pressurised leather sphere into an onion bag, you really haven't got anywhere else to be.

And where else would anyone possibly want to be? A 4-0 win qualifies for a post-match celebration, and back in the Blues Bar the mood is buoyant, although resident naysayer APJ attempts to dampen spirits by suggesting that Sutton thrashed us 0-4. As we have established, goals are all that matter. We scored some, and they didn't. I very much doubt that we'll be hearing from Sutton United or their manager again this season.

Attendance: 1,625   Position: 16th ↑

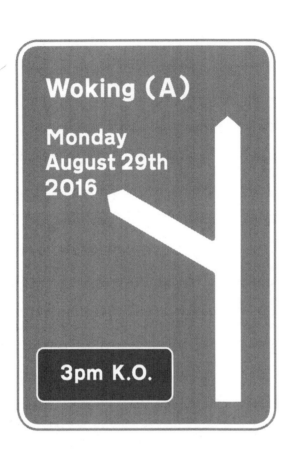

Game 7 of 50 →

Coming off one day's rest, this is game seven of August. It's a gruelling schedule that has already taken a physical, emotional and financial toll. We haven't even made it home since Saturday, simply remaining in a holding pattern at the House of Doom between matches, spending Sunday basking in the afterglow of an unexpected four-goal victory.

In theory, it should be just over an hour from Milton Keynes to Woking, but at my insistence we build several hours into the schedule. The reason? Three words that strike terror into the heart of any travelling football fan: Bank Holiday Monday. It is my understanding that this involves people who normally have to go to work not having to go to work for a day, instead choosing to sit in their cars in their millions not going anywhere. Why they do this is beyond my comprehension. Where are they attempting to go? And why? Please remain in your homes. Unless you live in a car, presumably you have accommodation. Why not sit in that and enjoy your day off? Or if it's sunny, sit in the garden or designated green space. Do not pile into your hot sweaty car and clog up the motorway system for decent right-minded people who are attempting to get to a live sporting event with a non-flexible start time.

But of course that's exactly what has happened, with radio reports suggesting that the M1 is fucked and the M25 is super-fucked. In terms of anger management, being stuck on a motorway as the clock ticks towards kickoff is sub-optimal. At least on the A-roads you have options. As such, I bite the bullet and select 'Avoid motorways' on our prehistoric satnav. This obviously adds a chunk of time to the journey, but it is time that would otherwise be spent stuck on the motorway staring at the back of a family estate in a state of unfettered rage.

As it turns out, we get hopelessly lost on a number of occasions due to the satnav not recognising any road built in the last decade. We do eventually reach Surrey, which is at least the correct county, and are treated to an unscheduled tour of various extremely smug villages. Apropos of nothing, Her Indoors announces that she could never live in one due to the overbearing culture of driving an expensive sports car to the tennis club and then having a gin and tonic through a rictus grin.

Woking itself is somewhat earthier, and could be described as a satellite of London. Famously, it is where local author HG Wells envisioned the Martians landing in *The War Of The Worlds*, a fictional event commemorated by a vast metallic alien structure in the town centre. Of far greater cultural importance is the fact that The Jam were formed in Woking, and indeed played a gig at the football ground as early as 1975. A mere seven years later, on my birthday, they played their last ever gig before Paul Weller split them up, meaning I never got to see them. I still haven't forgiven him. I saw him one night on Charlotte Street in London, smoking a fag. I gave him a look that I like to think conveyed the decades of disappointment.

Woking's Kingfield Stadium is also famous as the venue for The Boy's first ever football match, aged two and a half. On a freezing Tuesday night in January, I was faced with the option of missing the game or taking The Boy. As such, we drove directly there from his nursery and enjoyed a slap-up pre-match meal at a nearby snooker club, where my younger brother joined us straight off a flight from Marrakech before we all got thrown out for not being members.

Managing the child was far more stressful than the match, although pleasingly, almost 30 years after I witnessed a debut win with my dad, The Boy was rewarded with a debut win with me. Wearing an oversized replica shirt and wrapped in a Chester scarf, he was asleep with a smile on his face before we'd even left the snooker club car park, resulting in a pang of what I believe humans refer to as emotion.

That was half his life away. He's now asleep in a hot car in a pub car park near Woking train station while the grownups hastily ingest burgers, chips and pints at a nearby table. Walking distance from Stanley Road, where Weller grew up, The Sovereigns is a vast all-purpose drinkery-cum-eaterie. Both inside and out, there are Chester here, Chester there, Chester every-fucking-where. The pub has also been designated as the official meeting point for The Chester Exiles, at least one of whom has turned up.

On a separate table, gently listing in the sweltering heat is the non-exiled Azza, who nods in recognition at our rapidly expanding group. Something of a maverick, he lives in Chester but rarely attends home games, preferring the extended supping of an away day, subsidised due to the fact that he's a ticket collector on the trains. He generally travels with a dog-eared Wetherspoons brochure, ticking off the individual pubs as he visits them — at last count he was most of the way towards having had a drink at every one in the country. It would be an extraordinary achievement, and a worthy rival to The Card. The Spoon, perhaps?

I have previously named a random 'Spoons of my acquaintance and Azza has been able to instantly confirm whether he's been there, and even what civic building it was before being assimilated by the Wetherspoons behemoth; numerous old cinemas, libraries and schools now converted into cheap alehouses for the terminally unhurried. Despite being a vocal pioneer of the PMG (pre-match gallon), Azza never appears overtly drunk. In fact I have only seen him in trouble once, at Radcliffe Borough during an FA Cup tie when they put a beer tent in the away end and he threw his ring up on the side of the pitch.

Following some frantic speed-drinking, kickoff is almost upon us. The original plan was for the family to abandon me in Woking and head home, but after some gentle cajoling they agree to attend the match, which means I get the pleasure of their company and a lift home. Dumping me at the turnstile with minutes to go while they park the car, I am surprised at being able to pay in by debit card for the first time ever, a rare nod to modernity in a typically old-fashioned ground.

There are still a couple of minutes to kickoff, which of course means time for another pint. A man after my own throat, Azza is already at the bar, about to enter the realms of the PMDF (pre-match double figures). A Real Aler by habit, perhaps swayed by the heat, away from the watchful eye of the purists he suddenly breaks rank and announces, "Fuck it, Wainwright's not here," before ordering himself a Stella. A mutual acquaintance, the honourable Wainwright once admonished me as "scum" for enjoying an ice cold lager prior to a sweltering season opener at Hednesford. Following Azza's cue, I pour a Stella into my neck in about three gulps, like a 1970s darts player.

Blinking into the sunlight as the players run out, I take a seat in Woking's huge stand behind the goal. Sadly, it's not the goal that we are attacking, so in time-honoured fashion I simply change ends, taking a place on the terrace behind the other goal, now reunited with my friends and family, the latter presumably horrified to witness me in my natural state.

Despite being world beaters (or at least Sutton beaters) a mere 48 hours ago, the manager has needlessly tampered with the team, even though Woking's record consists of five defeats and a draw. Nevertheless, they are all over us like a soup sandwich, and take an early lead. We equalise shortly afterwards, and I toss The Boy into the air in celebration. The jubilation is short-lived however, as Woking immediately retake the lead.

Re-swapping ends at half time — via the bar — I am in dire need of a sit down. With no segregation in place, much of the chat among the Woking fans centres around how shit Sutton must have been. By now emitting a Stella-fuelled stream of consciousness, one Woking fan politely suggests that I wind my neck in. It reminds Her Indoors of an incident at Nuneaton years ago when I treated her to a Friday night game en route to Liverpool to see England take on Finland at Anfield the next day (won 2-1). Again, I found myself gibbering ceaselessly in an unsegregated area. One Nuneaton fan could take no more and simply stood up, announced, "I can't listen to any more of this" and promptly marched off in disgust. Won 2-1, in a game marred by late arrival due to train malfunction, and also notable due to the turnstiles being operated by candlelight.

Back at Woking, we are atrocious and they eventually make it 3-1 to secure their first win of the season. We never get anything here, apart from that one time when we did, but it's still a kick in the nuts and the manager later assumes responsibility, admitting that he got it wrong. At least it's a short journey home. We now wait to see what September brings.

Attendance: 1,271 Position: 18th ↓

Forest Green
Rovers (H)

Saturday
September 3rd
2016

3pm K.O.

Game 8 of 50 →

Drip, drip, drip, drip. In something of a departure from the norm, I awake on match day in a wet tent. In a wet field. In a wet country. Fear not, I haven't been kicked out of the house (yet), I am at Festival No. 6 in the Welsh village of Portmeirion. Something of a hybrid festival, you awake under canvas yet can be sitting on porcelain within minutes, and indeed taking your morning tea from same. I've been to Portmeirion a few times, but this is my first visit to the festival, having blagged a pair of free tickets on the pretext of writing a magazine feature about *The Prisoner*, the baffling 1960's TV series that was filmed in the village.

Chester is 70 miles east, but first I have to escape the village, something that is easier said than done, as Patrick McGoohan's titular character discovered half a century earlier. And he was probably in a better state.

The Friday night is sketchy, but at some point I watched cosmic northern songstress Jane Weaver crooning over a 1982 Hungarian animated film. I also interviewed, and then got murderously drunk with a McGoohan-obsessed actor from Wigan who randomly used to live on the same street as me in Chester, albeit at a different time. It became apparent that we had been out too long when we found ourselves in a marquee watching 1974 Spanish zombie film, *The Living Dead At The Manchester Morgue*, until they finally turned it off for our own good. While I retired to my canvas shelter in time to give me a live chance of making the match, I left him wandering in the woods waiting for his 6am train to Manchester, hopefully not the morgue. Be seeing you.

My journey to the North West is scarcely more orthodox. First I have to slide down a muddy hill, then board a shuttle bus (local service only), which takes me to my car. Thankfully, due to my exalted status, I have not parked in the public car park, which is already partially submerged. Instead, the car is on the firmer ground of Porthmadog Football Club, facing the token perimeter fence. It's a rudimentary stadium to say the least, and I'm not sure if or how they charge an entry fee, as if the occasion arose I could simply watch the match from my car.

Setting the satnav for the infinitely more luxurious Deva Stadium, I tentatively set off, remembering first to swap my wellies for more vehicle friendly footwear. The plan is to pick up my Cheltenham-based older brother from Chester station, stick it up Forest Green, then drive back to the festival for the Saturday night festivities followed by Super Furry Animals and Echo & The Bunnymen on the Sunday. That's living all right.

With the aforementioned Super Furries roaring out of the car stereo, I set about traversing the northern section of their homeland in order to get to England. It's ostensibly the same journey that my family made in 1982 when we left a tiny fiercely inbred village in Wales for the bewildering metropolis of Chester – escaping back to England via the nearest exit - a move that ultimately led to the lifestyle that I currently enjoy today.

Arguably even more rural than the Lake District, it's a majestically bleak journey, accompanied by the obligatory ceaseless drizzle. At one point I find myself driving across the top of a mountain, with the occasional sheep the only other living creature. If I break down here, not only is the match in jeopardy, but I may never be seen again. All the same, it's an improvement on the M6.

It does feel mildly deranged, leaving what is literally a festival of entertainment in order to witness something that has a strong chance of being actively upsetting. Every time you attend a football match, you are effectively taking a gamble with your emotions, and today's odds don't look good. In American sporting parlance, Forest Green are "7 and 0" against Chester, in so much as they have won all of our last seven encounters. If you were to throw a dart at a heat map of my recent life, there is a distinct possibility it would find me watching Chester lose 2-1 to Forest Green. It's almost my default state.

But of course today will be different, as I remind myself when cruising into Chester's fair city with a couple of hours until kickoff. Still reeling from the previous night's festivities, I am in dire need of rancid food and carbonated drinks. As such I head for the 24-hour McDonald's, only to find that it's not open, as in they're still building it. This does nothing to improve my mood, but I head for a regular chippy near Bache station, Chester's almost superfluous second station, from which I used to sometimes walk the two miles or so to the ground having first taken the Hooton 3 Car from Liverpool.

I'm so hung over that I can barely park. My impeded spatial awareness sees me pull up too close to a hedge, meaning that I have to squeeze out of the driver's door as the aforementioned hedge deposits its accumulated rain all over my face, neck and torso. I then have to make the reverse journey, with the same effect, albeit now clutching a paper-wrapped meal.

Sitting in the car drenched, eating a particularly sweaty sausage and chips, I stick on local radio station Dee 106.3 and catch an interview with Chester manager Jon McCarthy, who describes Forest Green as the Barcelona of The National League. A glorified village team from Nailsworth, near Stroud, near Gloucester, near Cheltenham, they were once a yardstick of how far we'd fallen. Now we're cowering to them before the game has even started.

We may as well just roll out the red carpet, or more appropriately, the green carpet. Bankrolled by eco-warrior millionaire Vince Dale — who really did once live in a car — Forest Green are deeply unpopular within the division for their policy of buying all the best players. In fact it later transpires that the amount they spent on agents' fees alone was roughly half of Chester's entire budget for the season. We don't stand a chance.

I couldn't be more cross if I tried. And then an advert comes on the radio, impelling listeners to get down to the official Liverpool FC Club shop — in Chester — to buy the new shirt, the new Liverpool shirt. What's the fucking point? Sadly, it was ever thus. When I was at school in Chester in the 1980s, a straw poll of a class of 30 revealed 27 Liverpool fans, one Everton fan, one Manchester United fan, and one Chester City fan: me. People genuinely didn't believe me and assumed it was a wilful act of rebellion, like spoiling your ballot paper. Having not grown up in a football household, nobody had told me that you're simply supposed to support the best team at the time.

Tossing the chippy wrapper into the footwell in disgust, I head to the real station and pick up my older brother, who has turned up for a festival in one of the wettest countries on earth sporting a pair of plimsolls. This will be his first home game for a few years. He used to go to Sealand Road back in the day, and even the odd away game, including when the coach got bricked at Halifax. But crucially he didn't come to that home win in 1984 that I dragged our dad to, because he had to go into town to buy some trousers. When he did make his debut shortly after, it was for a defeat. Denied that initial heady taste of success, I sometimes wonder if that may have subconsciously resulted in a more casual level of support. Or maybe he just can't be arsed.

After driving past the house in which improbably we briefly once shared a room as adults, we rendezvous with The Driver at Telford's Warehouse for a loosener, then hit the home end mob-handed. It has not stopped fucking raining since I stuck my head out of a canvas hovel early this morning in a different country. That said, technically we may actually be back in Wales. While the club offices are in England, and it is absolutely an English club — albeit one that used to play in the Welsh Cup — gallingly much of the stadium and pitch is in the principality. There was a rumour, since debunked, that you could take a corner in one country and score in another.

We'd take it at the moment, as Forest Green are all over us like a hi-vis bib, their ghastly luminous kit a direct result of Swampy's financial involvement with the club. They get a free kick on 25 minutes. Jon Worsnop aka Parsnip appears to have it covered but it clips his arm at a macabre angle and bounces sickeningly into the roof of the net. He concedes another long-range effort early in the second half and that appears to be that, not least for his Chester career, as this proves to be his penultimate appearance.

Forest Green are clearly the better side, but when we stop doffing our collective caps to them and actually get in their faces, they buckle like a belt. For all their inflated transfer fees and hefty wage packets, they are just another bunch of alehouse footballers. In fact my older brother recognises one of their defenders as a regular drinker in the nite-spots of Cheltenham. With ten minutes to go, Durrell lashes one in and it's all set up for a grandstand finish, which of course never materialises.

Speeding back across the mountain, it even stops raining for a couple of minutes. Despite a concerted effort to run out of petrol in the middle of nowhere, we make it to the festival in time to catch veteran punk poet John Cooper Clarke: "What kind of creature bore you? Was it some kind of bat? They can't find a good word for you, but I can… TWAT!"

Attendance: 1,820 Position: 19th ↓

Aldershot
Town (A)

Saturday
September 10th
2016

3pm K.O.

Game 9 of 50 →

Fuck The Shots. It's a horrible little military town, we never get anything there, and a section of their fans took great pleasure in relegating
us in 2009. Furthermore, it's pissing with rain and I am faced with a
momentous decision that will go on to define the rest of the day: train
or car. Train? Car? Car? Train? If I get the train I can speed-drink four
pints of strong European lager, watch the game through one eye, get
unnecessarily drunk with some vague acquaintances, roll home for
Match Of The Day and then spend the rest of the weekend wallowing
in a pit of despair.

Fuck it, I'll drive. It's cheaper, and there's less chance of having to talk
to somebody. When we were relegated in '09 I faced the double whammy
of spending the entire journey back to Waterloo with APJ lecturing me
about "the problem with Chester" when all I wanted to do was stare out
of the window in mute despair, and then go to see The Fall on my own.

London Traffic, going nowhere, the chat on 5Live is all about the
upcoming Manchester derby, how it's the most expensive game ever
played, and how most of the known solar system will be watching it.
Weirdly, there's no mention of The Mighty Chester attempting to stop
the rot with a tricky trip to The Recreation Ground, where the home
team currently boasts a 100% record.

Gleefully finding a free parking space outside the nearest pub to the
away end, I bowl into the fancifully named La Fontaine and nod to a
group of disparate Chester fans. I order a "driving lager" (Foster's in
a plastic glass) and a Clingfilm-wrapped cheese roll, taking a stool at
the bar in time to see Manchester City's Kevin De Bruyne slot in the
opening goal on the big screen. A nation roars, as does a bloke at the
bar, presumably a lifelong fan.

I am soon joined by The Hack and Wife, the drive from Sussex falling under his self-imposed two-hour radius. The Hack hates La Fontaine, and declares it Britain's Worst Pub, largely on the basis that they have no Real Ale, and indeed openly advertise the fact on their website. I see this as a bonus, as my route to the bar is unencumbered by bearded men with questionable hygiene sampling three thirds of Nutty Slack and then sharing their innermost thoughts with a moleskine notepad. Fuck Real Ale. It all comes from one giant vat of slops somewhere under Middle-earth. It's simply marketing, an attempt to convince 50-year-old men that just because they have a rudimental understanding of specific gravity it's acceptable to still live with their mothers. In protest, The Hack orders a pint of Guinness, basically Real Ale with black colouring. That'll show them.

The Driver soon rocks up, completing The Gateshead Three, and gets stuck into the Amstel, maintaining his 1970s approach to the drink-driving laws. He is soon accosted by The Curious Case Of Benjamin Button, who makes the fundamental error of attempting to discuss something other than the forthcoming match, a previous match, or general club business. I am forever in his debt as he gave me and The Evertonian a lift to Swansea when they dicked us in the play-offs in '97. As such, I nod politely and affix my gaze on the screen.

The population of the pub is comfortably doubled when about 15 Clone Island-clad Chester Youth pile in, fresh off the 7:55am train. We get chatting to a young shaver, notionally the brains of the operation, and a key witness to the Boreham Wood incident. There's talk of my ambitious stab at The Card, and he casually mentions that he hasn't missed a match for four and a half seasons, the only blemish coming when his Mum insisted that he go to school instead of North Ferriby.

Mid-sentence, the pub suddenly empties, and we look out of the window to see a pitched battle in the street, all baseball caps, rabbit punches and haymakers. Wielding an umbrella, the La Fontaine security guard joins in, as do a couple of locals, defending the honour of their pub as opposed to showing any regional allegiance. Nowadays, most so-called football hooliganism is largely non-contact, running backwards and forwards, arms outstretched as if tickling imaginary trout. It arguably has more in common with historical re-enactment, all costumes and posturing, the Sealed Knot Society in Aquascutum.

This seems to be the real deal though, with strangers punching each other hard about the face and head for a good few minutes, the fan known as Alan Carr overseeing matters from a safe distance. In his defence, he does wear glasses.

They either get bored, someone 'wins,' or the police turn up, but the Chester eventually repair to the pub and carry on as if nothing has happened, despite one youngster sporting a sideways nose and a freshly red polo shirt. Apparently, some Chester Youth were having a quick fag outside when a group of Shots threw a bottle at them, hence the ensuing mayhem. "I hope my car's all right," jokes The Driver.

The barmaid promptly declares the bar closed, before reopening it two minutes later. While some see it as a noble and fitting response to an unprovoked attack, Pauline, the Chair of The Chester Exiles, is shaking with rage, convinced that the skirmish will earn the club a fine. Of course it won't, but whatever the rights and wrongs of the incident, further shame is to follow when one of the combatants — a ringer for Gary Cahill — strolls up to the bar and orders a Dubonnet and lemonade, despite the fact that he doesn't appear to be with an elderly relative, and it's not Christmas.

The walking wounded are tended to by the landlord, and repay his kindness by ripping the hand dryer off the bog wall. Ten minutes after the event, the police come into the pub, presumably in search of troublemakers. Predictably they don't acknowledge our existence — once you're over 40, women and policemen don't even see you. Following all the excitement, there is of course still a match to go to, but not before The Driver checks his car, a regular pre-match ritual at the best of times. Returning with a look of concern, he asks if mine is the Blue Golf, specifically the Blue Golf with a dent in the passenger door and a detached wing mirror placed on the windscreen. Yes. Yes it is, and as well as the aforementioned damage it now sports a note from the local ambulance service. Presumably they turned up to treat a bloody nose and careered into my perfectly parked car. I'd very much like to personally thank the little prick that threw that bottle.

A policeman gives me permission to drive with one wing mirror, but first there's the small matter of sticking it up The Shots. The entrance to the away end of The Recreation Ground is one of the strangest in football, accessed only by walking through the tree-lined path of a public park. The arboreal theme continues inside, with a selection of trees actually growing within the ground. Paying at the turnstile, the match ticket has the words 'Tranmere Rovers' scribbled out with felt tip pen. Once inside, I treat myself to a limp pat of gristle in a rubbery bap from the catering van, and spot my younger brother and my dad. They've driven up from Bournemouth, as ever unannounced, safe in the knowledge that they'll see me there.

The match kicks off and almost immediately my younger brother's face is contorted into a twisted vision of hatred, spitting venom at the linesman over a mildly dubious throw-in decision on the halfway line. He intersperses the rage by live-tweeting such insights as 'Corner #ChesterFC', but mainly spends the whole match in a state of apoplexy, so much so that we have to move away from him at half-time. As for my dad, he seems happy to be out of the house, able to enjoy the match without necessarily knowing who the manager is, the player's names, our league position, or the intricacies of the new offside laws.

It's a first half that unexpectedly sees Chester on top, on-loan midfielder Ryan Lloyd twatting the post with such ferocity that the entire away end bucks as one, the width of a cigarette packet defining the success or otherwise of the weekend. At the interval, The Driver is recognised by an old schoolmate who lives locally, works in horse racing, and is attending his first Chester match in about 20 years.

It is no surprise to learn that football fans often need a piss at half-time, a side effect of hours of pouring lager into their faces, and being mammals. As such Aldershot have laid on three Portaloos for the 132 travelling fans. Christ only knows what they did for the visit of Tranmere. One of the bogs, theoretically the Ladies, is deemed unusable, and a steward leads the female contingent into the bowels of the main stand. It's a dignity of sorts.

The second half sees Chester endure extended pressure, but they hang for a 0-0 draw, which is widely deemed a decent point. Hugging the hard shoulder, I nurse my battered vehicle home in time to catch the end of the Liverpool match, as they stick four past Champions Leicester in front of 50,000 at Anfield. Good for them.

Attendance: 2,445 Position: 18th ↑

Guiseley (H)

Tuesday
September 13th
2016

7.45pm K.O.

Game 10 of 50 →

With the first nine games under my belt, we are now in uncharted territory. In Chester FC's debut season back in the Conference a few years ago, I managed the first eight, holding my nerve after five consecutive defeats to be rewarded with an historic 2-0 win at despised rivals Wrexham. For what it's worth, I have actually managed two home Cards in the past, coincidentally both promotion seasons, one in the 1980s under legendary manager Harry McNally, and another in the 1990s under Graham Barrow. I may have to consult the rulebook for the second one, as I did it while being employed as a steward at the club, although I claim a bonus for completing it while living in Bournemouth for the latter part of the season. No prizes.

In general though, doing The Card is a young man's game, specifically a young man who lives in the Chester area and has no responsibilities. Responsibilities such as being the primary carer for a five-year-old son who goes to school in London, for instance. As well as his Woking debut, there have been a few other occasions when I took him straight from school to a match, and I did have to question my parenting abilities when The Boy, The Driver and I were sat in a chippy in Welling at 10pm on a Tuesday night with school in the morning. Lost 2-1.

A midweek home match is a step too far however, and is simply not feasible within the current truancy laws. It is normally at this stage of the season that I concede defeat, settling in at home to follow the match remotely via text, tweets and latterly full audio commentary. It's a nerve-wracking business that involves pacing up and down, barking unheard instructions into the ether, and generally getting into a bit of a tizz about something that you have absolutely no control over. If things don't go our way, the soft furnishing can take a pummelling, and if things do go our way it is not unknown to perform a celebration lap of the garden. Win, lose or draw, The Driver habitually rings from his car on the way home for post-match analysis and it is at this point that I am extremely grateful not to be sat next to him with hundreds of miles of motorway between me and my bed.

This season feels different though. Given The Driver's utterly selfish emigration plans, I am still harbouring ambitious, nay ludicrous, thoughts of attempting the full Card. As such, I pull in a favour from another dad at school who agrees to pick up The Boy and take him swimming, even though he can't swim. I later have visions of him drowning and having to explain that I wasn't there because Chester had an early season six-pointer at home to bottom of the table Guiseley.

The Driver has no such restrictions and has canvassed for an early start on the basis that if you don't get round Birmingham before rush hour you're screwed, a theory that he has been attempting to drum into me for well over a decade. In the event, he's late, as he's had to re-alphabetise his CD collection at the last minute. As such, I sit in the car at Ardley reading Brix Smith Start's autobiography, specifically the bit where she describes Gary Lineker shitting himself at Italia '90 during a match and having to scrape his arse on the turf like a dog before mercifully being substituted.

I later read the offending passage to The Driver through tears of laughter, almost causing him to slew across the M40. Birmingham is successfully circumnavigated, followed by the time-honoured route of M54 then A41, the bleakest road in Britain, a succession of boarded up pubs, burger vans, a prison, a chippy and an airfield. And presumably dozens of undiscovered bodies — this is not the sort of place where you want to break down and have to knock on a door for help.

Having erred on the side of caution, The Driver delivers us to Telford's Warehouse for 5pm, bearing in mind that kickoff is at 7:45pm. This provides ample time to eat and drink, and I order a vast burger and chips, washed down with a raft of lagers. Meanwhile, The Driver sneaks out to his car and eats his carefully prepared sandwiches. Parking near the ground to avoid the £2 car park fee, as ever he tucks in his wing mirrors, something that I had always considered an affectation until one of mine was sheared off by an ambulance at Aldershot.

Walking the last few hundred yards, it is apparent that we're not in Kansas anymore. Having set off in blazing sunshine sporting shorts and T-shirt, I am woefully underdressed for a wet September night in the North. As such, I duck into the club shop on the off chance of purchasing a warm garment and am delighted to discover a rack of on-sale items. I am considering parting with £20 for a long-sleeved training top when finance director Laurence appears like Mr Benn and announces that everything is a fiver. It's a deal breaker, and I immediately buy it and put it on in the shop. In fairness, I may have to grow into it, as it hangs on my bulk like an artist's smock, with only a paintbrush behind the ear required to complete the picture.

As well as making me look a tit, the training top represents the first Chester shirt I've ever bought, having never been sucked into the annual polyester treadmill, unlike The Driver, who owns over 50 replica shirts — good luck taking them to France. Over the years, I have been given the odd shirt as a gift, or acquired them through extremely random means. In the late 1990s, The Evertonian and I appeared on cult cable channel L!ve TV — home of *Topless Darts* — representing Chester City in a football-based quiz show cunningly entitled *A Game Of Two Scarves*. Heavily refreshed after a few looseners in Canary Wharf, we began by singing the full version of "If you were born in Wales/You must have heard the tales/Of Chester boys/And what we do to you" before heroically winning with a record points tally. Keeping score on the day — with some difficulty — was a frisky young model who promptly whipped her Chester top off and gave it to me to keep, along with one of the titular scarves. As a footnote, a mate of mine later had a threesome with her, and indeed courted her for a few months.

Less interestingly, I was once obliged to wear a Chester top for a tenuous magazine photo shoot, and so expensed the away shirt for the 1999/2000 season, the latter stages of which were dubbed The Great Escape, something of a misnomer given that we were relegated out of the Football League for the first time since the 1930s. A hideous orange monstrosity, it was almost unwearable, not least due to a thick felt logo emblazoned with the words 'KWIK SAVE', one of which isn't even a word. As well as proving an eyesore, it always reminded me of a telephone interview I did with Kevin Ratcliffe, who began that doomed season as Chester manager before being replaced by despotic club owner, the eccentric American Terry Smith aka 'Coco The Clown'. At the start of the season, Smith had presented Ratcliffe with a raggle-taggle group of players, including an Icelandic triallist. According to Ratcliffe, "He couldn't cross it, couldn't head it, couldn't finish, and a shout went out, 'OK, he's from Iceland, where's the lad from Kwik Save?'"

Thankfully, the club is now owned and run by the fans, some of whom are supping in the Blues Bar. As soon as we walk in, a young Chester fan bounds towards us wielding his mobile phone, which is displaying a photo of a television, which is in turn displaying a photo of a man. It's a familiar man, who just over three weeks earlier had humiliated me in front of my peers and threatened to throw me out of Boreham Wood Football Club for using a minor swearword. I am understandably confused, but the lad explains that he took a snap of that week's *Crime Watch*, as the police are interested in talking to the man in question in regard to financial irregularities in the Borehamwood area. You couldn't make it up. I'm very tempted to tell them exactly where he'll be on alternate Saturday afternoons, recognisable by the fact that he'll be wearing a hi-vis bib and admonishing moderate foul language. What a prick.

In a game that lives in the memory almost as long as it takes us to get to Stafford Services, we overcome Guiseley 2-0 with a brace of second-half goals in front of The Harry McNally Terrace. I can clearly be seen in the highlights, punching the air with an oversized smock flapping round my groin. Stick it in the books: ten games down and we're unbeaten in the last two without conceding a goal. What a time to be alive.

After a midnight Ardley switch, I attempt to listen to *The Sports Bar* on talkSPORT, but it is beyond banal so I stick on a Portishead CD and tread on the accelerator. One minor panic attack. Home for 1am, I sit in the sweltering garden and watch the moon go down.

Attendance: 1,578 Position: 17th ↑

Braintree
Town (H)

Saturday
September 17th
2016

3pm K.O.

Game 11 of 50 →

I have made a big decision. Thus far, I have disguised my 100% record as early season enthusiasm, but can hide the truth no longer. Over a Friday night curry, I take an emboldening swig of Cobra and break the news to my family that I am intending to do The Card. Pleading my case, I explain that due to The Driver's forthcoming self-imposed Brexit, this season represents my last realistic chance of achieving immortality. If I don't do it now, I will live to regret it, maybe not today, maybe not tomorrow, but soon and for the rest of my life. Yeah whatever, pass the poppadoms. It's difficult to gauge the reaction, but the news appears to be greeted with a combination of confusion, horror and ultimately resignation.

Awaking the next day with renewed vigour, the family waves me off and wishes me luck with what seems like genuine sincerity. While London sleeps off its hangover, I am resplendent in my new smock, tearing through empty streets like a scene from *28 Days Later*. Sticking on the car stereo, there's some kind of jazz collage on Resonance FM, interspersed with snippets of The Beatles from another station with a stronger signal. This has the unfortunate effect of momentarily reducing me to a fugue state, unaware of where I am or what I'm doing. Allied to the previous evening's chicken jalfrezi, I am, as they say, drifting into the arena of the unwell. My mind begins to race. What if I get ill? What if I can't complete The Card? What obstacles abound between here and the end of April?

At this stage I should point out that I am not by nature what is known as a morning person. Unless I have to get up for a match, I generally have no truck with them, and am firmly of the belief that there is only one ten o'clock in the day. Nevertheless, The Driver has designated a

10am meeting, and what The Driver wants, The Driver gets, mainly because he's driving. I am there exactly on time, and he is of course late, having spent the morning trying to get through to John Major's Cones Hotline.

"We should not be playing the likes of these," he announces, for neither the first nor last time. With respect, nobody had ever heard of Braintree before The Prodigy. That said, they did make the play-offs last season under PE teacher-turned-manager, Danny Cowley, since snaffled up by Lincoln City along with his assistant and brother, Nicky.

For reasons we may never know, The Driver contradicts his own edict and takes the dreaded M6. As such, we find ourselves next to a car full of Cherries on their way to The Etihad to watch Bournemouth take on Manchester City in the Premier League in front of 54,000 people. Spotting the Chester car-scarf and the vision in polyester in the passenger seat, they give us a filthy, contemptuous look, despite it being less than eight years since we played them in the league.

I lived in Bournemouth for a few years, possibly the biggest test of my Chester support to date. Shamefully, there was a season when I only managed to get to The Deva once, the last game of the campaign, just to ensure that I had never had a blank year. But as a bonus, when we were in the same division as them, my younger brother and I would travel incognito on the away supporters coach to the Chester v Bournemouth fixtures. While in exile at Macclesfield between stadiums, there was a famous FA Cup tie, notable not least because before the match a local pub was smashed up in a scene reminiscent of the Wild West. On the pitch we came back from 2-0 down and were all set for a replay on our doorstep when a goalkeeping howler gifted Efan Ekoku a last-minute winner for The Cherries, thus consigning us to a six-hour coach journey pretending to read the programme amidst sickening jubilation.

I even went to a few random Bournemouth home games, but it didn't take. Suffice to say, a 0-0 draw against Mansfield was not enough to sway my allegiance. How different things could have been. Or indeed, how similar. I was actually on the bench at Dean Court writing a feature for *FourFourTwo* magazine when Bournemouth beat Shrewsbury to stay in the Football League. It is, as they say, a funny old game. And as I never tire of telling people, I was the first journalist ever to interview Eddie Howe, then a 16-year-old youth team player, now the most successful manager in the club's history. He initially thought it was a wind-up, but proved to be an extremely levelheaded young man with a big future ahead of him. I bet he's never done The Card though.

Back in the car, The Driver flicks between talkSPORT and 5Live. Pat Nevin comes on the radio and I am reminded of the time I saw him in the Chester branch of Our Price, casually browsing the vinyl — indie section of course — the day after scoring a hat trick for Everton. Something of a haven for Merseyside's finest, Jan Molby lived in the city for a while, and Ian Rush can still occasionally be spotted in town, the best part of four decades after we sold him to Liverpool for £300,000.

Merseyside's other team, Tranmere Rovers, are in action today in the early kickoff away to Sutton United, live on BT Sport. As such, due to the wonders of modern technology I am able to watch the match in the car on my mobile phone, or at least ten minutes of it, which uses up my entire monthly data plan.

Hitting Telford's in good time, we sit in the sun by the canal on the next table to a pair of alers of no fixed nomenclature.

"A bit early for you two," observes one of them, before complaining to his mate that nearby building work is obscuring his view of the buzzards. Furthermore, he hasn't seen a kingfisher on the canal for some time, presumably referring to the bird, not the Indian lager of the same name.

All day long I have been bombarded by social media urging me to buy something called the Cestrian10, effectively a mini season ticket that gets you ten games for the price of nine. In the scheme of things, it's a drop in the ocean, but as a statement of intent I decide to buy one, handing over £135 to the volunteers in the office, who unprompted remind me that I can't buy a ticket for Wrexham away until after the match, presumably as that would be too easy.

The transaction itself is a minor circus, but worse is to come when I present a voucher to the turnstile attendant who claims to have no knowledge of a Cestrian10, tacitly suggesting that I have somehow printed my own full colour perforated booklet with ten tickets, a list of conditions and a cardboard back. With minutes until kickoff, he insists that I'll have to go back to the office, something that would kill The Card stone dead — to be officially recognised you have to attend every minute of every match.

Pleading with him that it's been all over Twitter, he claims "We don't get Twitter down here," somehow suggesting that he lives in the turnstile. With both The Driver and the man behind verifying my story, he mutters, "They don't tell us jack," and finally lets me in as the teams run out.

With Braintree's all-orange kit clashing with the stewards' coats, offside decisions prove tricky, but they twat the post from close-range early doors. We respond with a flurry of corners, and in the 12th minute youth team graduate Sam Hughes bundles the ball over the line for the only goal of the game. That young man will go a long way, I think to myself retrospectively.

In other business, one hapless Braintree fan keeps a cone on his head for the duration of the game (presumably to The Driver's chagrin). And the match programme features a photo of our merry bunch on the terraces at Aldershot, replete with comedy speech bubbles. I am saying to The Hack, "IT'LL BE A 'SHOT' IN THE ARM IF WE CAN WIN TODAY" and he is replying "IT WASN'T FUNNY THE FIRST TIME MATE".

Lovely stuff, although perhaps no need for the shouting. Annoyingly, it does mean I have to buy a programme, something I usually try not to do on the basis that you then have to spend the rest of your life moving them around. The Driver gets one for every game, and subsequently has shelves full of them, all neatly stacked in chronological order. When I stay with him, I'll sometimes surreptitiously swap a Mansfield '87 with a Rotherham '90 to see how long it takes him to notice.

He's keen to get going after the match, but I insist on queuing for a Wrexham ticket. They could post one, but I don't trust them not to fuck it up. With The Card at stake, I'd rather have it in my hand. Sprinting to the ticket office on the final whistle, I am in the front 10% of the queue. Half an hour later, I finally get served and have to give my address to a man with a hearing aid and a pint. He writes it down, then another man takes the payment and another one finally gives me the voucher.

The Driver is cheerily furious, but at least we've missed the traffic, and we spend the early part of the journey home overtaking coach after coach of Cherries, smarting from their 4-0 defeat. I don't seem to recall them bringing that many to Chester.

Finally restored to my own vehicle, I spend the last leg of the journey hallucinating wildly all over the motorway, like Matthew McConaughey in series one of *True Detective*. Nevertheless, I manage to make it home for *Match Of The Day*. Only a week to go until we stick it up The Goats.

Attendance: 1.590   Position: 15th ↑

Game 12 of 50 →

"We hate Crewe Alexandra/We hate Wrexham too — they're shit!/We hate Tranme-er Rovers/But Chester we love you.../All together now!"

It is one of the ancient rules of football support that you must hate the teams closest to you, hence the advent of the local derby. Presumably with some deep-rooted foundation in territorial pissings, when it comes to football, it is truly a case of hate thy neighbour. And we really do hate Wrexham. A mere 13 miles separates the clubs, and crucially that short distance straddles the border between England and Wales. There is also a perceived cultural difference, with the historic Roman city of Chester seen as a glamorous tourist destination blessed with designer shops, fancy restaurants and of course *Hollyoaks*, the shit soap opera. Conversely, Wrexham — aka Poundland — is the home of feral six-fingered bin-dippers, riddled with unemployment, misery and low-grade drug abuse. The truth is probably somewhere, or nowhere, in between, but suffice to say the two respective sets of fans rarely see eye to eye.

The hatred even appears to predate organised sport, as according to an ancient bylaw/urban myth, Welshmen are prohibited from entering Chester before the sun rises, and have to leave again before it sets. And technically, you are still allowed to shoot a Welshman on a Sunday inside the city walls, providing it's after midnight and with a crossbow.

That I have not seen, although I have seen many things in the cross-border derby. On my first ever visit to The Racecourse, a Wrexham fan impressively ran the entire length of the pitch wielding a Welsh flag before being robustly tackled by our goalkeeper. Over the years, insults, fists, bricks and seats have been thrown, the latter even commemorated in song: "There ain't no seats in the Border Stand/ Do Dah/Do Dah/There ain't no seats in the Border Stand/Do Dah Do Dah Dey/Chester ripped them out/Chester ripped them out/There ain't no seats in the Border Stand/Do Dah Do Dah Dey (repeat to fade)."

What this charming little ditty lacks in grammar, it gains in a tiny semblance of veracity. While the vast majority of seats are in fact still intact, one of the defining sounds of any visit to The Racecourse is the unmistakable crack of plastic, often followed by a hefty shard of red seat sailing over your head.

For as long as I've been watching the derby, and indeed for time immemorial, there has been an undercurrent of violence, to put it mildly. In 1985, a charity game between the two teams was arranged at our then home Sealand Road in order to raise money for victims of the recent Bradford fire. Grandly dubbed the Duke Of Westminster Cup, in honour of the club's patron, it was intended to be an annual event. Following a minute's silence, within seconds of kickoff rival fans invaded the pitch and kicked the living shit out of each other as guest player Mark Lawrenson looked on in concerned bemusement. Unsurprisingly, the Cup was never contested again.

The fixture often crops up in lists of 'World's Tastiest Derbies' along with the likes of Celtic v Rangers, Liverpool v Manchester United, Millwall v West Ham, Southampton v Portsmouth and Boca Juniors v River Plate. It's what Danny Dyer might describe as "proper naughty," despite the significantly smaller crowds. That said, in the 1970s the fixture once attracted a remarkable 19,000.

With both clubs languishing in non-league, and Wrexham's former international stadium now partially derelict, the attendance today will be barely a quarter of that. The fact that it's being broadcast live on BT Sport will also provide an easier option for a few stragglers, particularly among the Chester contingent who have to face the dreaded bubble.

Introduced when the reformed Chester FC were promoted to non-league's upper echelon, and hence resumed hostilities with Wrexham, the bubble — aka safe travel — fixture essentially involves compulsory designated transport. With no independent travel allowed, supporters have to go on official coaches, for which they have bought a voucher.

They are only issued with match tickets once safely inside the cordon at the other end, thus negating any chance of rival supporters meeting.

It's the only non-league fixture ever to have had these restrictions imposed upon it, and indeed this season sees it as the only bubble match remaining in British football.

With police outriders stopping the traffic and a helicopter hovering over the convoy, it's an operation that would be more suited to transporting murderers between prisons than taking twitchers and alers to a sparsely attended non-league football match. In the good old days, going to Wrexham would entail a 15-minute train journey. Or on one occasion when it got so lively that the police shut down Chester station, we simply jumped in a cab.

But these days, to add insult to injury, the coaches take an arduous route that even my satnav would reject as outlandish, taking well over an hour to get there. Throw in the obligatory early kickoff, and suffice to say, the bubble is a massive pain in the arse. Many fans choose to boycott it, some claiming that it infringes upon their civil liberties. I've done all of them so far, and this will be my fourth.

Awaking in unfamiliar surroundings at an obscenely early hour, I recognise the Chester double duvet cover. A unique item of merchandise, the club shop only sells single duvet covers, the suggestion being that it is a children's item. Unperturbed, The Driver bought two and had them professionally stitched together to create the Frankenstein's Duvet under which I have just slept. He brings me a tea in a McNally mug, adorned with the iconic photo of the late, great manager taken by our mutual friend Parky, for which he has never received a penny, much to his chagrin and our delight.

A rudimentary breakfast is served and then we are on the road, destination Deva, from where our prison coach will take us into the belly of the beast. If you miss the coach, you miss the match, hence the safety first approach. We're not the only football twats on the road at this vile time, and Warwick Services is teeming with Man United, including a pair of grown men that The Driver overhears having a discussion in the bogs about a Bobby Charlton teapot.

At 9am we drive past Wrexham, somewhat frustratingly. The Hack comes on the phone, his voice tinged with regret at having sacrificed the derby for something as trivial as his 10th wedding anniversary. Settling in at home to watch it on the box, he says he'll listen out for my traditional war cry of "Come on Blues, these are garbage!"

Pulling into the Deva car park, we are among the first to arrive, along with the CEO, with whom we have a brief chat. He seems mildly impressed at how far we've come, geographically at least. As has become a bubble tradition, we have a bacon sandwich and a cup of splosh, and give ourselves an unauthorised tour of the ground, reminiscing about certain goals and where we were stood when they went in.

The players haven't even left yet, and are gathered in the Blues Bar, looking relaxed as they wolf down beans on toast and peruse the racing pages. Classy midfielder Tom Shaw strolls outside and bids us a good morning.

"Stick it up the Goats, Tom," I say.

"Thank you," he replies.

On the coach, the atmosphere is muted, the novelty of the bubble having rapidly worn off since it was instigated. Where once people would sing and chant en route, it now has the air of a reluctant works outing. Seated across the aisle from us is a pair of old lags of The Driver's acquaintance, one of whom famously slept under a car during a pre-season tour of Scotland. Even as we leave the stadium car park, the coach is being filmed, which leads to a discussion about coach spotters, and subsequently an anecdote about train spotters, specifically concerning a renowned Chester hooligan walking up to one and giving him a porn mag in an attempt to cure him of his locomotive affliction.

The journey is tiresome as usual, wending into Wales, back into England, and back into Wales again. At one point we drive past Big Al's house. He's on a different coach, presumably seething, his natural match day state. Wrexham's massive floodlights eventually loom into view, and we are issued with tickets and funnelled into the archaic turnstiles by a phalanx of robocops. For the second season running, there is no alcohol on sale, the final kick in the teeth in a series of Draconian measures. Football without beer is good, but it's not right. Robbed of the basic human right to pour bottles of tepid fizzy piss into our gaping maws, we have no choice but to simply stand and watch the mediocre pre-match entertainment, replete with ear-splitting bilingual announcements. At one point, it all becomes too much for Big Al, who snaps: "There's no-one

Welsh here, you cunt!"

Disappointingly, Chester have opted for their yellow away kit instead of traditional blue, something that fucks me off no end. Wrexham versus Chester should always be red versus blue — the Red Dragon of Wales slayed by the Royal Blue of Deva. Anything else is a mockery. Even when we won here 2-0 it was in some ghastly purple kit, since consigned to history. You would never see Everton turn up at Liverpool in anything other than their correct colours, and vice versa. It is disrespectful to the fans, and makes us look like a two-bob outfit.

As usual, Wrexham's idiots are housed to our right, and mutual insults are hurled with a modicum of gusto. But with the smallest ever away following, and the life crushed out of us by the early start and monstrous travel arrangements, it's a pale shadow of previous meetings. The bulk of the ire is reserved for John Rooney, who left Chester in the summer to join Wrexham, despite intimating otherwise. This of course makes him a dirty little Judas shithouse and he receives a dog's abuse throughout, not least when he plants his studs into the chest of a former teammate, a challenge for which he is fortunate to only receive a yellow card.

It's one of the few incidents of note in an absolute shit sandwich of a game that must have viewers turning over to Man United v Leicester in their droves. With scarcely a shot on target in the entire 90 minutes, it dribbles towards a goalless conclusion, which is still infinitely better than losing here. Back on the coach, the dads and lads of Wrexham town line the streets to give us the traditional two-fingered send off, making something of a mockery of the bubble arrangements. And with no police outriders to be seen, mercifully our driver breaks ranks and gets us back in roughly a third of the time. He even allows lads to pile off on request, including at Chester Racecourse where a meeting is in full flow, with 20,000 people allowed to attend under their own free will and drink as much as they like.

On the way back south we overtake a coach full of Kettering Reds, presumably overjoyed at having seen their local team Manchester United win 4-1. Stafford Services is full of them, including a grown man in an Ibrahimovic replica shirt. He looks enviously at my £5 Chester smock, or it may have been disgust. Switching cars back at The Driver's village residence, I am dangerously tired and almost career into a Vauxhall Zafira outside Acton Town station. Twenty-five hours door-to-door for a 0-0 draw that was on the telly.

Attendance: 5,058 Position: 15th →←

Game 13 of 50 →

Despite a printout of the fixtures being clearly displayed in the kitchen since the start of the season, Her Indoors is off to Portugal with a load of mates from school. In fairness, the trip was booked BC (Before Card) but nevertheless presents a significant logistical problem: what to do with The Boy. He can't go with her, so he'll have to come with me. As a further spanner in the works, The Driver has refused to take me to the match, despite the fact that he is driving there and back on the day. It's not because he hates kids (he does) but due to work commitments on Saturday morning he cannot guarantee getting me there for kickoff, and is not prepared to risk sabotaging The Card: every match, every minute.

As such, I manufacture a Friday night stopover near Watford Gap, at the home of one of the aforementioned school friends of Her Indoors. With perfect synchronicity, they can drive to Luton Airport in the morning for a weekend of sunshine and talking, while I head north with The Boy to stick it up the Dover, a far more appealing prospect.

By the way, contrary to a common misconception, Watford Gap is nowhere near Watford in Hertfordshire. It's essentially a service station at junction 18 of the M1 in Northamptonshire, near the tiny village of Watford, hence the name. Effectively the Gateway to the North, as such I have relentlessly abused our hosts' generous hospitality over the years in order to pursue my monomaniacal football-based agenda.

To add further confusion, the husband does actually support Watford (in Hertfordshire). This manifests itself by him attending the occasional match, shouting at the telly, and having the club badge tattooed on his lower leg. Effectively treating his body like the door of a pub toilet, it's one of a swathe of sports-related inkings that includes Wigan Warriors, Northamptonshire County Cricket Club, Miami Dolphins, Detroit Redwings, and San Francisco Giants. He even has the name of a Bulgarian midfielder tattooed on his upper arm on the basis that he saw him have a good game at the USA World Cup in 1994. You couldn't make it up.

He frequently asks me why I don't have a Chester tattoo, and I have to repeatedly explain that I have no interest in permanently defacing my body via a painful process that I have to pay for. Furthermore, I remind him of the cautionary Dahl-esque tale of the Chester fan who had the club badge tattooed on his back many years ago. Over a number of sittings, a huge replica was inked into his skin, a perfect pair of seals frolicking above the CHESTER FC logo, pristine and ready to be unveiled for the forthcoming season. At which point the club changed its name to Chester City and completely redesigned the badge.

Hitting the M1 on Friday night, we arrive under cover of darkness, primarily because it's dark and their village has no streetlights, something that the residents are apparently particularly proud of. Northamptonshire's most tattooed man has already been kicked out of the house for bellowing at a rugby league match, and is forced to watch it in his adjoining man cave. A converted barn, it boasts a full-sized snooker table, plus pool table and dartboard, and is strewn with trophies, Watford tat, scrapbooks of England cricket tours, and all manner of sporting memorabilia. There is also an extensive A-Z of VHS movies, mainly from the 1980s, including the sheer decadence of two copies of *Tron*. I have told him about Netflix, but I don't think he was listening.

As I let myself in to the barn, it sounds like he is committing an act of self-asphyxiation. Charging up the stairs, I am mildly relieved to find him on his feet, pacing up and down while roaring at some perceived injustice on the screen. Helping myself to a beer, I sit down and watch the spectacle, while occasionally glancing at the match. At one point he gets so cross that he slaps his open palms on the windowsill while baying at the moon. If it's that important, I suggest that he could have actually gone to the match. There appear to be plenty of empty seats.

Some time later, back in the house, I manage to convince him to put on highlights of the Premier League Friday Night game, Everton v Crystal Palace. It's a turgid 1-1 draw, but after being subjected to hours of rugby league, it's like coming up for air. I don't really buy into the whole Beautiful Game shtick — football is a vile sport played and watched by vile people, myself included. But after the onslaught of egg-based brutality it suddenly seems imbued with an elegance and grace. As my son often says, "rugby is just putting people on the floor".

In the morning, The Boy is ready to go, in so much as he's openly sobbing at what his weekend holds. It's not the first time he's cried at the prospect of watching Chester. On the way home from school one Friday, I informed him of the following day's plans, at which point he burst into tears with the Costello-esque riposte, "I don't want to go to Braintree".

Strapping him into the car, I attempt to second-guess the satnav and we spend an age circling Tamworth, scene of an epic 4-3 win a few seasons ago. Finally locating the A41, we stop for petrol and marshmallows, and get to within four miles of Chester when the car inexplicably loses power. In a state of panic, I pull over and switch it on and off again, which seems to do the trick.

In the Blues Bar we share a table with a pair of rival fans in the form of a dad and his sullen teenage son, the latter of whom drags the former everywhere, including this hefty 271-mile journey. I sup up my beer and wish them good luck, although obviously I don't mean it.

This is not The Boy's Deva debut, having previously sat in the main stand, and indeed had his name read out at half-time, at which point, to his horror, I had to explain that there was now a break, and then another half of similar length. This is however his first visit to the McNally Terrace, standing up with the big boys. As such, I warn him that he may be subjected to concepts and language with which he is unfamiliar, and introduce him to Big Al, with whom he respectfully shakes hands.

You can normally tell from the opening minutes if this team are up for it, and there is no sign of a post-Wrexham hangover, with outbreaks of football all over the pitch. Seven minutes into the match, The Driver nonchalantly strolls in, still suited and booted from spending the morning teaching a dead language to privileged children from the Home Counties.

As we're playing well, most of the action is up the other end of the pitch, proving a test of The Boy's concentration, which is flimsy at the best of times. After the initial flurry of excitement, including high-fiving Lupus the Wolf, ennui begins to set in. "I'm bored," he informs everyone, not for the last time, as I shove another marshmallow into his face. He then swings perilously on a crush barrier and I make it clear that I will not sacrifice the game in order to take him to hospital.

Somehow it's goalless at half-time, and The Driver makes his traditional rounds, pressing the flesh with a cross section of the crowd like a visiting dignitary. Meanwhile, I placate the child with Haribo (and myself with a nice pie). The timing could scarcely have been better. As the sugar hits his brain, Chester hit two goals in the space of a minute. A third follows — a penalty — then a fourth and a fifth, all right in front of us, the home end by now in a state of giddy delirium and near incredulity. There's something happening here. The Boy loves it, grinning like a mule and bouncing up and down uncontrollably. As each goal goes in, he gets tossed into the air, a well-rehearsed indoor celebration now getting a rare live outing.

It finishes 5-0. At the end, an old-timer ruffles his hair.

"It's not always like this," says the auld fella.

"He can come again," says his mate.

The car eats up the motorway as the Ryder Cup unravels on the radio. In the back, a small boy in a replica shirt sings, "Stick it up the Dover..."

Attendance: 1,686 Position: 12th ↑

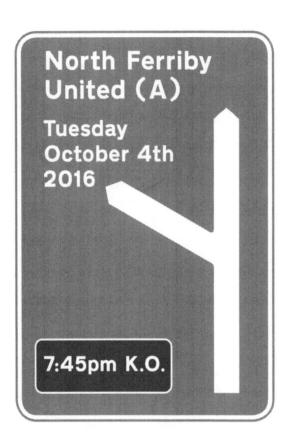

North Ferriby
United (A)

Tuesday
October 4th
2016

7:45pm K.O.

Game 14 of 50 →

Barely 48 hours after leaving Watford Gap, I'm here again, the man with The Card in his eyes. I only really left so that The Boy could attend school, apparently a legal requirement. He's there now, but I won't be picking him up. Having spent weeks grooming the Yummy Mummies of NW10, I have convinced one of them that I have important business in the North, and she has agreed to look after the child. His mother is making her way back from Portugal, having been burgled of everything she took within minutes of arriving at the villa, yet another reason not to go on holiday. The decent thing to do would be to meet her at Luton Airport with sympathy and a lift. Admittedly, I do feel a twinge of guilt as I drive past it, but I don't set the fixtures and I don't make the rules.

Strategically arriving in early afternoon, The Watford Gap has recorded the Wrexham v Chester game for me, and I put my feet up in the barn and watch the entire fucking thing as live. Robbed of the tension of not knowing the outcome, it makes for even grimmer viewing, but I still find myself shouting at the screen. I am mildly impressed at Tom Shaw screaming, "That's a fucking penalty" when it clearly wasn't, and even more astonished that Rooney was allowed to stay on the pitch. The build-up is arguably more interesting than the action, and Big Al appears so many times that he should consider getting himself an agent. The Driver and I also get our fair share of screen time, stood front and centre like a pair of polyester-clad buffoons.

Conveniently, he has Tuesday afternoons off, and arrives on cue to pick me up. As we leave, I jokingly ask The Watford Gap if he wants to come. It's a huge mistake as he starts listing the things he has to do instead. With no end in sight, we simply drive off and leave him

talking on his doorstep. The M1 takes us to the A46, through Lin-
colnshire, where cabbages grow and no motorways go. The flatlands
are largely uninspiring, and the outstanding feature of the county is
that it is the epicentre of the coleslaw industry.

The Humber Bridge looms large, with the bargain fee of £1.50
offering a panoramic view of Hull and its impressive sporting stadia.
Long since dropped from the tour, instead we turn left for the village
of North Ferriby, the entire population of which could comfortably
fit into our stadium. The team has nevertheless played at Wembley,
and even won there, memorably beating Wrexham on penalties in the
FA Trophy, something that we take great pleasure in reminding them
about. Incidentally, South Ferriby is the other side of the estuary. It's
even smaller, and has no football club.

The Driver has memorised a free parking spot from a previous visit,
and we take a stroll down a doggers' lane that gives us a decent view
of the bridge and the estuary. With dusk creeping in, it feels like we're
a long way from home. Pausing to applaud the arrival of the team
coach, we find the only pub in the village, a large mock Tudor affair
called The Duke Of Cumberland, where a few elderly Chester fans are
dotted about having a scoff. After wolfing down some rudimentary
pub fare, we are joined at our table by a pair of familiar faces, namely
Chas, Club Historian and Statistician (and prolific TV extra), along
with Rick, the *Chester Standard* photographer, who always manages
to get a snap of The Driver's gurning visage. As is their wont, Chas
'n' Rick have spent the afternoon geocaching. I'm not entirely sure
what that is, and I don't want to ask, but I imagine it be somewhere
between dogging and an adult version of *Pokémon Go*.

Kickoff approaches, and we get in the ground in time to have a
scoop in the club bar. A hardcore of Chester Youth have made the
trek, including Four Cards who we spoke to at Aldershot. As I have
my elbows on the bar, he proffers a couple of quid and asks if I can get
him a Carlsberg. I tell him to put his money away — the poor prick
hasn't missed a game in four years. In fact, the last one was here. The
least I can do is buy him a pint of piss, especially at northern prices.

At the other end of the scale, a pair of old-timers survey the scene
like Waldorf and Statler from *The Muppets*. They were old when
everyone else was still young, and while he almost certainly doesn't

know it, one of them was immortalized in print in a fanzine I used to write for in the early '90s. There was a section called 'The Man Behind Me Said', and the man in question was quoted due to his outrage at Darlington when he discovered that it was "A pound for a pie! A pound!" A pound!

Our away form has been shocking, and as the players come out I encourage them to "pretend it's a home game," which gets a laugh from on-loan midfielder Ryan Lloyd. Assuming position behind the goal that we're attacking, I am intrigued by a wire gate behind us with a steward guarding it. Further inspection reveals that it leads to an allotment, and I'm uncertain whether the steward is there to stop people getting into the match or to safeguard the rhubarb from those already here.

This is North Ferriby United's first season in The National League, and it's fair to say that they haven't immediately adapted to the higher level. In fact they have scored a grand total of one goal in their previous eight games, which is *Ripping Yarns* territory. The surroundings are equally substandard, and this is probably how people who have never been to a non-league match imagine one to be. The sparse crowd is so stereotypical that they could almost be extras in some shit Sky comedy, only needing the obligatory one man and his dog to complete the scene.

The Driver can't relax until I have bellowed "Come on Blues, these are garbage!" but the atmosphere is so intimate that it would feel like shouting it at a funeral. And we're wearing yellow. Instead, I half-heartedly mutter it as the game gets underway. The players have no such reservations, however, and after we are awarded an early free kick, their keeper yells "Fucking switch on!"

"Language, Watson!" I reprimand him. "Children here."

To his credit, he holds his hand up by way of apology.

The usual suspects are milling around, and appear to be more interested in the railway line that runs close to the ground, with The Train Driver routinely identifying the 185 each time it cuts through the darkness, and reminding us, uninvited, that he is qualified to operate it. Despite their lowly position, Ferriby are all over us like flies on shit and we are fortunate to get to half-time goalless. Changing ends, the Chester fans group together in an attempt to instil some atmosphere, but no breakthrough is forthcoming. Ferriby have a man sent off for a second yellow, and we make a concerted push for a winner. It doesn't look like it's going to come, and you never really believe that it will. But with 15 minutes left, suddenly James Akintunde is bearing down on goal. He slips his shot past the despairing dive of Rory Watson, there's a split second of uncertainty, but it's in, it's a goal, it's an actual fucking goal in the actual fucking net. There's an absolute bounce, and in the midst of it someone lets off a smoke bomb, with plumes of thick blue mustard gas enveloping the away end. It's technically more of smoke pellet, barely an indoor firework, but an off-duty Chester steward marches over demanding justice, and claims that the club will face a points deduction. He is given short shrift, and the celebrations continue to the final whistle and beyond as we hold on for our first away win of the season. Whisper it softly, but we are tenth in the league.

Perhaps dizzied by the result, I splash out on a reduced-price bag of out-of-date North Ferriby-branded sweets to take home for The Boy as appreciation of his understanding at this difficult time. Back in the car, an M1 closure is a kick in the balls, and it is well past the witching hour when we reach Watford Gap. The Driver fucks off immediately, but I stay for a drink, rapidly rendering myself too tired to drive home. After a vat of red wine and a couple of episodes of *Bullseye*, I pass out in a child's bed. I've been to Hull and back.

Attendance: 476 Position: 10th ↑

Game 15 of 50 →

This is the return of The Park. The one and only Parky, aka Sydney Blue, is back in Blighty for a three-match tour. Just as things are looking up, this is all we need. Chester's most pessimistic fan, he is a bitter, bitter man, who routinely refers to his own club as Dog Shit FC. Nevertheless, he plays a significant part in the story: no Parky, no Driver, no Card.

It was late 1997 when I first encountered this happy-go-lucky character, at a party to which I wasn't invited. One of the major manufacturers of fizzy lager (either Carlsberg or Carling) had organised a football-themed do at Dingwalls in Camden, and I blagged my way in with some employees of the short-lived *Goal* magazine, which I penned the occasional tale for, and with whom I had recently been to Rome to see England qualify for the '98 World Cup with a 0-0 draw against Italy. Incidentally, that was a match that saw me sprint onto the pitch at the final whistle — sporting a photographer's bib and borrowed camera — to shake hands with David Batty and buff Ian Wright's sweaty head. That, as they say, is another story, and indeed one that appeared in the magazine.

Coming at the arse-end of Britpop, other guests at the party included two of The Boo Radleys, with whom I had an animated chat about a mutual musical acquaintance whose group I once saw them support in Chester, and who they informed me was now dead, having committed suicide while in prison for matricide. There may also have been someone there from Shed Seven, and probably Howard Marks. That made sense. What didn't make sense was seeing a random Chester fan bowling about, unmistakably recognisable from his shiny pate and hangdog demeanour.

Seeing Chester fans out of context in Chester itself was a rare and bewildering experience; spotting one at some wanky media do in Camden Town was unheard of, and required further investigation. Parky — for it was he — presumably felt the same, as a mutual nod became a chat, and it transpired that he worked on *Match Of The Day* magazine and lived in Wimbledon. What I didn't know at the time was that he had been at school with The Driver, who he would later introduce me to, and who would go on to spend a significant chunk of his life touring me round the country while breathing in my fetid arse gas. By the way, I should probably also mention that it was at the same party that I met the mother of my child. And as a footnote, Parky, a Real Aler by default, won a year's supply of lager.

Having emigrated to Australia, we believe in order to avoid a parking fine, he has been back to The Deva since, appearing for the fake relegation game in 2014, when macabre circumstances saw us go down in the last five minutes of the final match, only to be reprieved some six weeks later when Hereford United went out of business, news that saw me performing Mick Channon windmills round my back garden.

Despite the geographical chasm, Parky remains as attached to the club as ever, having replica shirts shipped over, getting daily snippets online, and lying in bed listening to live commentary on headphones in the dead of night, mainly so that he can phone me up the next day to tell me how crap we were. He even managed to get a question asked at a meet-the-manager event in London, inquiring from the other side of the world as to why Rooney should be allowed to take corners given his inability to get the ball above knee height.

Sat in The Bouverie Arms with his tonsorially converse friend, Curly, it's like he's never been away, and the piss-taking begins almost immediately. News of The Card has spread Down Under, and he can't believe that I'm allowed to get away with it with a young child under my charge. Whereas most people offered heartfelt congratulation, as soon as my son was born, Parky gleefully pointed out that my life was now ruined and that football would be but a distant memory. This was of course his own experience, with fatherhood reducing him to a handful of appearances per season. So rare were they that whenever he was allowed to attend a game he styled it as Parky's Big

Day Out. The biggest of all of these big days out came at Gillingham one season when he attempted to keep pace with a regular aler, and ended up spewing and shitting on a South Eastern train, eventually having to be led home by the hand by then fellow Wimbledon resident APJ. He still blames the bottle of lager that I bought him at half-time. Lost 2-0.

Perhaps with this is in mind, he has been cautiously sipping some dank brew while watching Tranmere v Wrexham, live on the pub TV. Apparently, a Chester fan had earlier addressed the screen, and asked of Rooney, "Is it wrong for me to want him to die?" All things considered, it probably is, despite him fucking us over to join our deadly rivals, and taking substandard corners when he was with us. Later on, a few Wrexham fans returning from defeat at Tranmere make it into Chester city centre, having, according to the police, got off at the wrong stop. A couple of very drunk ones even make it into the Torquay end without the aid of a bubble. Thanks for the donation.

Today's opponents give Parky the perfect opportunity to regale us with one of approximately eight stories that he recites on heavy rotation. In the 1984/85 season, long before I knew these pricks, struggling Torquay were managed by former Chelsea defender David Webb, and so threadbare was their squad that he squeezed himself into a pair of shorts and named himself on the bench at the age of 38. Bear in mind that this was a man who had scored the winner in the 1970 FA Cup Final replay, and had latterly been working as a salesman. Guess the rest. With the game goalless, he brought himself on, and with minutes left on the clock found himself in our half with the ball at his feet. Unable to run, he instead attempted an audacious lob, which of course sailed into the net for the winner, his last ever goal. This sent Parky into such a tailspin that on the way home he apocryphally attempted to throw himself off Chester's Grosvenor Bridge, and had to be restrained by The Driver.

Where I live in fashionable North West London, a nearby tyre shop has a faded photo in the window of the 1975/76 Queens Park Rangers squad: front left, seated, one Dave Webb. I always stop to look at it. Staring back at me, little does he know that in nine years time he'll be making a bald man cry.

The current Torquay outfit are in similarly dire straits, and player-manager Kevin Nicholson has had to drive the team up to Chester on a minibus, a mere 250 miles. The Driver takes us the final mile, but not before Parky is recognised and subsequently abused in the street by some alers spilling out of a weird new pub called the Goat & Munch, basically someone's front room with a few barrels in it. In the more civilised confines of the Blues Bar, Curly's sister, sadness in her eyes, says to me, "I hear you're doing The Card. Congratulations, or commiserations..."

The game gets underway, and as is his wont, Parky spends much of it identifying every player's footwear. This is man who can pretty much tell you who wore what make of boot and in what season. He is also obsessed with kits, and describes our keeper's flamboyant garb as "Electric Salmon".

Torquay are largely the better side, but in the 26th minute our tricky winger Craig Mahon is felled in the area. Penalty! Durrell steps up. Saved! Lloyd on the rebound. Scores! With nine minutes to go, the 36-year-old Torquay manager brings himself on. Surely history can't repeat itself — that would finish Parky off. With seconds left and Torquay in the ascendance, he picks up the ball... and takes a foul throw. Full time 1-0, astonishingly our seventh consecutive clean sheet. Of course, Parky isn't happy as he feels that we could have easily not won, despite the fact that we did. His long-standing recipe for a good day out involves a couple of pints, a hint of trouble, and a cheeky win. Two out of three ain't bad.

Leaving Parky and Curly to catch up with some old faces in the Blues Bar, The Driver and I hit the Bache chippy and I eat a fish the size of my lower arm. With uninspiring commentary of England v Malta on the radio, I lapse into unconsciousness. Bucking awake, I am disappointed to discover that we are only at Stafford. By the time I drive past Wembley, it has emptied of 82,000 England fans, presumably buoyant at having thrashed Malta 2-0. Fuck that shit.

Attendance: 2,201 Position: 11th ↓

Southport (A)

**Saturday
October 15th
2016**

FA Cup
Fourth
Qualifying
Round

3pm K.O.

Game 16 of 50 →

We've never won the FA Cup, and in all probability we never will win the FA Cup. Yet every year we all shit the bed when the FA Cup comes around. And rightly so. A decent FA Cup run can galvanise the team and the supporters, as well as earning the club a few quid, crucial at this level. More importantly, it's an absolute tear-up. Fans you haven't seen for years come out of the woodwork, the draw is televised, sometimes the games are televised, and you get to visit grounds that you don't normally see, all accompanied by the obligatory hint of trouble.

The furthest Chester have got on my watch was a Fourth Round replay in 1987 against Sheffield Wednesday at Hillsborough in front of more than 20,000, the culmination of a seven-match cup run in the days when teams simply kept playing replays until somebody won. In the Third Round that year we memorably came from behind to win 2-1 at a snowbound Wrexham, with Gary 'Psycho' Bennett scoring twice with an orange ball. If pressed, it may well be my favourite ever game.

That same season, we had a run to the semi-finals of the Freight Rover Trophy, which still represents the closest I have ever come to getting to Wembley, only three years into my tenure. In total, we played 16 cup games that term, so if you were doing The Card it would have represented an extra third of a season. There is a man who actually did do The Card that season, the venerable Wainwright, arch druid of Real Alers, who once reprimanded The Driver for having a Tetley's at Doncaster. Wainwright also produced the sorely missed fanzine, *The Onion Bag*, a surrealist slice of humour that included such regular features as 'Great Doodled Goals' and

'Scored Against The Wrexham.' As far as I know, Wainwright also first coined the phrase 'doing The Card' and has now done a total of four. He'll doubtless be here today, as despite the lack of any real history, Southport v Chester is something of a local derby, in geographical terms at least.

It's not so handy for us southern pricks, and The Driver has already ruled himself out. No one said it was going to be easy, nobody said it had to be fair. Another avenue has opened up though, bearing in mind that the match represents the second instalment of Parky's trilogy, potentially his *Empire Strikes Back* moment. He is staying with his brother near Warwick, but I do have options in the form of his mate Curly, an arrogant prick who lives in the South and drives a Porsche. Not my words, the words of his best friend, Parky. Two of these attributes are extremely useful to me, and we spent much of the previous match haranguing him about making it to this match, emphasising that it's the FA Cup and that if he has any shred of decency there's nowhere else he should be. Three days before Southport, he finally relents, telling me to be at St Albans station at 8:30am, where he'll either be in a silver Audi or a blue Porsche.

I think we both know it'll be the latter, and true to form he pulls up in a five-year-old's fantasy and sets the controls for the heart of Warwickshire. I've never really had a hard-on for cars, at least not since puberty, viewing them as little more than an extremely dangerous way of getting from a house to a stadium. This is clearly a superior vehicle, however, sticking to the road like shit to a blanket and drawing looks from law-abiding motorists as we leave them in our wake. Curly occasionally presses what appears to be a turbo button, giving us an extra boost of speed. I'm quietly impressed, and he's quietly impressed that I'm impressed.

The Porsche eats up the road, and we convene with Parky in good time, snatching him from the bosom of his family, some of whom take great delight in mocking our convoluted trip. Yeah bye, have a great day sitting round the house while we seek glory in the North. Sadly, the expensive Porsche only has two seats, so we have to switch to Parky's cheap and cheerful hire car for the next leg.

Having initially dismissed it as Cup Fever, I am in the grip of a filthy cold, and by the time we get to Southport, snot is simply pouring out of my face like an open tap. I throw pints at it to no avail while we enjoy a champion luncheon in a nearby pub, girding myself with a nice bit of fish. Cup Fever does eventually kick in on the walk to the ground and I am riddled with nerves, despite our exceptional form and Southport's lowly position. As a further twist, they are now managed by our former boss Steve Burr, who I spoke to on the phone in the build-up to the match as part of my debut article in *The Non-League Paper*, going for a Master v Servant angle as he pits his wits against his former assistant Jon McCarthy for the first time. McCarthy didn't answer his phone.

Haig Avenue is swarming with Chester, and we make up roughly half the crowd. We've simply got to stick it up The Sandgrounders, bearing in mind that victory will get us into the First Round Proper of the FA Cup and hence the chance of a tasty draw. And of course if you get to the Third Round there's the chance of a massive payday against a Premier League club to take the edge off the patronising coverage and inevitable humiliation.

That all appears a long way off though, as we come out of the traps like a three-legged whippet, a pale shadow of our recent league form, as reflected in the dismal atmosphere. Southport are scarcely any better, but after half an hour one of their players has a long-range dip that bounces off a defender's arse and into the gaping net, bringing to an end 700 minutes without conceding a goal, and giving them a half-time lead.

The facilities are woefully inadequate for a crowd this size, and all food appears to be long gone. This doesn't deter one enterprising Chester fan who takes heed of a Domino's Pizza advert, dials the number on his mobile, and orders a meat feast to be delivered to the away terrace gate, which promptly turns up in the second half. Another fan convinces a steward to let him out in search of chippy, and is never seen again.

He doesn't miss a great deal, as while we huff and puff, there appears to be no way back, and that familiar frustrated feeling returns, replete with a tight chest and churning stomach. We do have the odd shot, one of which threatens to interfere with another match being played behind the stadium. Depressingly, it finishes 1-0, and the FA Cup dream is over before it really began. While it is scant consolation, in terms of The Card it could be considered a kindness, and I certainly wouldn't have relished a Tuesday night replay.

The mood in the car is bleak and after stopping at a garage to buy a bag full of cold and flu treatments, I spend the entire journey self-medicating. Apropos of nothing, Parky informs us that he has never once had a shit in a football ground, or indeed at school. Curly pretends to be asleep. The hire car is considerably more comfortable than the Porsche, and I do actually pass out, yet again bucking awake at Stafford. Thoughts turn to a previous FA Cup game at Stafford Rangers when the traffic was so bad that people simply abandoned their vehicles and marched across the fields, with the official supporters' coach arriving deep into the second half. At least we won that day.

Astonishingly, Parky only charges us a fiver each for petrol, arguably the high point of the entire day. Back in the Porsche, the inbuilt satnav informs us that the M40 is closed and reroutes us to the M1, past The Watford Gap, who is probably shouting at the telly. Without Parky as a buffer, chat is sparse, and I simply stare into the rainy blackness while battling the torrent of mucus pouring from my head. On talkSPORT, there's an extensive and utterly mind numbing interview with Gary Neville in which he literally goes through his diary and explains what he's going to be doing on what date, at what time, and where. At one point I consider opening the door and throwing myself onto the hard shoulder, Card or no Card.

When we eventually reach St Albans, a Saturday night is in full swing, with people eating, drinking, chatting and laughing. Losers. Curly generously waives the fee, and drops me at the station, where it becomes evident that I am reeling from a cocktail of meds. A weird redneck fancy dress party is taking place, but they pay little heed to the spluttering man in a smock. I peruse the tourist information, finding myself drawn to a leaflet advertising a nuclear bunker in Essex, replete with mushroom cloud.

Waiting on the southbound platform, I raid the vending machine for a Lucozade and a Bounty, in the vain hope that the fruit will help my cold. On the northbound Thameslink, an all-female 40th birthday party is in transit, and they appear to be pointing and laughing at me. I somehow make it home for the second game of

Match Of The Day and tuck into a fish pie with a gin and tonic and Lemsip chaser. Four trains, two cars, no goals. Fuck the Cup. Let's concentrate on the league.

Attendance: 1,674

Game 17 of 50 →

He's finally flipped. Still haunted by a minor half-term delay on the way to Stockport two years ago, The Driver has insisted on an 8am start at Ardley, and will not budge. As such, I leave my house under cover of darkness, navigating to Willesden Green Tube station by moonlight. Trains have barely started running, and the only other people around are teams of Polish builders — lazy bastards — and a man asleep on a skateboard. From there I take the Starlight Express to the scenic suburb of Hillingdon, where the M40 meets the M25 and all hope dies. The Hack is waiting in his car, having presumably left Sussex half an hour before he went to bed. A minor Tube delay has thrown the schedule into turmoil, and one of us has to break the news to The Driver that we're running slightly late. He appears to take it well, and takes himself off to Cherwell Valley Services for a frothy coffee. In fairness, we could probably get to New York for 3pm.

He's not angry, just disappointed, whereas I'm sulking at having to get up in the middle of the night. Wedging my head between the backseat headrest and the left rear door, I put on an eye mask and attempt to resume my night's sleep, all the while my phone buzzing with wickets as England collapse in Bangladesh. Drifting into unconsciousness, I hear The Hack predict a bottom-six finish despite being currently in touching distance of the play-offs, followed by an unfamiliar adult conversation about restaurants or holidays.

Bucking awake to the harmonic sounds of the new Teenage Fanclub CD, peeling the eye mask from my face I discover that we are entering Derbyshire. It is not yet 10am. I could still be in bed and comfortably make the game. We take a built-in pit stop at an anonymous service station, and I spend my entire allotted time in a cubicle, birthing a particularly combative stool to the cacophonous accompaniment of a wall of Dyson Airplane V hand dryers versus an ersatz cover version of *Paved Over Paradise*. I genuinely don't know where I am. Outside we spot an absolute ringer for Zimbabwe President Robert Mugabe, replete with military uniform and a chest full of medals.

"Mansfield North has fallen," observes The Hack, solemnly.

The Driver's predicted Trafficageddon has yet to materialise, although there is a warning of 'ANIMALS IN ROAD' near the Rotherham turnoff. Some mild congestion on the A1(M) almost has him reaching for the atlas, but he holds his nerve and delivers us into York city centre for midday, where we immediately spot Wainwright and The Colonel, already deep into a pub crawl, the former back in his university town.

Spotting a decent looking pub adjacent to some traffic lights, The Hack and I make the split second decision to jump out of the car, leaving The Driver to park up by the ground, a good mile or so away. Fuck him.

It's a vast sprawling boozer with all human requirements available, so we find a room showing Bournemouth v Tottenham and order a full English breakfast. I wash it down with a weird hybrid ale, which is a mistake. In due course, we find ourselves squeezed into the corner by an ever-increasing cross-generational gaggle of northern women, evidently regrouping after the previous night's revelry, with tales of nightclubs and taxi ranks impressively interspersed by pints and vodkas. Some girls are bigger than others; some girls' mothers are bigger than other girls' mothers. The Driver eventually joins us and we see out the Premier League match, an absolutely turgid 0-0 of no interest whatsoever, and certainly not worth getting out of bed for.

Parky is holed up in a pub ahead of his final match before returning Down Under, so we stroll through the city, bathed in autumnal sunshine and teeming with tourists. Drinking in the splendour, we are interrupted by the unmistakable sound of garden furniture hitting a solid surface. As veterans of multiple England tours, it is instantly recognisable, and we instinctively head for the source. True to form, we turn a corner to see a pub forecourt alive with flying chairs, overseen by baffled Japanese tourists who perhaps mistake it for impromptu street theatre.

Chester's finest are in evidence, including our top boy, who is face to face with what appears to be their top boy, the latter flanked by a pair of weasely baseball-headed underlings.

"You called it on, then ran off," accuses our top boy, perhaps channelling Weller in *The Eton Rifles*: "Loaded the guns then you run off home for your tea/Left me standing like a naughty schoolboy."

What follows is less lyrical.

"Knobhead."

"You knobhead."

"You and me, now."

With the sound of police sirens growing louder, Grandad, Chester's oldest hooligan and evidently director of operations, advises, "The job's done. We move".

Melting into the crowd like Keyser Söze, our top boy suddenly displays a hitherto uncultivated interest in Roman brass rubbings. It's good to explore the more cultural aspects.

Parky has had a couple of pints and is thrilled to hear about the hint of trouble, just needing a cheeky win to complete the fêted triumvirate. It's a formula that he came up with at Rochdale one year, when all three fell into place, the day only sullied when he later dropped me off on the side of the M1, eight miles from where I needed to be. He also slightly ruined his own day when he missed a goal as he had gone to buy a Topic.

Approaching the ground, it's my first visit to Bootham Crescent, a proper old school stadium flanked by terraced streets. There are Chester here, Chester there, Chester every-fucking-where. One seasoned York fan offers us hope when he proclaims the home side to be the "worst City team in 64 years, got beat 6-1 b' Gizlee," thus ensuring that Guiseley will forever be known as Gizlee.

Turkeying for another pint, we duck into what appears to be a working men's club. Basically a room full of heavy-duty trellis tables with a bar, it's like the Miners' Strike never ended, a snapshot of another century. It could be a scene from *This Is England*, including the beer prices, and for once I am happy to buy a round.

The away turnstiles are teeming, and one particularly officious female steward is having an animated argument with a Chester fan, accusing him of being on drugs, simply because he is frothing at the mouth and has lost control of his limbs. Bearing in mind that I am legally drunk, I tactically switch queues to avoid any Card-threatening intervention. Safely in, we're on an open terrace behind the goal, a mass throng of Chester, and indeed a bigger turnout than at Wrexham, the cross-border derby temporarily supplanted by the Roman derby: Eboracum versus Deva.

Everybody and his wife seems to have made a weekend of it, York being one of the few places on the tour that you can realistically take your family to. As a rule of thumb, if it's got a cathedral or is by the sea, you're OK, although the jury is still out on Dover. All kinds of faces are in, and I'm fairly certain that I spot my older brother's mate, Ben, who came with us to my first ever gig, The Damned at Chester Northgate Arena. But it's testament to the size of the crowd that I don't see him again.

After all the driving, eating, drinking, fighting and shouting, there is of course a game of association football to watch, and it's a zinger, with Chester threatening to put their cup disappointment behind them and continue their rampant league form. York give as good as they get, buoyed by the reinstatement of former manager Gary Mills, freshly sacked by Wrexham, which of course earns him a dog's abuse, including one Chester fan bellowing: "Return to barracks, Agent Mills, your mission is complete!"

Goalless at half time, Chester pile on the pressure, but in the 70th minute a York corner is headed onto the line, and apparently over. It's the first league goal we've conceded since the 3rd September, when I was still living in a tent. Undeterred, and roared on by the febrile away following, Chester swarm forward. Durrell free kick — post! More pressure. And Richards must score — post! It's exhaustingly exhilarating to watch, but still they come forward. As the game creeps into injury time, Parky announces that he is going to stand at the back. Minutes later, Lloyd crosses, glancing header from Richards — it's in! Absolute fucking bedlam. Some people celebrate by rabbit-punching stewards, whereas I instinctively run to the front and call their keeper a cunt. The Driver and The Hack are lost in the mosh pit. It feels like I'm having an aneurysm, but this is what you live for. This is the hit that the addict craves. But where's Parky?! He's halfway down the road, having snuck out early to beat the traffic, mistaking the roar for a second York goal.

The realisation that he wasn't there for the equaliser is the icing on the cake, and prompts a double celebration. Ten thousand miles and he's missed the highlight of the season to save five minutes on the road. It's not beyond the realms of possibility that he may never see another Chester goal. Still, he did get back to that family do in Chester notionally earlier than he may otherwise have. Apparently nobody noticed.

Attendance: 2,639   Position: 12th ↓

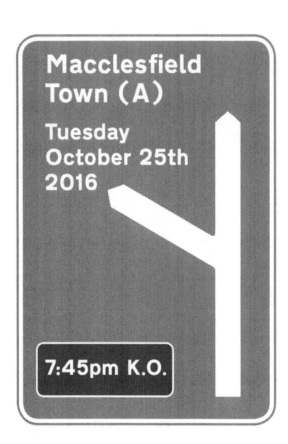

Macclesfield Town (A)

Tuesday October 25th 2016

7:45pm K.O.

Game 18 of 50 →

My three most visited grounds: 1) Deva Stadium, Chester. 2) Sealand Road, Chester. 3) Moss Rose, Macclesfield.

Why? Homelessness. Not me, but the club. For two seasons between 1990 and 1992, following the sale of Sealand Road and before the completion of The Deva, Chester City was a club without a stadium, something of a prerequisite for football. A number of ground-sharing options were looked at, with Wrexham, Crewe and Tranmere summarily dismissed along with more geographically outlandish suggestions.

Step forward non-league Macclesfield Town, who nobody had ever heard of until we played them in the FA Cup the previous season. While technically in the same county, it was — and still is — 45 miles away by country road. With public transport proving even more prohibitive, the club would lay on a convoy of double-decker buses, turning Saturdays into a football-themed version of *Wacky Races*. Prior to the advent of satnav, nobody really knew the best way to get there, and it was not uncommon to see another car full of Chester fans coming the opposite way down the road.

Understandably, attendances plummeted, reaching a nadir against Bury in the Leyland DAF, watched by a mere 409 paying customers. Sadly, I wasn't among them, but I believe members of the 409 Club still meet up to commemorate that inconsequential 2-0 victory. Miraculously though, the late Harry McNally kept us in Division Three alongside the likes of Stoke, Swansea, Huddersfield, West Brom, Birmingham, Fulham and Hull, all of whom were presumably horrified to turn up at this tinpot ground.

Obviously it was shit at the time, but in retrospect there were some great memories, mainly of standing behind the dugout and listening to McNally growling at his charges. If you were brave enough you could even beat on the roof and demand a substitution, which was sometimes forthcoming, although on one occasion he turned around and terrifyingly roared, "What do you know?"

Moss Rose is now transformed, and these days we go to Macc as equals, at best. I drove there on my own last season, and did something morbid that I'd been meaning to do for the best part of three decades. I first became aware of Joy Division by taping John Peel's *Festive Fifty* every Christmas, initially baffled by this austere yet spellbinding music. It seems inconceivable that something so otherworldly could come from such humdrum surroundings as Macclesfield, yet somehow it's entirely appropriate. 77 Barton Street — where Ian Curtis lived and tragically died — is an unassuming terraced house, and when I drove past it there was an estate agent's sign offering 'VIEWING BY APPOINTMENT', an even more morbid option. From there I drove to Macclesfield Cemetery, wandered around aimlessly, gave up, then suddenly spotted the memorial, took a picture, felt weird, got back in the car and went to the match.

It's a more orthodox build-up this season, the year of The Card. Meet The Driver at Ardley. Switch cars. Have inane conversation. Slag off Parky for missing a goal at York. Slag off Parky in general. Listen to radio. Listen to a selection of The Driver's CD's. By extreme fortune, The Driver and I have broadly similar music tastes, crucial when spending six hours in the car. Imagine spending 15 years sat next to a Sons Of Mumford fan. You'd throw yourself into the road.

There is a slight deviation to today's schedule, however. Due to the labyrinthine mysteries of Cheshire we are meeting The Driver Senior in a hitherto unheard of village called Wistaston on the outskirts of Crewe, who we hate, although it's been so long since we played them that we have to remind ourselves of the fact. The Rising Sun is our destination, and we're barely out of the car when The Driver and father embark on a lengthy, animated and detailed discussion of local roadworks.

Inside, the barman clocks the Chester FC smock.

"Chester Football Club," he reads out loud, "We don't get many of them in here."

"I'm from Chester myself," he continues.

"I'm a Liverpool fan to be fair," he ends.

"How original," I judge.

For no discernible reason I drink something called IPA, which is mainly unpleasant. The Driver and I each order a cheap meal, much to the barman's chagrin, who tries to shame us by describing it as the pensioner's deal. Meanwhile the pensioner has a vast fish platter, which he duly demolishes.

To get to Macc, we have to drive through Crewe, and it is no exaggeration to say that every single street we go down has a chippy on it. What a plaice. As ever, The Driver has erred on the side of caution and we are the first people at the ground apart from Chester midfielder Tom Shaw, who tells us that he's fit to play but uncertain if he's in the team.

The Driver has pre-ordered a ticket to save two quid, but can't pick it up until 6pm. I haven't, but have missed the 5pm cut-off by minutes. Denise in the office will not budge on the price — the computer genuinely says no — but does print me out a full-price ticket. I'm naturally furious, but a Card in the hand is worth two quid in your arse pocket. Following the transaction, we wander unfettered around the innards of Moss Rose. What access.

There's a perfectly good pub next to the ground, but The Driver insists on schlepping halfway down the hill to The Railway Inn as it's in The Good Pub Guide, the weighty tome by which true alers swear. Not of course to be confused with The Good Beer Guide, although there is presumably some crossover.

To the untrained eye, it's not even a good pub. In fact, it's more like someone's house, specifically a hobbit's, that is if they had pool tables in Middle-earth. We eventually track down the landlord, who appears to have been getting high on his own supply, and sip a pair of frothing pints of mead by a crackling log fire. Apart from the combatants in a seemingly endless game of pool, we are the only customers. Eventually a Macc fan turns up and sinks pints on his own, staring into middle distance. A pool player eventually asks us who's going to win. The Macc fan says Macc, the Chester fans say Chester, we all say we'd take a point and move on.

With nothing to say to each other, The Driver asks the landlord if he can make sport come on the telly. The landlord in turn asks me if I can draw the curtains in case a representative of Sky happens to walk past. He then fiddles with an unfamiliar black box until Scottish football highlights appear. The picture intermittently freezes for a few seconds and the entire pub appears to stop in unison like a prototype mannequin challenge. Pints remain untouched, pool balls unstruck, the silence only breached by the crackle of the fire.

On the stroke of 6pm, The Driver jogs up the hill to claim his ticket, still scarred by an incident a few seasons ago when he and Big Al missed a sizeable chunk of the game due to Macclesfield Town's policy of having one person to feed tickets to the 500. They humiliated themselves further when they both leapt on goalscorer Gareth Seddon for an extended celebration, all three locked together in man love, blissfully unaware that the goal had been ruled out for offside and the game had restarted.

There are no such ticket woes this time round, and he returns triumphant, celebrating with a cold pie after the landlord mistook his mild interest for an obligation to purchase. Following more mead, as tradition dictates we bid the Macc fan good luck after tonight's match, which is reciprocated, and march to the top of the hill again. Moss Rose under lights, a big away following, there's magic in the air. Someone even unveils a shiny new flag proclaiming Hobson Magnifico, in tribute to the departed striker's magnificent injury time winner the previous season.

Tom Shaw is indeed in the team in the absence of captain Luke George who has mystifyingly picked up an eight-match ban for biting an opponent in the opening game of the season at Gateshead. It's a baffling development as nothing was mentioned at the time and there is no evidence that the offence took place. Indeed the ban is later reduced to six matches on appeal, which makes little sense as either he did it or he didn't.

Elsewhere, we have a debutant in goal in the shape of Alex Lynch, who once played in an FA Cup Third Round tie for Wycombe Wanderers against Aston Villa, live on the box. It's game that I watched in La Fontaine, Aldershot — Britain's Worst Pub — oblivious to the fact that the floppy-haired young buck between the sticks would one day go on to greatness. He has his work cut out tonight, as Macc bombard us, hitting the post not once, not twice, but thrice. It finishes

0-0, a decent point, but for the sake of a cunt hair, a flea's eyelash and a Rizla paper, it could have easily been a 3-0 thrashing. A truly preposterous sport.

All the way back I am wracked with the fear that I have left my car lights on, envisioning sitting at Ardley waiting for the RAC, or spending the night at Cherwell Valley Services with tea-making facilities and basic Freeview. The tension mounts as we turn the corner to find the car shrouded in darkness, which I interpret as meaning that I either imagined the whole thing or that the battery is dead. In the event, neither scenario is true. I did leave my lights on, but due to ruthlessly efficient German engineering, they turned themselves off.

I almost punch the air in celebration, gratefully dismiss The Driver, and hit the M40 with renewed gusto. Even listening to *The Sports Bar* on talkSPORT cannot dampen my mood, despite a perfunctory phone-in about people doing runners. I am about to switch over when a caller grabs my attention with the story of how he and his mates once had to rapidly leave a campsite due to an indiscretion. Returning back heavily refreshed one night, they spotted a railway sleeper, which they decided to mindlessly throw down a mineshaft. Unbeknownst to them, it was attached to a chain, which was in turn attached to a live goat, something they only realised when they fleetingly saw its startled expression as it disappeared into the blackness. Bucking with laughter, I can barely see, and it's as much as I can do to keep the car on the road. Take a point, move on.

Attendance: 1,922   Position: 12th →←

Game 19 of 50 →

Now this is a test, both on and off the pitch. The selfish prick has gone house hunting in France and not even left me his season ticket. The train is prohibitively expensive, and The Hack isn't up for a car share. Looks like me, myself and I then. All the same, with The Card at stake, a door-to-door trip is inadvisable so I tactically invite myself to stay at Watford Gap. With the family waving me off on Friday night, it feels like going on another tour of duty, and I promise that I'll make it home safely: Daddy's on The Card, it doesn't mean that he doesn't love you.

In the car in time to listen to live commentary of Queens Park Rangers versus Brentford, it's a fixture that I could comfortably walk to. Indeed, Her Indoors has previously asked why I don't just support QPR. It's a perfectly logical question. After all, whenever I feel like looking at caged animals I don't drive 200 miles to Chester Zoo. I simply go to the nearest one, in Regent's Park. But supporting a football club has never been about logic otherwise nobody would do it.

And I wouldn't be tearing up the M1 on my own on a Friday night at 100 miles per hour listening to increasingly crackly commentary of a meaningless football match: ultimately, they're all meaningless. I finally lose reception at Billing Aquadrome, a place better imagined than visited as I discovered to my cost some years ago.

As ever, The Watford Gap is pleased to receive me, and the evening follows a familiar pattern of drinking alcohol while bellowing at televised sport. The key is to drink enough to ease the passage into unconsciousness but not so much that I render myself incapable of operating heavy machinery in the morning. I seem to strike the right balance and am up and about to watch more televised sport in the kitchen with my breakfast. I also have a chat with a visiting builder who coincidentally used to go and watch Lincoln City but has now lost touch with them, something that seems almost unfathomable.

Yet again the M6 proves unfit for purpose as a viable thoroughfare, so I take a random non-Driver approved route. With time on my side, I ease in like a cruise ship, even stopping on the A51 to enjoy a petrol station meal deal while watching a cow slowly lift its tail and empty its load. An omen, perhaps?

Unusually, I don't even bother with a pint, simply taking my place on the terrace with a nod to all and sundry, followed by the obligatory "Come on Blues, these are garbage!" even though they're third in the table. With a decent following from Lincoln, for once the away end is open and there is almost the feel of a proper football match, as reflected in the biggest home crowd of the season so far.

It is one of the great Parky-isms that we always fuck it up in the big games, and relatively speaking, this is a big game. If we are remotely serious about competing in this league we have got to be sticking it up the likes of these. Amazingly, that seems to be exactly what we're trying to do, even having the temerity to take the lead. It doesn't last long, but then we do it again, and it lasts even less long, with Lincoln equalising in stoppage time to go into the break 2-2, thus ensuring that my half-time pie is not as nice. At least I make it to half-time, unlike one hapless Lincoln fan, who has already been thrown out. No Card for him.

With The Driver lost in France, there is a marginally different dynamic in our section of the home end and I find myself stood perilously close to The Strangler. Before he acquired the nickname he was mainly known for wandering around with a transistor radio and headphones, relaying arbitrary scores to nobody in particular: "Arbroath still goalless". Then one August day in 1999, at home to Rochdale, something snapped. Referee Chris Foy sent off a Chester defender for a second bookable offence, a decision that resulted in an irate Chester supporter invading the pitch and dragging the official to the ground by the neck. I wasn't there, but The Driver witnessed it and had to admit to his dad, who was making a rare appearance, that he actually knew the assailant.

Chris Foy went on to become an established Premier League referee, whereas The Strangler served a three-year ban. He would still travel to matches, but simply remain in the pub while the game was on. You quite possibly couldn't make it up. The Driver once gave him a lift from Telford's Warehouse to The Deva — as he sat behind me, I feared the icy grip of his fingers round my neck. Thankfully, he is now a reformed character, his interaction with referees going no further than persistent demands for a "booking," pronounced "boo-king."

Three minutes into the second half, Lincoln take the lead. As ever, it is sickening to see the entire away end erupt with joy as three sides of the ground remain in mute despair, almost in denial at what they have witnessed. With ten minutes to go, they make it safe with a fourth, and for good measure, leather in a fifth.

Back in the car, I now face a 200-mile drive on my own, having agreed to attend a friend's birthday party in Shepherd's Bush. Numb from the result, there is very little to ease my pain, although I do at least have free reign of the radio. The Driver usually insists on listening to 606 on 5Live, whereby a witless cavalcade of angry men phone in with one-eyed views of the day's action and are summarily dismissed by Robbie Savage, Wrexham's answer to Oscar Wilde. It can be entertaining in small bursts, but can also make you question the future of the human race.

Instead I opt for live commentary of Crystal Palace versus Liverpool. It's an absolute humdinger, focusing my mind and detracting from the fact that I am hurtling through space in a metal box and that one minor misjudgement could result in instant death. I only passed my driving test about ten years ago, primarily because I had to get to a tricky midweek fixture at Salisbury. Before then I spent decades on the trains, ritually shoving a baguette into my maw at Crewe Station. Even in the early stages of The Driver era, he would pick me up and drop me off at Oxford, with midweek games becoming a nerve-racking race against time to make the last train at 12:22am, or else face the mysterious Oxford Tube. Remarkably, I never missed it, although we never got there with more than five minutes to spare. Someone, somewhere must have done The Card on public transport, and they have my full respect.

Palace v Liverpool finishes 4-2 to the Scousers. This takes me past the physical and psychological barrier of Birmingham, a vast sprawling metropolis plonked in the middle of the country that I have been through several hundred times more than I have been to. Angry music eases me down the M1 and back to the bosom of my family. It's a quick turnaround, and minutes later I'm in a cab that goes directly past QPR's ground, Loftus Road, 24 hours after their game finished.

I am late to the party, and set about playing catch-up in earnest. In attendance are one Crystal Palace fan and at least four Liverpool fans, including the birthday boy, none of whom have been to the match that I have just listened to. Perhaps it's me that's doing it wrong. Indeed, when I tell people where I've been, what I've done, and what I plan to do, they look at me with a mixture of confusion, pity and disgust.

Back in a cab in the early hours, it finally sinks in that we have been dicked 5-2 at home. It feels like a turning point. But it's also a foothold in The Card, as with no involvement in the FA Cup, I now have two weeks off to reflect. Winter is coming.

Attendance: 2,586 Position: 12th →←

Tranmere Rovers (A)

Saturday
November 12th
2016

3pm K.O.

Game 20 of 50 →

The Driver cannot guarantee getting me to Prenton Park for kickoff and suggests that I make alternative arrangements with The Hack. These arrangements lead to me standing outside Hillingdon Tube station in the pissing rain on a Saturday morning with a Club Wembley-induced hangover, having been given a ticket for England v Scotland the night before. The 3-0 home win represented my first live football match in 13 days, a period that also included my first Saturday at home since July. Naturally I made the most of that precious day in the bosom of my family by watching televised football and seething at all the clubs who made it to the first round of the FA Cup.

Elsewhere during my time in the wilderness, I squeezed into the smock for an appearance on a live television channel called FANTV. Sharing the sofa with a fellow Chester fan to preview the Tranmere game, we both optimistically predicted a 1-1 draw. There was also some chat about doing The Card, an explanation of The Driver's ersatz double duvet cover, and a nonsensical quiz in which I deliberately misidentified Kim Kardashian as recently deceased Dead Or Alive singer Pete Burns.

Back to Hillingdon and I have been standing here so long listening to Aphex Twin that allied to the roar of the motorway and the driving rain, I briefly consider that I may have discovered a new type of 3D ambient music. There's a burst of Card-oriented panic when The Hack's arrival time comes and goes but I hold my nerve and the silver Audi looms into view. The M40 is closed due to a crash and the M25 is closed due to a crash; it's like the apocalypse is taking place in our rear view mirror.

Not feeling at my absolute best, chat is perfunctory and largely traffic-related. The Hack tells me that he has recently interviewed Graham Taylor, his go-to football personality for a quote. Apparently, Taylor revealed that one of his pet hates is people using their mobile phones in restaurants, something that he and his wife Rita find immensely annoying.

On the way up I receive a phone call from the manager of Half Man Half Biscuit. I pitched a half-arsed idea to *The Non-League Paper* about interviewing lead singer and lifelong Tranmere fan Nigel Blackwell about the former Championship club's fall from grace and subsequent adjustment to non-league football. But as I am informed, it's not going to happen for the dual reasons that he cannot be located and is not interested in doing interviews.

I did manage to snare a rare interview with him years ago and felt obliged to ask about the near-mythical occasion when the group were invited to appear on Channel 4's Friday night music show, *The Tube*. Famously, they refused as it clashed with a Tranmere home game, even turning down the offer of a helicopter from the Newcastle studio.

This is what Nigel said: "We were happy to do the thing at first, naturally, but then I realised it would involve missing the match which I didn't really feel comfortable about so the offer was amicably declined. To be honest, it was no big deal as far as I was concerned — I used to watch *Crossroads* anyway — but the show's producer was seemingly 'impressed by our priorities' and the story proceeded to interest, albeit mildly, some of the newspapers. I reckon if we had waived the opportunity in order to watch a much bigger club then the whole thing would have been forgotten come the next set of traffic lights and I suppose I should slightly resent the somewhat patronising stance some people take whenever the thing's mentioned. There is nothing twee or quaint about supporting your local team! I don't follow Tranmere for their 'perrenial underdog' status, what absolute rot that idea is. I follow them because they're the team my father and his father watched, because they were the nearest club! Indeed it possibly may have been more satisfying to have been brought up in Salford or Walton but we've had our moments — like all clubs — so I can't complain. And anyway it did garner some unexpected publicity for the band, which irrespective of our nonplussed attitude at the time, helped to sell some copies of our record. They did genuinely offer the helicopter but it would only have got us to the ground at half-time and not being ones for a fuss we weren't particularly sold on the idea of what may have been perceived as the antics of 'Big Time Charlies'. The perhaps surprising, though pleasant, footnote to it all is that we won the game — against Scunthorpe Utd — with what in those days was a fairly desperate side."

Presumably not quite as desperate as the one that fell out of the league two season ago — to cheers in the Blues Bar — thus enabling them to resume hostilities with The Mighty Chester for the first time in a generation. And it always was fairly hostile, not least when I was once chased to Rock Ferry station by a knife-wielding youth. The good old days...

Hopefully there will be no repeat of that today, as I'm not as quick as I used to be, and we're in the car. Ably deputising for The Driver, to his credit The Hack gets us there in good time, but slightly sullies it by driving around Birkenhead for 20 minutes looking for a free parking space. Nevertheless, we make it into Tranmere's bespoke marquee for a solid 90 minutes of pre-match, giving me a decent run at the München lager while he sups something out of a keg.

The marquee is a fantastic idea, with fans of both clubs milling about with no suggestion of windmilling in. There is meat and drink for all, and the music is exemplary, with Ramones, Bunnymen, Mondays and Roses blaring out like an indie disco meets Oktoberfest. It almost makes me nostalgic for the North West — the natural home of football and music — and at one point I even find myself questioning my compulsory hatred of Tranmere.

At one end of the tent is a huge wall of scarves, a tribute to late manager Johnny King, and we lurk there to avoid any unnecessary conversations with over-opinionated Chester fans. A man comes over handing out leaflets about banning *The Sun* newspaper because of its despicable coverage of the Hillsborough disaster. Spotting the Chester smock, he asks if he can take a photo of me holding one and I am happy to oblige. I tell him that a kid from my school died there, and surprise myself at how upset simply saying it makes me feel.

Half an hour before kickoff, The Driver strolls in with a shit-eating grin and a synopsis of traffic updates. Impressed by the set-up, he sinks a pint and we head for the away turnstiles in an atmosphere of civilised conviviality. Turning the corner we walk straight into the police escort of Chester fans, and it suddenly feels like a proper spite-filled football match. We are not few, we are legion, with the best part of 1,200 Chester in attendance, occupying a large stand behind the goal.

There's a bar underneath and The Driver is playing catch-up, insisting on a double round of pissy bottled lager even though it's five to three. Heading for the action, we are stopped in our tracks by the traditional Remembrance Day tribute, and I spend the entirety of an impeccably observed minute's silence trapped on the steps staring at the crease in the back of the head of the man in front. Less than 20 hours earlier, I was trapped outside the door at Club Wembley as a bugler played a baleful lament, which was about as exciting as it got.

Watched by almost 8,000 fans in the best stadium in the league, this is very much a big game, and we very much look like fucking it up, conceding a brace of scrappy goals around the half-hour mark. With half-time approaching, thanks to the excess lager, my bladder is at breaking point, and I hover near the steps desperately hoping for the whistle. The stand is in a constant state of unrest and a shaven-headed steward gets all up in my grill, repeatedly barking, "Kanye fanda sheet? Kanye fanda sheet?"

I can find a seat, thank you, but it might involve pissing down my leg. With a player down injured, I make the gamble of running to the bogs, unleashing a torrent of warm lager into the urinal before sprinting back in time to see Kane Richards crash the ball against the underside of the bar. Technically I have missed some of the action and may have to get a ruling from the elders as to whether The Card is still intact. Mercifully, the general consensus seems to be that as long as you're in the ground you can do what you like. Nevertheless, Wainwright warns me of the many pitfalls ahead, still banging on about the five replays that he had to endure during one of his Card seasons.

The second half kicks off and the atmosphere is hugely toxic. At one point a little Chester scrote calls one of our players, James Alabi, a "black cunt". The Driver, who hears it, is rightly incensed. This is clearly unacceptable, and an incongruous throwback to the good-old bad-old days. Chester may paint itself as a nice place, but in the early '80s the home end at Sealand Road was a despicable hotbed of racism, with monkey noises and vile language routinely directed at visiting players. In 1985 we signed the mercurial midfielder Milton Graham, and on his home debut, a veteran racist thug — and friend of The Murderer — made a defining keynote address. Turning to face the home end, with fist aloft he warned, "We've got one now. The next one to give it 'ooh ooh' gets this". Not exactly Martin Luther King, but it had the desired effect.

Back to the action and a deft Tom Shaw header quickly makes it 2-1. It's on for young and old. A Tranmere player goes down looking for a penalty. He's dived! Second yellow — he's off! Throughout his walk of shame, Tom Shaw follows him closely, repeatedly shouting "FUCK OFF!" directly into his face. It's one of the greatest things I've seen on a football pitch.

Enjoying a man advantage, Chester pour forward, roared on by a febrile following. With five minutes of injury time announced, gargantuan defender Ryan Astles is summoned forward like a Titan. The ball is launched into the box, he swings his left wand at it, and fuck my life it nestles into the bottom corner. There's a split second of incredulity followed by sheer abandon. I unleash a primal roar, The Driver takes a punch in the face, while Big Al and The Hack practically consummate their relationship. People are rolling down the aisles and tumbling over seats with glee. Absolute scenes.

Heading south in convoy, we don't want the day to end. Reconvening in The Fox and Hounds at Ardley for a pint, we spontaneously order sirloin steaks all round, forever known as the Ryan Astles Steak. What a man. What a day.

Attendance: 7,790   Position: 12th →←

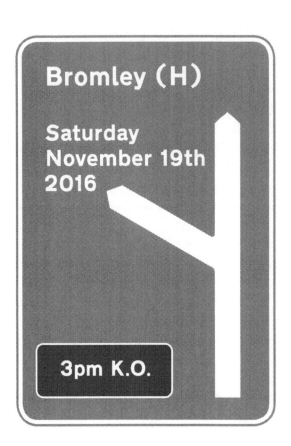

Game 21 of 50 →

Following the euphoria of Tranmere, there was a minor bombshell in the week when assistant manager Ian Sharps promptly announced that he was leaving to start a better job at Walsall. It's easy to say in retrospect, but he did look slightly sheepish when we saw him outside Prenton Park after the game. In other post-Tranmere news, reports that a Chester fan suffered a fatal heart attack proved unfounded, whereas reports that a pair of Tranmere fans in the hospitality area glassed each other proved true. Lovely stuff.

Bromley at home should hopefully provoke no such incidents. But while it's not exactly a fixture to get the blood racing, they all count towards The Card. You can't pick and choose, that's the point. Opening the blinds in the morning like *The Prisoner*, the moon is still out and there's a hint of frost on the lawn. We are now well out of the sun-kissed foothills of The Card and deep into the climb, albeit with the distant summit still shrouded in cloud and mystery.

And so the ritual begins. Blue pants, blue socks, blue T-shirt, blue jeans, blue trainers and, of course, blue smock. Yes I know it makes absolutely no difference to how well a football team will play several hours hence, but I still do it, almost self-mockingly as opposed to through genuine superstition, which is in itself a contradiction. Perhaps it provides me with a psychological shield for the travails ahead; perhaps I've just got a lot of blue clothes, the sartorial equivalent of Picasso's blue period, if three decades longer.

Bowling into the kitchen, a vision in polyester, there's some rare football chat on Radio 4, which stops me from immediately switching to 6 Music as convention dictates. Adrian Chiles is talking to Cyrille Regis about a testimonial game of black players against white players, which astonishingly actually took place at West Brom in 1979. Six years later, I saw Regis score five goals for Coventry against Chester in a League Cup tie at Highfield Road that finished 7-2. At one point, the scoreboard read: 'REGIS 5 CHESTER 2'. A decade later, he finished his career at Chester, scoring seven goals in the entire season, one of which I missed as I got to Orient late, something that I regret to this day.

Some thoughts there, as I get in the car and hit auto-pilot for another *Groundhog Day*, albeit one where absolutely anything could happen, within the confines of the rules of football. That said, I was once at Salisbury away when a parachutist landed on the pitch during open play. Footage is available, to prove I didn't imagine it.

The Driver is marginally late as he's had to iron his laces, but the journey is textbook, passing Walsall's Bescot Stadium on the right for the umpteenth time, with some special words reserved for our departing assistant manager. He made the usual noises in the week about opportunities and travelling distances when, like every single person to ever move jobs in football, what he really meant was "they offered me more money so I said yes". And why not? Players and managers are not fans — it's strictly business.

Delivering us into Chester's fair city with hours to spare, we hit The Bouverie Arms to watch Manchester United v Arsenal on the big screen. I feel slightly uncomfortable ordering a ciabatta, a request that would have been greeted with bafflement and ridicule when the pub was a smoke-filled hovel in the 1980s. Free Wi-Fi would also have caused some confusion, but progress can be a good thing, and this enables me to watch the day's real football story on my phone. While Arsenal grab a late equaliser at Old Trafford, Lincoln come from 2-0 down to win 3-2 at Forest Green, a huge result at the top of the table.

In the Blues Bar, I am mobbed by readers of *The Non-League Paper*, which this week published the first instalment of *The Card Trilogy*, essentially my manifesto statement and précis of the season so far. Well, one person casually mentions it, but nevertheless the article gives the quest something of an official status and spurs me on for the winter ahead. The piece also inspires a reader to write in with the story of a Weston-Super-Mare supporter who has completed

26 consecutive Cards, the majority of them on public transport. Additionally, he has attended every under-18s game over a similar period. As the email said, "There can't be a better football supporter anywhere in the world." Not for me, Jeff.

Winter is already here. The big coat is on, along with scarf, hat and optional gloves, the staple protection for the next three months at least. Grim as it is, astonishingly some people manage to get through the British winter without the distraction of football, seemingly oblivious to the fact that the sporting calendar is the only thing that makes living in this godforsaken country bearable. To quote myself: "Without football, there is only weather."

Compared to the massed ranks of Lincoln fans for the previous home game, the Bromley contingent appears to have come on a skateboard and consequently the atmosphere is more Russ Abbot than Joy Division. Despite being born in Chester — and allegedly going to my school — you never see Abbot at a game. Although when we were bottom of the league the Sealand Road DJ, presumably with his tongue firmly in his cheek, used to play Abbot's top ten hit, *Atmosphere*, with its catchy refrain, "Oh what an atmosphere! I love a party with a happy atmosphere..."

None of those things are in evidence here, particularly when Bromley take a first-half lead following a farcical defensive mix-up. It's a dismal affair, but the second half is a minor improvement with Chester attacking the McNally End. Penalty! Emphatically dispatched by Shaw for the equaliser, it's greeted by relieved applause all round, with the exception of one large-coated man who sprints down the steps and attempts to join the players' celebration. It's not quite my Strangler moment, but I'm not sure what comes over me, perhaps an attempt to inject some excitement into an otherwise dreary day. In the event, I manage to get a glancing glove on Shaw before buffing Alabi's head.

The game finishes 1-1, very much a case of After The Lord Mayor's Show compared to the euphoria of Tranmere, although both results earn a point. Afterwards, we sneak into the Legends Lounge above the Blues Bar, mainly so that The Driver can help himself to one of the discarded programmes left by an uninterested corporate guest. I bump into my fellow sofa sitter from FANTV who, it transpires, is some kind of brain doctor. His brother asks how The Card is going. Word is spreading: we're halfway through November and we've still got a man on The Card. As we leave, APJ slaps me on the back and grins, "Only 26 games to go…" I reserve my reply until we're outside.

On the way home we overtake a coach with its destination alternately flashing between 'MERRY CHRISTMAS' and 'HAPPY NEW YEAR'. This fills me with disgust, contempt and horror. At Ardley, I pay The Driver and take a piss on my onside rear wheel, which you are legally allowed to do. Driving through Storm Angus at breakneck speed, I sing along to the new Half Man Half Biscuit compilation CD. It's by far the highlight of the entire day.

Attendance: 1,827 Position: 12th →←

Game 22 of 50 →

Back-to-back home games is a massive kick in the balls, particularly at this time of year. It hardly seems worth coming home. If it wasn't for other responsibilities, and basic human decency, we could just live in the car for three days: Saturday night tear-up, a bit of Sunday lunch with the football on the box, look round the shops Monday, then you're into the pre-match on Tuesday. I'm joking of course, although we did used to talk about doing The Card in a camper van with me and Parky on words and pictures, and The Driver on driving duty, perhaps teaching a bit of Latin in the week. Unsurprisingly it never got any further than that.

Instead I cash in yet another childcare favour and set the controls for the heart of Ardley, arrival time 2:30pm. This is later revised to 3pm, which is of little use to me as I'm already on the M40. With time in hand, I treat myself to a cultural tour of Ardley-with-Fewcott. This essentially involves driving to the other pub, where we once celebrated promotion in the reformed Chester FC's debut season, and then turning round to resume my original parking space, stealing Wi-Fi from The Woman With The Dogs. I sit there for an age, listening to The National in the rain like a great big indie fop, albeit draped in a polyester smock.

The Driver eventually rocks up at 3:20pm, claiming to have been adjudicating an exam. Pathetic. I am beyond caring and simply want this over with, particularly as I am flying to Stockholm the next day on other business. Naturally I would have turned it down had it jeopardised The Card, but it's a one-night trip and I should be safely back for the weekend, unless I die in a plane crash, in which case The Card is off.

There was a time when I left the country on a more frequent basis, something that proved a stern test of my football loyalties, which often took priority. On one occasion I was booked to fly to New York on the Saturday to interview Tiger Woods on the Monday. So of course I changed the flight to Sunday so I could take in an away game at Stockport. After all, what is an all-expenses paid Saturday night in the Big Apple compared to a trip to Edgeley Park? Drew 0-0. Similarly, I gave up a night in Florida for a 2-0 defeat at Leyton Orient, flying out on my own the next day to baffled looks when I explained why I was 24 hours late. The list goes on, including missing a Saturday night in Los Angeles for a game that I can't even recall, although it seemed important at the time. Do I regret it? Absolutely, I regret it. Would I do it again? Almost certainly.

The A41 at night takes on an exotic sheen, almost Vegas-like, with the Newcott Chippy lit up like a palace of glittering delights. Straight to the Blues Bar, I get the round in while The Driver talks to his fan club who demand to know when he set off, how long it took, and what route he took, every single match. Arguably his keenest admirer is a man known only as Six Hours In The Car, a nickname he earned after a defeat at Dagenham one year when he berated the players by shouting "Six hours in the car for this!" while operating an invisible and hugely oversized steering wheel. He is friends with a bald postman that he calls Gandhi, who in turn calls him Frank Sidebottom. Fuck knows what they call us; they probably think we're in a civil partnership. And when The Driver is gone, does his band of nutters fall under my jurisdiction?

By the time I return from the bar, he has filled them in on the details, including my stab at The Card and pending trip to Sweden. An elderly gentleman of their acquaintance has read about the former, and also enthuses about the latter, instantly recommending a Stockholm nightclub called *Le Chat Noir*. By recommending, I mean graphically describing the activities that take place in there.

I thank him for his advice and take my place on the terrace in time to keep The Card intact. Having knocked us out of the FA Cup, former manager Steve Burr is back at The Deva for the first time since his sacking. He's one of a handful of Chester managers that I have actually met, pressing the flesh when he came down to London for a meet-the-manager evening prior to our fixture at Dover the next day. Taking place in the upstairs room of an East London pub — with butties laid on — it ended in mild farce when Burr's taxi to Dover sprang a puncture before departing, resulting in him coming back for another pint of lager, the bulk of which he gave to me when his driver summoned him, having changed the tyre.

For that act alone, I bear him no malice, but following a spate of draws we could really do with a win here, so if his team could just roll over that would be most helpful. It seems to be going to plan when a brace of headed goals sees us somewhat fortunate to hit the half-time break 2-0 up. Fuck knows what Burr says to his charges at the interval but they come out refreshed, pinning us back and leathering in a long-ranger on the hour mark to halve the deficit. Approaching ten minutes to go, they twat another one in from distance to equalise and send their paltry following into paroxysms of joy. They have done to us what we did to Tranmere ten days ago: football giveth and football taketh away. Worryingly, we have now gone seven games without a win.

As an extra kick in the balls, the M40 is closed and I am forced to take a diversion as mapped out by a series of sporadic and largely indistinguishable hieroglyphics. Gambling that the lorry in front is going to London, I lock on to its taillights, following it through sinister Oxfordshire villages on a moonless night. This is no way to live.

> **Attendance: 1,752 Position: 12th** →←

Eastleigh (A)

Saturday
November 26th
2016

3pm K.O.

Game 23 of 50 →

Beastly Eastleigh. The Boy hates them. On his only prior visit, he burst into tears at 3-0 down, with a full meltdown only averted by a couple of late consolation goals. He also made his home debut against them in a Haribo-assisted 1-0 defeat. He's in the car this morning, along with Her Indoors. The plan is that I drive to Eastleigh, get out, and then they take the car to my old dear's in Bournemouth, to where I get a lift with my younger brother after the game. It's an elegant solution that means they don't have to sit through the match, and I get to enjoy limitless drinking.

However, on the M3, to everyone's surprise Her Indoors has a sudden Damascene change of heart, perhaps lured by the thrill of a new ground or simply unable to be apart from me and my smock for even a few short hours. Either way, she is now responsible for the post-match driving, thus enabling me to still enjoy limitless drinking. This begins in The Cricketer's Arms near the ground, where there is already a smattering of Chester, including the *Crime Watch* kid, who it transpires is a junior darts champion.

With all manner of meal deals in place, they are practically giving away food and drink, and with The Boy lost to the iPad, we trough down on vast burgers and chips. The Hack and Wife roll up and do the same, followed eventually by The Driver, who has done a morning's work. Despite not qualifying for a two-for-one meal he somehow manages to ponce a free pint of swill, with British Lager Time now but a distant memory. Throw in free parking, and The Hack formally declares this as the template for future visits, presuming both clubs are still in the same league. He nevertheless maintains that Eastleigh is the worst day out in non-league, despite its relative proximity to his house.

It's certainly one of the trickier destinations on the tour, accessible via a country road that flanks a field full of horses. Situated mere walking distance from Southampton Airport, it's arguably easier to get to by air. As such, a number of Chester's finest have taken this option, flying from Manchester for as little as £60, with some of them even staying on for a double-header of Southampton v Everton the next day. The Hack and Wife are doing the same, as, perversely, she supports Southampton despite being from Portsmouth. They will however be spending Saturday night at a New Forest retreat as opposed to enjoying a lager-fuelled frenzy on the streets of Southampton.

As well as being in the arse end of nowhere, the ground itself is an absolute disgrace, a hotchpotch of portacabins and scaffolding. It's like a football match staged on the set of series one of *Auf Wiedersehen, Pet*. And this despite Eastleigh being one of the wealthier clubs in the league, with a huge squad assembled at vast expense thanks to a moneybags owner. Amid the squalor of the stadium is a brand new electronic scoreboard, which allegedly cost more than our entire team. We are not expected to unduly trouble it today, as Eastleigh are one of the favourites for promotion and we have never got anything here.

The usual faces are in evidence, including The Colonel, who commends me on my recent article in *The Non-League Paper*. We're pretty sure he's never been a real colonel, although it has taken me a couple of decades to realise that he bears a passing resemblance to Colonel Sanders of Kentucky Fried Chicken fame, which may provide the origins of his given title.

Chas, Club Historian and Statistician, has also read the piece, but while impressed at my commitment he has a technical query that threatens to throw the entire venture into doubt. It's a question that has challenged mankind throughout the ages: should The Card include the Cheshire Senior Cup? Chas says 'yes' on the basis that it is technically a first team competition. I say 'no' on the basis that I'm fucked if I'm driving 400 miles on a Tuesday night to watch the reserves play in front of 300 people. It's food for thought however, and if Chas is right then The Driver has been living a lie for almost three decades. We get a second opinion from Four Cards, who claims that a traditional Card is League, FA Cup and FA Trophy, albeit with the caveat that all of his Cards have included the Senior Cup.

An acquaintance of his, who has heard of my attempt at The Card, shakes my hand and congratulates me on my efforts. He says that he lives ten minutes away from The Deva, but finds it a pain to go.

One man who must literally find it a pain to go is The Curious Case Of Benjamin Button, who hobbles into the away end on crutches. I only catch half the story but it appears that he woke up in Brixton with a broken hip and no recollection of how he got there. Curiously it's not even the first lower body related injury that he has flaunted at an away game. He famously got hit by a car outside Cambridge United's Abbey Stadium prior to a league match. Despite openly bleeding, he heroically hauled himself into the ground, watched the game and then admitted himself to hospital. You possibly couldn't make it up.

The gang's all here, the players are present and correct, let the game commence. Eastleigh's expensively assembled team threatens to overrun us, but we gain a foothold in the match and even venture forward. A well-worked move sees the ball drilled into the box, Richards gets on the end of it, and shit the bed we've only gone and taken the lead. The reaction is more shock than elation, but it's a decent bounce and we enjoy it while we can. The presumption is that we've woken the beast, but we manage to make it to half-time intact.

I immediately head for a beer, which is served from a mobile bar at one end of a hastily erected mini-marquee behind the away terrace. I don't need it, I don't particularly want it, and there isn't really time to enjoy it, as unlike almost every other sport, at football you're not allowed to drink alcohol within view of the pitch, a despicable piece of utterly biased legislation. As such, I hastily pour a pint of fizzy muck into my face on the basis that if I'm not driving I may as well be comfortably over the limit. Meanwhile, The Boy's half-time treat is a Mars Bar courtesy of The Hack's wife, something that results in him running around like a lunatic for the next half hour.

On the pitch we are slightly more circumspect, frustrating the home team and looking to pick them off on the break. On one such occasion, Richards is clattered and the ref points to the spot. Gathering behind the goal for the penalty, it's saved, but an almighty scramble ensues and it's eventually stabbed over the line for 2-0, something that the expensive scoreboard fails to acknowledge for a good few minutes, earning the obligatory ironic cheers when it eventually does so.

My younger brother, who is there with a random Cherry and child, starts a chant of "2-0 in your building site!" which gets some traction. By way of response, a handful of Eastleigh schoolchildren embark on an extended routine that involves singing, "Let's pretend we've scored a goal!" followed by a mock celebration and chanting of the imaginary scoreline. The fantasy score gets as high as 4-2 in their favour, even going as far as to mock-bait us with "2-0 and you fucked it up!" An embarrassment to themselves and their club, it's one of the most pathetic things I've ever witnessed in a football ground or a building site.

With the clock running down, it becomes apparent that we are almost certainly going to win, something that is confirmed when substitute Jordan Chappell bursts forward in the 90th minute and leathers it in for 3-0. It is, as James Alabi later observes on social media, a "big boy win". As convention dictates, the jubilant players come over to applaud the fans, albeit from a respectable distance. When they were growing up dreaming of being professional footballers, they can't have envisaged winning for 119 alers, twitchers and junior thugs in a ground full of scaffold, sadness in their eyes.

Back to The Cricketer's, we brave an outside table for a celebratory pint. Attempting to pacify the feral child, it's at this point that we realise we have lost the iPad. Her Indoors heads into the pub more in hope than expectation, but remarkably retrieves it from exactly where we left it at lunchtime, prompting a double celebration.

With the scent of victory in our nostrils, we go our separate ways in German cars. On the way home the following evening, as I pull out of an M3 service station, Her Indoors announces that she needs the facilities. This untimely and infuriating request proves directly responsible for me driving at 80mph in a 50 zone, which in turn causes a speed camera to flash us. With The Card at stake, I simply cannot afford to lose my licence. And so the wait begins.

Attendance: 1,932 Position: 12th →←

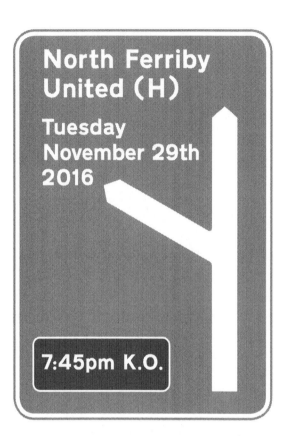

North Ferriby
United (H)

Tuesday
November 29th
2016

7:45pm K.O.

Game 24 of 50 →

Didn't we play these last month? A Tuesday night, the Humber Bridge, nicked a 1-0 win? All true. Nevertheless, the mysterious fixture computer has swiftly paired us again, which at least gives us the chance to get an early double on the board. If you support Manchester United or Chelsea, a double generally refers to winning the league and the FA Cup in the same season. For us, it involves beating a village team home and away. We'll take it.

Having managed only one full day at home since the last match, I again entrust The Boy's childcare to one of his friend's mothers and hit the road, enjoying the freedom to drive while I can, the speed camera incident still hanging over me like the sword of Hercules, or possibly Damocles. Leafless trees flank the M40 as autumn's rusty hues yield to winter's frigid grip. It ain't warm, and with the temperature dropping by the minute this is absolutely a game to miss if I wasn't on The Card.

Even The Driver has expressed doubts, claiming that he's only here as part of The Card campaign in his role as unofficial sponsor. He's talking through his hat of course, he goes everywhere come rain, shine, or as is looking increasingly likely tonight, frost, which is putting the game in doubt. The postponed match is the bane of the long distance football fan — if there's one thing worse than driving the length of the country for a shit match, it's driving the length of the country for a postponed match.

Particularly at this level, it comes with the territory, and The Driver has experienced postponements in all four corners of the country. Only last season, he was bedded in with The Driver Indoors at a guesthouse prior to Torquay away when the game fell to a waterlogged pitch. The Hack and Wife were also in the vicinity, and they all had to spend an utterly pointless weekend in Devon at no little expense, as did a bus full of Chester Youth. Prior to that, The Driver got almost all the way to Workington — in the northwest of the Lake District — before the game was called off, simply turning around and going to a meaningless neutral game at Accrington Stanley (who are they?). Back in the league days, he once got the train to Darlington, discovered that it was off and got on the first train back, only to be kicked off at York as his pre-booked ticket wasn't valid. This was the same season that Big Al did The Card, heroically returning for the rearranged fixture so as not to blot his copybook.

I have fallen foul of the weather a few times myself, not least when my younger brother and I drove to Plymouth on a sodden day to discover an abandoned Home Park, despite regular reassurances on the phone that it was on. But for a combination of expense and sheer improbability, some years ago I treated Her Indoors to a week in Wales prior to the opening game of the season at home to Grimsby, in August. Biblical rain accompanied our journey on the Saturday morning, followed by a radio report telling us that the Deva pitch was waterlogged. Suffice to say I did not take the news well, although The Driver still finds it amusing to this day.

Neither of us will be laughing if it's called off tonight, and as we gingerly navigate the A41, the dashboard at one point reads minus 1.5 degrees. I attempt to Google the temperature at which soil freezes. At an opportune moment I even get out of the car and tread the crunchy turf at the side of the road, otherwise known as The Parky Test, whereby he would ascertain the likelihood of a game going ahead based on whether his back garden could take a stud. All avenues of investigation prove inconclusive, and we have no choice but to continue. The official Twitter feed claims that the game is definitely on, the missive echoed minutes later by The Hack who is gleefully tracking our progress from afar. It's vaguely encouraging news, although as experience has taught us, everything is definitely on until it's definitely off.

Arriving at the ground, the Blues Bar is sparsely populated. One punter suggests that people didn't know the match was scheduled, although as the barman says, it's been on the fixture list since day one like every other game. What's more likely is that people have got better things to do on a Tuesday night than freeze their bollocks off at The Deva at the risk of not even seeing a match. Since we set off, both Stockport and Macclesfield have been called off, and they're in the same county. It's as if the weather is encroaching upon us, like in *The Day After Tomorrow*, and at any second The Deva could be encased in ice. I think that's what happens in the film anyway; I saw it in warmer climes, in a Portuguese cinema during Euro 2004 while sharing a hotel room with The Driver and The Evertonian.

Despite the arctic conditions, no announcement is forthcoming so we take our place on the terrace, overlooking a pitch that has a light dusting of frost but is apparently playable. We have finally appointed an assistant manager in the shape of former Scotland striker, and indeed former Chester striker, TV's Chris Iwelumo. He must wonder what he has got himself into, patrolling a frozen touchline instead of sitting in a warm studio delivering platitudes to a frisky blonde.

Also present for no discernible reason is a sizeable representation of the armed forces, sitting in the main stand bedecked in full camouflage gear. It's an open goal for resident mirth makers, with jokes revolving around the premise that whatever traumas they may have endured in military service, little can have prepared them for the horror of North Ferriby at home on a Tuesday night in November. The crowd is encouraged to applaud their presence, presumably as a show of gratitude for arbitrary acts of lethal violence. The Driver chooses not to take this option, instead singing a snippet of *Wasted Life* by veteran Belfast punks, Stiff Little Fingers: "Stuff their fucking armies/Killing isn't my idea of fun".

Following several hours of weather-based stress, it is with some relief that the game finally kicks off. Infuriatingly, Chester are attacking the home end first, having presumably lost the toss. This razzes me off no end. By all means toss a coin for kickoff, but it should be an immutable law of football that the home team always attacks the home end in the second half, as this is when the majority of games are decided; the first half is often little more than foreplay. Liverpool should always attack The Kop in the second half, and Chester should always attack The Harry McNally Terrace. Because it makes it more exciting. As we are often reminded, football is in the entertainment business. And we are actually paying for this, in my case, to the tune of thousands of pounds over the course of The Card.

Playing the 'wrong' way gives us an early chance to resume the baiting of Watson, Ferriby's foulmouthed albeit apologetic goalkeeper from the away game. For reasons unfathomable he is sporting an extraordinary combination of kit that gives him the appearance of a wine waiter. It's almost evening dress, but he takes the light-hearted ribbing with a friendly thumbs-up. He also keeps our strikers at bay, maintaining a clean sheet for the entirety of a half during which North Ferriby's fans continue to flood in, finally numbering six. Six people. It's not a huge turnout, admittedly, although one tabloid newspaper later does The Villagers a huge disservice by reporting the away attendance as two, a genuine case of fake news.

Rock bottom in the league, North Ferriby have never scored against us in their history, and we really should be beating the likes of these. As one wag points out, at least we're attacking the home end in the second half. Except, of course, we're not. We score an early goal anyway, Richards apparently, although as it's down the other end it's hard to tell. It's followed immediately by a penalty that Alabi dispatches with such venom that nobody else should ever be allowed to take one. He rounds off the evening with another thunderous strike late on to give us back-to-back 3-0 victories. With exactly half of the league season played, we have somehow crept into 8th place. What a season to be on The Card.

The journey back is moderately life threatening as we weave between giant juggernauts on a treacherous surface. Stopping at Warwick Services, I treat myself to a vegetable samosa at half past midnight, becoming increasingly aware that we are existing on the fringes of society. When I finally reach my car, it is almost unrecognisable, effectively a solid block of ice. Prising the door open, I scrape a porthole into the windscreen and tentatively manoeuvre onto the M40. Naturally a section of it is closed, but I somehow make it back to London, almost falling asleep on Harlesden High Street, where I spot that some tit has already got their Christmas tree up. Pulling into my drive at 2am on the dot, I am near collapse. Four months down, five to go.

> **Attendance: 1,392 Position: 8th ↑**

Game 25 of 50 →

This is arguably the key fixture of the entire Card, and the one to cause me the most anguish. Not because it's a pain to get to (it is), but because of an email I received literally the day after the fixtures were announced. Subject: Save The Date. The date: December 3rd. The occasion: my cousin's wedding. The location: Heathrow (ironically where this all began on 6th August).

As with any invitation proffered for an event during the football season, the first thing I did was check the fixture list, which in this instance was barely dry. In the normal scheme of things, an excuse not to go to Guiseley could be considered cause for minor celebration. With respect, while it has a certain rustic charm, it's not the most alluring destination on the tour, and there's occasionally a hint of trouble. It's in Yorkshire by the way, basically Leeds.

So while missing it would not be the end of the world, it would definitely be the end of The Card. Although when the invitation was first received, The Card was not really a genuine consideration beyond the obligatory annual braggadocio. Yet it must have been at the back of my mind, as I persistently deferred my response. Having formally committed to The Card, it was not until October that I finally sent this mealy-mouthed reply: "Due to work commitments in the north I am only able to make the reception, and it will just be me, not my family. Also, I will be slightly late, probably nearer 8pm. I hope this is OK."

What else could I say? "Please accept my apologies. I'm on The Card and we've got Guiseley away. The Driver is emigrating and this may be my last realistic chance of immortality."

Fuck it, it's done. Sacrifices have to be made. Besides, if people have to get married, there is the entire summer during which to do so. That's what it's for.

This twist in the tale adds a further level of jeopardy to the day, with the post-match journey now almost as important as the pre-match. Looking for any kind of time-saving option, I consider all combinations of planes, trains and automobiles. Leeds Bradford Airport is ten minutes by road from Guiseley's Nethermoor Park, but sadly there's nothing doing for Heathrow, which is a shame, as flying in for the wedding could have been perceived as the antics of a Big Time Charlie. There's little to gain by letting the train take the strain, so my best bet is the traditional two-car shuffle via The Watford Gap, who has again extended a generous welcome.

Remembering to pack my suit, I set off on the Friday night, leaving the FA Cup tie between Macclesfield and Oxford United on the telly, and picking up Nottingham Forest versus Newcastle on the radio. It's possibly the longest journey in the country that I am able to make without recourse to the satnav: get on the M1, get off at Watford Gap Services, take the secret exit, thread across the fields to the house using visual cues committed to memory. I sometimes get there quicker than my texts, which has the effect of confusing everyone and making them think I have either teleported or discovered time travel.

The evening follows a familiar pattern, but amidst the rugby league, golf, American things, and old episodes of *Bullseye*, we stumble across highlights of Notts County versus Watford from the 1983/84 season. Watching it with the result unknown, The Watford Gap retrospectively celebrates a frankly sensational 5-3 win for The Hornets. Arguably more remarkable is the absolute state of it, the whole thing proving barely recognisable as either a sport or a leisure activity. Played on what resembles an oil slick, it's to the players' credit that they manage to conjure a contest, further hampered by shorts so tight that their genitals visibly undulate. But off the pitch is an even greater disgrace, with fans caged like an East Midlands tribute to Guantanamo Bay. And all this from the first season that I ever went to watch football.

As a footnote, no mention of Notts County is complete without me wheeling out the story of how I essentially blackmailed Her Indoors into driving me there on New Year's Day 2007 in return for a tepid New Year's Eve. She slept in the car outside Meadow Lane while we turned them over 2-1, then drove directly to The Circus Tavern, Purfleet, Essex, for the final of the World Darts Championship between Phil Taylor and Raymond van Barneveld, widely regarded as the greatest game ever played. What a time to be alive.

The blackness comes swiftly, and before I know it The Driver is pulling in and we are pulling off and pulling G's on the M1. He feels that he could have done a better job of circumnavigating Leeds, but delivers us to the usual pub in time for the bulk of Manchester City versus Chelsea, which is vying for attention with some kind of rugby. Nobody is really watching the football, except when a skirmish breaks out and the entire pub turns as one to enjoy the melee. I chase down a burger and fries with pints of pissy lager as The Driver has a cursory chat with Four Cards who is here with the usual rabble.

Also joining us is an old friend who I have invited at short notice, the honourable Seffers, a Leeds fan who lives in nearby Saltaire. While working for a computer games magazine, he and I once simultaneously urinated on Hugh Hefner's lawn during a party at The Playboy Mansion. It's a slightly less glamorous assignment today, and as we approach the ground he asks, in all seriousness, "Is it a cup game?"

Sadly not. This is the level we are at, playing in front of a three-figure crowd in a ramshackle stadium with some kind of chemical tank in the away end. Bringing a neutral to a game can be a chastening experience as it lets you see it through their eyes for what it is. And it's not pretty. It's a bit like taking someone dogging for the first time, I imagine, and the tone is immediately set when a minute's silence is breached by a squeaky fart.

As is their wont, the Guiseley fans are hung up on the whole Welsh thing, geography clearly not being their strong suit.

"Sheep! Sheep! Sheep shaggers!" they chant, seemingly oblivious to the irony that they are surrounded by fields full of sheep. By way of riposte, Chester offer up a round of "Ingerland, Ingerland, Ingerland..." followed by the more thought-provoking, "Jimmy Savile, he could be your dad..." as well as an unsuccessful, "Peter Sutcliffe, he murdered your mum..." Banter, they call it.

To his credit, Seffers manages to stifle a yawn, and only checks his watch a few times. He's actually rewarded by one of the goals of the season when James Alabi produces an athletic overhead kick to give us a half-time lead. It's soon cancelled out when the referee awards Gizlee a dubious penalty, a decision that he later admits was a mistake. Fat use. It finishes 1-1. Take a point, move on.

There are times when The Driver's aggressive approach to his vocation prove useful, and this is one of them. He is that Audi driver who is trying to get into your boot, cutting you up at roundabouts, overtaking at blind spots, and generally risking the lives of all road users in an attempt to shave a few minutes off the journey, which is often accompanied by a flurry of middle fingers and wanker signs from other motorists. Nevertheless he delivers me to Watford Gap in time to give me a fighting chance.

Without even saying goodbye, I get in the car, retrace my steps through the Services and floor it. Within the hour I am tearing anti-clockwise round the M25 before cutting in on the M4 to Heathrow. Taking the final parking space at the Radisson Blu Hotel, I am Super-man in reverse, shedding the spandex smock for less ostentatious garb. Dodging any familiar faces, I pick up a key, head to my room and swiftly put on my suit. Composing myself, I sashay in just as the first dance begins. Spotting an empty seat, I dive in and immediately order a curry and a lager.

Commending everybody on a beautiful service, I seem to have got away with it until somebody mentions the horse. Being an Indian wedding, the groom apparently arrived on horseback, a small detail that I overlooked due to the fact that I was watching a non-league football match in Yorkshire.

I eventually get to chat to him, and talk turns to his former class-mate, Bournemouth's Eddie Howe, with whom he organised the fateful interview that arguably kick-started my moribund career, if not his. What I didn't know was that my cousin and the then future Bournemouth manager fell out due to an argument involving the dissection of a frog. If he ever becomes England manager, there's a tabloid story in the making.

I have at least salvaged something from the day, other than taking a point at Gizlee and keeping The Card intact. Throw in a solid five-hour run at the free bar and it's been a largely successful operation. I eventually retire to bed and have a gin-fuelled stress dream about trying getting to Aldershot on a variety of planes and boats. Of course the funny thing is we've already played at Aldershot.

Attendance: 957   Position: 7th ↑

Witton Albion (A)

Saturday December 10th 2016

FA Trophy First Round

3pm K.O.

Game 26 of 50 →

What more could a man want for his birthday weekend than a trip to Witton Albion? There's nowhere else I'd rather be, and of course there's nowhere else I can be: as established, the FA Trophy is formally considered part of The Card. Apart from the play-offs, it also represents our last route to Wembley, which would provide the dream finish that I have envisaged since the outset of this frankly unhinged venture.

The Driver has pulled his 'can't guarantee kickoff' routine, and The Hack doesn't lower himself to the Trophy. As such, accommodation is booked and the family is bundled into the car on the Friday afternoon, picking up The Boy from school and press-ganging Her Indoors from work. Hit The North. Nothing's Gonna Stop Us Now.

'STOP!!!' Not my words, but the words of the violently flashing dashboard in front of me. This isn't something that you want to see at the best of times, and definitely not while travelling at 100mph on the M40. In a blind panic, I attempt to get off the motorway and swerve into the next junction. Unfortunately, the next junction is that with the M25. Under increasing pressure from an aggressive automated message, I have little choice but to pull onto the hard shoulder. Statistically, it's one of the most dangerous places on earth; juggernauts skim past, rocking the car and disgorging acrid smoke. I try to read the fucking manual, but it makes little sense. The car has apparently become sentient and will not accept reason.

"Open the pod bay door, GOLF."

"I'm afraid I can't do that, Steve. I need coolant, Steve."

What the fuck is coolant? Why is this happening? We can't stay here in case we die, so we defy the instructions and limp on, eventually leaving the motorway system and stopping at a pub car park, at which point The Boy runs off, convinced that the car is going to explode. Reassuring him and ourselves that this is not the case, we crawl to a nearby village garage. They recommend that we give it water, and that quietens it for a while. Eventually rejoining the M40, during the time that we have been pissing about there have been at least two accidents ahead of us. We sit in static traffic for hours, the only consolation being that we are not the people who have had the accidents.

Regularly stopping to allow the beast to drink, it takes a painstaking six hours to reach Cheshire. I am already resenting the players for their inevitable fuck-ups the next day. To add insult to injury, the official Twitter account cheerily tweets about making the short journey to Witton Albion. The drama continues on the rain-slicked streets of Northwich when I lose control of the car and embark on a mildly terrifying skid.

It is therefore with some relief that we finally pull up at a seemingly abandoned converted farmhouse and let ourselves in. Randomly, we have been designated the Oriental Room, mid-Cheshire's tribute to the mysteries of the East. It's like an interior scene from *Monkey*, the room littered with so much faux-Chinese tat that simply moving around is a logistical quandary. To my mind, a hotel room needs a bed, a flat screen TV, and rudimentary tea-making facilities. It doesn't need 16 ornate scatter cushions, a bamboo plant and a gong. Immediately heading out, we find a huge family-oriented pub and I ease the pain with a sirloin steak and pints while feral children roll around on the floor.

This tides me over until breakfast — full English of course — where we are joined by a smattering of fellow diners. They include a couple who it transpires have come away for the weekend to go shopping. Shopping? When did that become a leisure activity? They've already spunked the best part of £100 on the guesthouse. Mindless.

Kicked out of our padded cell at ten bells, we have five hours to kill until kickoff. In the normal scheme of things, this would involve three hours and 55 minutes in a pub, but we are having a family day out and we are going to explore the more cultural aspects. First port of call is the Anderton Boat Lift, a restored Victorian hydraulic engine that transports boats between a river and a canal. I refuse to pay to

The Deva Stadium's pristine playing surface is a credit to the ground staff.

Chasing rainbows at York City's Bootham Crescent. But where's Parky?

The Hero enjoys Tranmere's excellent pre-match marquee. One of these scarves is not like the others…

Prenton Park from the away end. Cometh the hour, cometh the man…

An elevated view at Dagenham & Redbridge. "Come on Yellows, these are garbage!"

Chas, Parky and The Driver in happier times, lifting the Conference trophy.

"Three points for Christmas please." The Boy meets Santa before sticking it up The Shots.

Tense times on The Harry Mac. The Boy ripped to the gills on Haribo.

The sins of the father will be visited upon the child. A rare wash for the smock.

The Chester Exiles at the home of The Bromley Boys.

Boreham Wood at home. What a time to be alive.

Ingredients: hope, misery, despair. Bake for nine months and serve cold.

Every good boy deserves cake.

Au revoir to The Driver.

On the bench at The Deva. The dream team of the Blues Bar boys, The Driver and The Hero.

go in on the basis that we can simply look at it for free. Instead we take a stroll down the canal where, unprompted, Her Indoors makes it clear that she would never have any interest in living in Cheshire.

The thrills continue apace with a visit to the defunct Lion Salt Works, which now functions as a frankly improbable salt museum. Again, I refuse to go in, although much of the excitement is taking place in the car park where a collection of moustachioed middle-aged men are showing off their respective miniature steam engines. One is even offering rides for a quid, and The Boy shares a trailer with a girl with a facial disfigurement. I ask Her Indoors if she would prefer that I did this sort of thing with my Saturdays, and she says that she would leave me immediately.

One enthusiast in full costume is spraying his machine with water, and I take the opportunity to fill a bottle to feed the malfunctioning car. The chap in question mutters something about "infernal combustion engines". Spotting the VW, he has a dig at the Germans and says, "Remember they came second," presumably in reference to a global conflict in which millions of people were slaughtered.

We really have stumbled across a hive of activity, and a nearby hut is host to Professor Mace's Cabinet Of Curiosities. Tentatively venturing in with The Boy, a Victorian explorer is displaying a table full of artefacts apparently collected on his travels, including a pair of shrunken heads — in Northwich. It's only when he shows me a yeti's ear that I realise he's a despicable charlatan, and that perhaps the chameleon that I couldn't see didn't exist.

We really are through the looking glass, and it's all too much to take in on a match day. Seeking respite, I retire to the nearby Salt Barge pub to drink alone while they visit the gift shop. After all, it is my birthday tomorrow, and everybody loves salt. They eventually join me, and The Boy shares his pre-match thoughts: "It might be a boring game when it's zero-zero, a sad game when it's four-zero, or it might be a happy game when it's 10-1. I think it's going to be 2-1 to Chester. I've never heard of a team called Witton."

The history of football in Northwich is long and complicated, and there seem to be more football clubs per capita than is strictly necessary, sharing grounds and drifting in and out of existence on a regular basis. We have played these before in our first season as a reformed club, but my solitary prior visit to the ground was for a rare cup final. On a balmy night in 2013, The Mighty Chester vanquished Stalybridge Celtic to lift the Cheshire Senior Cup for the first time in generations.

Heady days, but it will be eclipsed if we can lift the FA Trophy for the first time, and a decent turnout is expected for this first step on the journey to Wembley, with Witton graciously giving us the home end. Driving past Northwich station, we spot APJ and a selection of Chester Youth being disgorged, but it's not exactly a mass exodus, the Trophy failing to capture the imagination of the greater Chester public. Parking near the ground, we avail ourselves of the huge bar where Her Indoors spends the entire time on the phone to the RAC and then announces that she plans to sit in the car and wait for them during the match. It's a baffling thought process and it takes all of my powers of negotiation to convince her that the entire reason that we are here is for the match and that all other matters can be dealt without outside the allotted time. She begrudgingly acquiesces, but it sullies the day and I barely see her and The Boy during the game as they skulk at the back eating sweets. In fairness, sitting in the car may have been more entertaining.

I watch the action with The Driver — who bowls in before kickoff — and his mate Tom, who recently accompanied him to Kazakhstan to watch Bordeaux play in a Europa League tie. He's had a shorter journey today, getting here via a 40-minute stroll. Another hapless supporter has even cycled here from Chester.

They appear to have been rewarded when we take a first-half lead, but despite being three divisions below us, Witton give a good account of themselves and force an equaliser. It's a measure of how interesting the game is that The Driver's mate Tom commends the nearside linesman on the excellent positioning of his non-flag bearing hand. The official in question overhears and gives a stealthy thumbs-up behind his back.

A further highlight occurs when the rain dissipates the fog and enables us to see some of the action. Witton are all over us, and it appears that there will be only one winner. Although I naturally want to get to Wembley, I question whether a tiny part of me wants the dream to be crushed here, thus avoiding a replay and making it a more manageable Card. It doesn't really matter what I think; I have absolutely no control over what happens and simply have to accept my fate. Despite going down to ten men late on, we somehow hold on for the draw. We go again on Tuesday night at our place.

Back in the car, the mood is tense. A text arrives from the RAC saying that they can pick us up in six hours and put the car on the back of a lorry. Forget it. We load up on water and limp south to the House of Doom. Happy Birthday to me.

Attendance: 883

Witton Albion (H)

Tuesday December 13th 2016

FA Trophy First Round Replay

7:45pm K.O.

Game 27 of 50 →

This is the game that nobody wanted, particularly me. And if Richards had put that chance away I'd be sat at home in the warm watching Everton versus Arsenal on BT Sport. The same applies if Witton had scored instead of hitting the bar, or if Lynchy hadn't pulled off that wonder save. But football is full of ifs, and the reality is that I face the daunting prospect of driving from door to turnstile on my own. At least the car is fully functioning, having spent its solitary day at home having a new radiator fitted, yet another financial sacrifice in pursuit of the mythical Card.

With the Wembley arch silently mocking me, I set off in early afternoon. It's the kind of day that needn't have bothered, as grey swiftly turns to black. Even the self-styled Butty Man of the A41 is nowhere to be seen, which must be a great disappointment to people who enjoy al fresco dining in wet lay-bys. Released from the tyranny of The Driver, I am free to eat where I choose, and I choose Newcott Fish & Chips: frequently passed, rarely frequented. Primarily catering to visitors to the nearby Stoke Heath prison, calling it a chippy doesn't really do it justice. It's a one-stop shop including a mini-supermarket, restaurant and even licensed bar — what better way to wind down after a chat with a murderer?

Famous throughout the surrounding metres for its seemingly random bespoke meal boxes, I opt for the Lunch Box, which comprises 'Chips in a box with fish cake, a small sausage and a choice of either curry, gravy, mushy peas or beans'. Other options include Fish Box, Pie Box, and Off Your Box, which consists of a battered sausage, a Texan bar and a can of Special Brew.

Refusing to pay the indoor premium, I enjoy the latest in in-car dining, and it may be the best £2.95 I've ever spent. Obviously I go for the mushy peas — I'm not an animal. Girding my stomach for the remaining journey, I cruise into Chester with hours to spare. I drive past people on running machines at the Northgate Arena, where I saw my first gig, and circumnavigate the roundabout where I had my head kicked in by a pair of scallies. Good times.

There's no point going to the ground alone this early, so I park up near Telford's Warehouse and read *The Non-League Paper*. Draped in the smock and with a Chester FC foam hand on the parcel shelf of the car, a passer-by could easily mistake me for a non-league football fan, something I'm not sure that anyone really sets out to be.

Bucked into action by this prospect, I decide to take a stroll into town for the first time in years, retracing a chunk of my old walk to school. With my birthday out of the way, Christmas festivities are beginning in earnest and the area in front of the town hall is host to one of those twee German markets, including a pop-up Real Ale bar. With a handsome Christmas tree taking pride of place, it's all twinkly in the rain, and if I wasn't dead inside I could almost appreciate the heart-warming festive scene. Incidentally, the town hall only has three clock faces — the westerly side is blank, apocryphally because the good people of Chester won't give the Welsh the time of day.

Continuing the retro vibe, I visit the supermarket where I used to stack shelves for beer money, now a Poundworld, naturally. I also pass the location of the shop where I used to buy ZX Spectrum games, and the pizzeria where my parents once spotted Mike McCartney out of The Scaffold, very much the John Rooney of that brotherhood. Staring ghostlike into the windows of formerly frequented pubs, most of them now appear to be upmarket eateries; even The Liverpool Arms, always good for a flexible last orders on the way home, has been loftily rebranded as LA. I believe the actual LA is yet to break its silence on the matter.

Having got my *It's A Wonderful Life* moment out of the way, I park up near the ground, still with time on my side. I've been trying to get an interview with new assistant manager Chris Iwelumo for *The Non-League Paper* and send him another text. He agrees to a chat after the game, so whatever the result I can vaguely justify this monstrous trip. Buoyed by this news, I bowl to the ground and have a token look around the club shop, briefly picking up a copy of the latest *Football Manager* computer game. Over ten years clean now. What a senseless waste of human life that was.

I treat myself to a driving lager in the Blues Bar and spot a veteran fan who is now in a bad way, reliant on a walking frame. An original member of Sealand Road's famous Beer Belly Crew, he was in far better shape when he kicked me in the balls at the top of Walpole Street a few decades ago. We had spotted them in town late one night and instinctively chanted their trademark anthem: "B… B… BBC!" It was out of respect rather than any antagonism, but they seemed nonplussed and we moved on. We thought nothing of it until some time later when they piled out of a taxi and drunkenly attacked us. Good times.

I take my place on the sparsely-populated terrace next to Big Al. He's a link to the past in so much as he used to work with my old schoolmate Mikey, one of the original quartet who fielded a few haymakers from the BBC that fateful night. Mikey has a season ticket in the main stand these days, and we hardly ever see him. One season he was there, the next he was gone, a short but seismic leap into oblivion.

Season tickets apparently don't cover the FA Trophy, as we are graced by the presence of The Colonel and Wainwright, both making a rare appearance on the terrace tonight. The latter is pleased to see that I am taking The Card seriously and again warns me of the perils that lay ahead, still bleating about his godforsaken replays.

The game begins and after six seconds history is made. Astonishingly we concede what is believed to be the fastest penalty ever awarded in a football match. You couldn't make it up. You would struggle to deliberately concede a penalty in six seconds. If it was a pinball game, you'd just get your ball back. But concede it we have, as lumbering ex-Wrexham defender Blaine Hudson slips on his arse and clips the advancing Witton attacker. Lynchy heroically saves the spot kick, but the rebound is stabbed in to give the part-timers a very early lead. It's only the beginning of the madness. They have a man sent off. We have a man sent off. They have a goal disallowed. They have a coach sent off. They have another man sent off for conceding a penalty with four minutes to go.

As I deliver live commentary to The Driver on the phone, Alabi steps up and twats it against the underside of the crossbar... and in! With ten versus nine, and extra time beckoning, suddenly Durrell is rounding the keeper and slotting home the winner. It's an extraordinary end to an extraordinary game, described by Radio Merseyside's Neil Turner as the footballing equivalent of an episode of *Fawlty Towers*. Almost an "I was there" evening, one fan calls it the best shit game he's ever seen.

Regaining my composure, I text Iwelumo and wait for him in the deserted Legends Lounge. There's some contention among the Witton players, who were under the impression that a post-match meal would be provided, largely on the basis that they laid on pizza on Saturday. When it becomes apparent that no such reciprocal deal is in place, the most vocal of them, a Scouser with a full-sleeve tattoo, promises another young player that "I'll buy you a chip barm" on the basis that he's a student.

While this is going on, our opposition in the next round has yet to be decided as Truro have taken Forest Green to extra time. Following the match on my phone, Forest Green snatch a late winner, meaning we play them at home in round two. And we all know how that ends. Further bad news follows when Iwelumo sends an apologetic text from his car, as he was under the impression that I wanted a phone interview. Immediately heading to my car, I spot match winner Durrell getting into his, and offer him a cursory "well played".

The journey south has never seemed longer. Even the water feature at Stafford Services fails to lift my spirits. It's a constant blur of lights and rain, interspersed by glimpses of a perigee moon. I begin hallucinating around Coventry. Motorways are closing all around me, closing in on me. It is with numb despair that I learn that the M1 has fallen. I lose the diversion instructions instantly and simply point the car south, traversing a rain-sodden Rugby where I see a total of one person, a poor prick on a bicycle, who may or may not be having a worse night.

With sleep rapidly beckoning, I decide to seek respite at the House of Doom, via a 24-hour McDonalds. Clutching a Big Mac and fries to go, I let myself in and wolf it down. I then pour myself a large gin and tonic and mindlessly flick through the TV channels. It's the first time I've stayed here on my own. It's fine. Bricks and mortar.

Attendance: 921

Aldershot Town (H)

Saturday December 17th 2016

3pm K.O.

Game 28 of 50 →

There is no Xmas on The Card. The day before we face The Shots, I receive an email inviting me and The Boy to attend a "magical Christmas visit to Lapland UK" including door-to-door travel, free entry, and a personalised meeting with Father Christmas.

"Thanks," I reply, "but we have a magical appointment with Chester v Aldershot."

No further correspondence is forthcoming, and I don't tell The Boy what he's missing. Instead I groom him in preparation for taking on The Shots at The Deva. It's the only solution to a logistical quandary that has arisen due to an extraordinary fixture clash that sees the final of *Strictly Come Dancing* being played on the same day as Chester v Shots. For purposes of work, Her Indoors is obliged to attend the former, and for purposes of The Card, I am obliged to attend the latter. So at least one of us gets to watch twinkle-toed prima donnas prancing around like tits, the key difference being that The Boy comes with me.

He's not overtly happy about the arrangement, particularly when he's wrenched from his mother's arms and bundled into the car on the Friday night. And by not happy, I mean that openly sobbing thing. To give ourselves a fighting chance, we are once again abusing our key to the House of Doom, Her Indoors' former family home rapidly becoming a portal to the North West.

After a false start because I forgot to pack a coat for The Boy, the journey goes from bad to worse, not helped by thick fog. A diversion after Dunstable requires me to drive eight miles to a roundabout, go round the roundabout, and then drive the same eight miles back. Attempting to second-guess it, I go off-piste, end up back in Dunstable, and have to do the whole thing again. Close to a breakdown (me not the car), the one blessing is that The Boy is now asleep. Stepping over junk mail addressed to the dead, I carry him up the stairs and place him in his mother's childhood bed. Following a cursory flick through what's left of the Sky channels, I tactically opt for an early night. We ride at dawn.

A rudimentary breakfast puts The Boy in good spirits. Strapping him into the car, I put an iPad in his face and head north, a mere four days after my last trek. It's reassuring to see that The Butty Man of the A41 is back, as ever brandishing his self-written sign: "TRY 2 DAY AND YOU WILL CALL AGAIN".

It's a powerhouse of advertising, but nevertheless we opt for the more established McDonald's near the ground. On the way there I show The Boy my former family home.

"Not good," he observes.

As we're awaiting a Happy Meal and an unhappy meal, The Driver sends a text from Montpellier where he is apparently basking in the sun ahead of the Bordeaux game. He asks me to keep him updated on events at The Deva, which is a bit like asking your wife to send you dirty messages while you're hanging out the back of your mistress.

With time in hand, The Boy drags me round Toys R Us, situated a goal kick away from the location of the old Sealand Road away end. Full of Christmas tat, he insists on showing me where he was bought that infernal pinball machine prior to our trip to The Lakes on that sizzling August day, half a Card away.

With free parking secured, we head for the ground and The Boy poses for a picture next to the incongruous Chester Rhino, a fibreglass statue of a creature with no historical association with the club. Part of a larger art project-cum-advertising campaign, the Rhino has stood there in full kit since 2010, the same year that it was due to be removed. If that were not excitement enough for his young mind, we then bump into Father Christmas outside the Blues Bar, despite being given assurances that he would be at Lapland UK near Ascot. It's a Christmas miracle.

Given that The Driver is lost in France, we decide to treat ourselves to a seat in the main stand — Big Al will have to entertain himself, free to use non-child friendly language in reference to the officials.

Taking a seat slightly nearer the away end, it actually works in our favour as we again kick off the 'wrong' way, attacking The Harry McNally Terrace in the first half. It also gives us a chance to witness some of the action, as seeing from one end of the pitch to the other through the fog appears increasingly difficult.

"We're probably going to lose," says The Boy, already in the grip of natural pessimism.

"I could have scored that," he claims as a chance goes begging.

"Why is football really quiet?" he asks, in all seriousness.

The atmosphere is ramped up when Alabi is clattered in the box and the ref awards us a penalty. As I prepare to toss The Boy in the air in the traditional manner, Alabi places the ball on the spot. He loves scoring against The Shots, having bagged four in the corresponding fixture last season, the freak 8-2 win that both The Driver and I somehow missed. Facing the same goal that he scored a penalty in on Tuesday night, perhaps mindful of clipping the crossbar again, this time he goes low, with power. A nation holds its breath as the ball strikes the inside of the left-hand post and ricochets across the face of the goal... to safety. Shithouse.

Half-time — aka Haribo time — is approaching, and we go into it with a bounce when the lesser spotted Jordan Chappell chases a lost cause, cuts inside and somehow forces the ball in for a 1-0 lead. The Boy gets his bag of chemicals and we briefly take a seat in the notorious H block, something that I instantly regret when we are subjected to a cavalcade of foulmouthed invective that makes Big Al sound like a choirboy.

Retaking our original seats, we kick back for the second half, a classic dad and lad pose, something that both warms the cockles of my arctic heart and fills me with dread at what future misery he may endure should he choose to pursue this desperate half-life. With adroit timing, Alabi gets his goal, slotting in from close range early doors and performing a knee slide in front of us as a small boy full of gelatin becomes momentarily airborne.

Aldershot are a decent side and they refuse to roll over, coming at us strongly as we sit back on the lead. It's a dangerous tactic and they come close on a number of occasions, twatting both post and bar. Almost of as much concern is the fog, now billowing over the walls like a horror film, specifically the horror film, *The Fog*. It would be a real shame for the game to be called off now, but despite the latter stages being played on what looks like the set of the *Thriller* video, the referee is happy for it to continue and we clinch a huge 2-0 victory. Whisper it softly, but unfathomably Chester go into the festive period in seventh place. What a season to do The Card.

The only downside is the pending 200-mile journey south with almost zero visibility. The M6 is little more than a rumour, and I am basically driving by satnav, with the taillights of the car in front a scarcely distinguishable reddish blur. Squinting through the fog at the overhead digital displays, I can just about make out the orange word 'FOG' as I drive under them. Slow and steady wins the race, and we take a deserved break at Watford Gap Services, where The Boy breaks into song, a self-penned ditty that goes a little bit like this: "Chester stuck it up The Shots two zero." I buy him a bouncy ball for his efforts.

It's been a big day for a small boy, and he drops off during the final leg of the journey. Thankfully I don't, and we make it home alive in time to see assistant manager Chris Iwelumo on Channel 5, having opted for a soccer sofa instead of a fogbound Deva.

I have been invited to a nearby Christmas party, but all attempts at finding a babysitter fall flat. This is life on The Card, watching *Match Of The Day* on my own while a nation revels. Her Indoors sends a text to let me know that she is dancing with Jamie Redknapp. I tell her to tell him that I saw him boss it as a 17-year-old playing for Bournemouth against Chester at Macclesfield. For some reason she doesn't bother.

Attendance: 1,937 Position: 7th →←

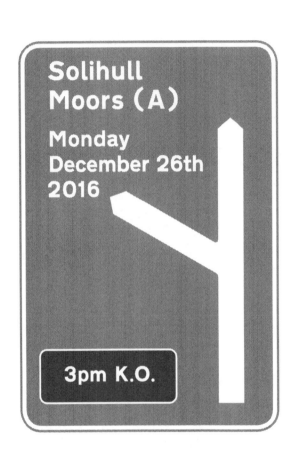

Solihull
Moors (A)

Monday
December 26th
2016

3pm K.O.

Game 29 of 50 →

So this is Christmas, and what have you done? Gone seven league games unbeaten and got to within two places of the play-off positions. Scenes. In the past our season has frequently gone to shit after the Christmas period, on at least two occasions in recent history resulting in such a collapse that the manager has had to be sacked. But of course this season will be different, because this is now, and now is all that matters.

It's clichéd to be cynical at Christmas, but it is an absolute pile of shit. Adults who profess to love Christmas are often the same kind of amateur drinkers who enjoy fancy dress and karaoke. If you watch sport, every day is Christmas Day, except for Christmas Day itself, which is garbage because there's no sport to watch. As such, having football on Boxing Day is a dream ticket, one of the few occasions where simply having a game to go to is almost as important as the result.

Before football was ruined, the Boxing Day fixture would always be a local derby. This was to make it easier to get to with limited public transport, and because everyone really enjoyed it, a currency that holds little sway in these wretched times. Such was the tradition that the occasion even had its own festive ditty: "Hark now hear/ The Chester sing/The Wrexham ran away/And we will fight for ever more/Because of Boxing Day."

So what do we get now? Solihull Moors away, a team with whom we have no history and who are situated in Birmingham, about 100 miles away from Chester's fair city. Mindless. That said, it's a touch for me as despite the circumstances we are continuing the tradition of having Christmas at Her Indoors' family pile near Milton Keynes, serendipitously within striking distance of the match. This means that I can still be absent for the bulk of Boxing Day without hugely inconveniencing myself. Win, win, and hopefully win.

I don't even need The Driver's assistance, a dry run for when he's gone, although he has come up with a cockamamie plan to meet in a pub in Solihull to watch Aldershot versus Woking, which infuriatingly is actually a local derby.

Tapping the details into the chunky satnav, I leave The Boy in tears and drive away in my capsule of solitude. It's at least ten minutes before I tuck into my turkey sandwich, slewing all over the road as I try to keep the cranberry sauce off the smock. After a minor tour of Solihull, I bowl into the pub at the same time as The Hack and Wife. After all the pissing about, they're not even showing the National League match and instead we sit in front of a huge flapping screen half watching Watford v Crystal Palace. It's a turgid game, regularly interspersed by extreme close-ups of recently installed Palace manager Sam Allardyce's massive head, like a freshly glazed Christmas ham. Ham Allardyce.

Time's running and we're nowhere near the ground. For reasons unknown, The Driver has parked miles away from both pub and ground. As such, this is a rare instance where I drive The Driver, poacher turned gamekeeper. Despite being Half Man Half Car, he's not a good passenger, as I once discovered to my cost when I took him to Forest Green as I couldn't be arsed switching The Boy's child seat. Mercifully, this is a much briefer journey, but with ten minutes to kickoff there is still no sign of the ground. We hold our nerve and it eventually appears, with a sign for Solihull Borough harking back to a previous incarnation that I once saw Chester City beat here in a Trophy replay. Heady days.

The good news is that we're at the ground. The bad news is that the car park is full. With panic rising I head down a nearby lane that is being used as an ersatz overflow. A graveyard car park offers hope, sadly shattered by a sign clearly stating that it will be locked at 5pm. Fat use. There really isn't a parking space, but in desperation we forcibly manufacture one out of an overgrown verge. Basically reversing into foliage, The Driver gets out of the car to direct.

"Back," he says.

"Back."

"Back."

"Forward."

"FORWARD!"

It transpires that the gentle bump I felt was his foot. Serves him right. Limping to the ground with eight minutes to go, we can see the pitch through a fence, along with a series of skips and industrial levels of building materials. Despite The Driver's presumably inadvertent attempt to sabotage The Card, we just about make it in before kickoff, and festively greet Big Al. The Hack and Wife eventually rock up, he incandescent with rage, having simply abandoned his vehicle on a dual carriageway. I make a mental note that in future, when The Driver is gone, we will get here on time, park in the club car park, and drink in the club bar. Not that we'll be in this shithouse league as we're obviously going to win the play-offs at Wembley and resume our rightful position in the Football League.

Further drama follows. As the low winter sun recedes, I remove my prescription sunglasses with the intention of putting on my actual glasses, without which I may as well be watching on the radio. Somehow the glasses slip out of my grasp and tumble onto the pitch, agonisingly out of reach due to a hefty perimeter fence. There are no stewards to help, and I can't climb over in case I face a Card-killing expulsion for what would technically be a pitch invasion. I could feasibly dangle over the fence with at least two people holding each leg, but it's not a particularly elegant solution and volunteers are at a premium.

Redeeming himself, The Driver has an idea.

"Lynchy," he shouts. "Lynchy!"

Lynchy, who is busy warming up in the Chester goal, looks round and is bemused to find two grown men frantically pointing at an area of turf. Trotting over, he delicately picks up the specs with his gloved paws and carefully passes them to me. Safe hands.

Vision restored, it's a sight to behold as Chester have turned up in numbers, some 700 strong, making up virtually half the attendance. A lot of people must really hate their families. The Boxing Day crowd is markedly different to the normal turnout, and arguably more unpleasant, with some people treating it as an annual festive tradition like going to a pantomime or having a fight in John Lewis. Improbably, even The Driver's dad and brother have made the trip, albeit from relatively nearby.

While there is officially no segregation in place, Chester have staked a claim to one end, gathering behind the goal and in front of a shiny new metal standing area. It would make far more sense to stand in the new stand — that's what it's for — but sadly it has yet to be awarded a health and safety certificate and so we are forced to dangerously mill about, craning for a view.

This may be a contributory factor to me missing the first key incident of the game when our left back is sent off after 16 minutes for an apparent lunge. It's a huge blow, albeit one that is assuaged when we immediately take the lead. It's an advantage that we hold until the cusp of half-time when Solihull are awarded a contentious free kick that is superbly dispatched into the top corner over Lynchy's despairing dive. I wonder if it's my fault for interrupting his meticulous pre-match routine, but the reality is that it's one fuck of a goal that no cunt on earth could have saved.

Investigating the bar at half-time, I am quizzed as to my allegiance, as unlike the viewing area, the drinking area is segregated. It's like a big old dance hall, replete with flapping screen, and looks like the scene of a proper festive tear-up, with some people having possibly been here throughout the match. A heavily inebriated Grandad is holding court, tooth missing, mashing a plastic pint pot into his face in an appropriation of events real or imagined. And in an act of almost heroic pointlessness, some tit has shoved an entire bog roll down the shitter, thus mildly inconveniencing his fellow supporters.

With a man advantage, the second-half Solihull onslaught is inevitable and they soon take the lead. They shortly make it 3-1, at which point almost the entire away following heads for the exits, perhaps wary of missing a repeat of *Only Fools and Horses* or that last slice of ham. Those of us who linger to the death are rewarded with a 94th minute consolation goal, but our race is run, and it's measure of our overall progress that it feels unusual to have lost a game.

Heading for our respective vehicles, the lane where I left mine is now entirely shrouded in blackness. Eking my way forward by mobile phone light, it's like a horror film, with silhouettes and murmurs of people doing the same. Systematically pointing my phone at number plates, I eventually identify mine, negotiate the foliage, clamber in, and wolf down a mince pie before setting off. There's a crash on the M1 causing a 30-minute delay. Of course there is. I shrewdly avoid it by taking the A5. Joy to the world.

Attendance: 1,475   Position: 7th →←

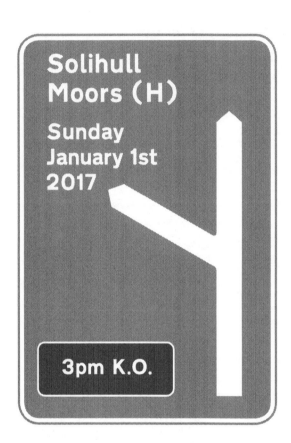

Solihull
Moors (H)

Sunday
January 1st
2017

3pm K.O.

Game 30 of 50 →

"Revenge is a dish best served cold," said Oscar Wilde. Or was it Robbie Savage? Either way, we have a swift opportunity to redress the balance with Solihull Moors following the freak Boxing Day defeat. It's the second part of a double header that nobody wanted, not least the Solihull fans who now have to make the arduous trip north, many of them presumably stinking of ale following the obligatory end-of-year celebrations.

New Year's Day football is something of a double-edged sword in that it's good to get out of the house and away from people, but not so good to be standing on a freezing terrace in a bleak northern outpost wishing you were dead. Hangover management is the key, along with pacing yourself through New Year's Eve, which like Christmas comes under the category of compulsory fun. It may be the end of the calendar year, but in football terms it's largely an irrelevance. Our year begins in August and (hopefully) ends in May, interspersed by a strange barren limbo where we wince at the heat and dabble with the sporting methadone of cricket, tennis and golf.

As has been traditional for a decade or more, we are to spend New Year's Eve at Watford Gap with an array of regular guests plus the odd squad member. The Watford Gap is obviously first on the team sheet, followed by my good self, then a Liverpool fan from Oxford and a Manchester United fan from London. I doubt they've been to more than one and nought games, respectively. I appreciate that the measure of a human soul is not the number of association football matches one has attended, but you know, get to fuck.

As happens every year, the evening begins with the womenfolk fussing about in the kitchen and reminiscing about that time they hid Clarissa Camden Taylor Maynard's hockey stick. Meanwhile the men, thrown together by marriage, repair to the pub and stay for one pint too many. And as he does every year without fail, The Watford Gap asks me incredulously if I'm really going to watch Chester the next day, and as ever is astonished that this is the case. Governments have fallen, children have been born, but every year he asks, and every year I go, apart from that one season when it was mercifully called off, allowing me to chuck my ring up without interruption.

There will be no such mistakes in this year of The Card, and I take it easy throughout the night, or as easy as one can take it when drinking constantly for eight hours. Having watched extended coverage of millions of pounds worth of fireworks going up in smoke, I volunteer to put The Boy to bed and tactically don't return. My reputation is in tatters, but The Card must come first.

The Driver has made his usual token protestations about going out of his way, but the sound of his car on the gravel cuts through the fug. Feeling only mildly nauseous, chat is nevertheless sparse and he puts on the new Nick Cave CD, presumably a Christmas present. Songs of death and despair soundtrack an entirely grey vista as horizontal rain lashes the windscreen in as bleak a scene as this or any season has mustered. We are only bucked out of our silent reverie when the car starts aquaplaning on the M6, forcing The Driver to take evasive action to avoid killing us and, by association, The Card. As usual, he has prepared a rudimentary Christmas hamper, and we tuck in greedily, grateful to be alive, if only to see us stick it up The Moors.

The Bouverie Arms is open for a spot of pre-match, and with cinematic timing I walk through the door as the jukebox contradictorily blares out, "All is quiet… on New Year's Day".

Somebody appears to have put on an entire U2 album, and when we attempt to watch Watford v Tottenham he makes himself known, checking that we're okay to view it with Bono bellowing over the top. A stocky thick-necked Scouser, he doesn't seem the sort of person to argue with so I tell him it's fine, at which point he immediately starts quizzing me as to my U2 allegiance. I am about to wheel out the time-honoured line that it's "music for people who don't like music" but shrewdly opt for the less confrontational "I can take it or leave it" which is at least half right. Occupying most of my personal space, he aggressively inquires, "Who do you like?"

Put on the spot, I blurt out "The Fall" to no response.

"Half Man Half Biscuit" draws a similar blank.

"Echo & The Bunnymen" elicits a flicker of recognition, but he accusatorily counters with "You look like a Leonard Cohen fan".

Barely 12 hours into the New Year, and I'm being accosted by a steroid-ridden psychotic U2 fan, randomly accused of liking a recently deceased iconic Canadian songsmith. You couldn't make it up. Backing away from the bar, I leave him to it and take solace in the big screen, where Watford appear to be not so much hung over as actively drunk, with Spurs seemingly scoring at will. I smugly picture The Watford Gap raging at the TV with a Bloody Mary.

Food is required, and as it's Sunday I am thrilled to order a Sunday lunch with all the trimmings. It's a champion luncheon, and allied to the hair of the dog I feel almost human again. Polishing off the last drop of gravy I reach down to loosen my belt only to discover that it has nowhere left to go, my bloated gut filling the oversized smock. Five months on The Card and I have reached my all time heaviest, breaching a monstrous 16 stone, with a gut like Phil Taylor. Never forget that this is a physical as well as a mental challenge.

The Blues Bar is teeming and the crowd is again bolstered by part-timers seemingly oblivious to the fact that football is not just for Christmas and that we play here every other week. On the terrace, New Year greetings are traded and even The Strangler proffers a handshake that I tentatively accept, all the while mindful of my neck.

Under a crescent moon, the game commences and we are absolute dog shit. A yard off the pace, the players look as though they've just rolled in from a two-bit knocking shop. There's no suggestion that this is the case, but if any of them have been swayed by the New Year festivities then they ought to be ashamed. If I can have an early night, then so can they. Any prick can get arseholed and sing *Auld Lang Syne*; very few have the privilege of being paid to play football.

The only football being played here is by Solihull Moors, who score one, two, and three goals without reply, prompting their paltry following to gleefully sing, "Can we play you every week?" It's probably the greatest week in the club's history, as they complete a momentous double over The Mighty Chester. It was cold, but there was no revenge.

A dry mince pie in the car does little to lighten the mood, and at Stafford Services The Driver snaps, kicking the fixtures and fittings in a moment of impotent rage. To add insult to injury, the water feature is switched off with no explanation given, an example of Broken Britain at its worst.

Charged a premium for the detour to Watford Gap, I throw an extra fiver through the car window and bid The Driver a two-worded farewell. Letting myself in, I take consolation in the bosom of my family. And more importantly, the darts.

Attendance: 2.244 Position: 10th ↓

Game 31 of 50 →

A mere four days after leaving, I'm back at Watford Gap. It's not the most obvious route to Essex, but we have a Friday night appointment at the Coventry Empire with the peerless Half Man Half Biscuit, their first of a handful of annual fixtures. Unlike football, entertainment is guaranteed, and I've seen them countless times all over the country, even in Chester where they played on the same night that Everton and Liverpool drew 4-4 in the FA Cup.

It's The Watford Gap's turn to drive, which means it's my turn to drink. We immediately bump into Chester fan Howie, who does the full Biscuit Card every year, but is surprisingly not going to Braintree, a confusing set of priorities. We join him in a nearby brewery-cum-pub where all kinds of fantastically named potions are fermented on the premises. It's a Real Ale fantasy, but I manage to locate a lively lager and go at it with gusto.

Randomly, The Watford Gap is faced by twin sporting nemeses with different shaped balls. Howie supports Warrington Wolves, sworn rugby league enemies of Wigan Warriors, and he's accompanied by a man who supports Luton Town, a team that The Watford Gap will only refer to as "Scum". In fact, The Watford Gap's one and only appearance at The Deva came against Luton, a game that he turned up to mob-handed from Wrexham, having watched a Rugby League World Cup quarterfinal at The Racecourse, eventually attending all four over the course of the weekend. Absolute idiocy.

"Creature. Wake up! Braintree awaits."

It's a rude awakening, but he has a vested interest in me continuing The Card, primarily getting me out of his house. Having secured cheap tickets, the entire family are off to Vicarage Road to see Watford take on Burton Albion in the Third Round of the FA Cup. Meanwhile, I'm off to deepest, darkest Essex: one man and his smock. How different things could have been, particularly as my maternal grandparents apparently first met at a Watford home game.

It was a typically strong Biscuit gig, but I instantly regret the six pints of heavy that accompanied it. I am hungry, thirsty, very cross, and very, very lost. Ye olde satnav has thrown me a bum steer and I fail to get onto the A14, instead going cross-country down rural lanes where people in Barbour jackets take dogs for walks and piss about with horses. Eventually getting back on track, I go past Kettering, scene of a solo train trip for a 4-0 drubbing, and past Cambridge, scene of a number of entirely random results that seemed important at the time.

Sitting in my own mess listening to sport, I am bucked out of my fug by a familiar vehicle on a dual carriageway. It's the official supporters' coach, about to begin its descent into Braintree, having departed Chester at 8:30am. Like a prison bus full of lifers, a bulk of the occupants must do The Card every year, not so much an achievement as a lifestyle choice. As I overtake the coach, they all have a thousand-yard stare, maybe a thousand-match stare. I give one dead-eyed passenger a fist-pump salute. No response. Resorting to the universal non-verbal communication of the football fan, I rhythmically toot the horn to the tune of "Der der der-der-der der-der-der-der City!" Nothing. Forget it.

In my three previous visits to Braintree, I have only ever been to the ground and the pub nearest the ground, The Orange Tree. Parking in its car park, I see no reason to change this routine, despite the fact that The Driver and The Hack and Wife have gone into town to sample the delights of whatever civic building Wetherspoons has assimilated. Perhaps wary of the Solihull debacle, I have no intention of joining them, preferring to sit in the car sulking, stinking of ale. The Hack even phones up and attempts to change my mind, claiming that it's a particularly nice Wetherpoons, an old cinema, no less, The Picture Palace. As I tersely explain, it could be the greatest Wetherspoons in the known universe; I'm not walking a mile in the rain through Braintree to find it.

Gathering my strength, I haul myself into The Orange Tree, where the Chester Youth have commandeered the pool table. Spitting feathers, I order a pint of Diet Coke and a double bacon cheese burger and chips meal deal that includes a pint for a pound. However, because I neglect to claim the pint at the time, the deal is negated and the barman informs me that there's nothing he can do as the transaction is closed. Absolutely livid, I wolf down the burger in mute despair. Restating my complaint to the plate collector, he takes pity and gives me a free pint to shut me up. This immediately lightens my mood. Whatever happens this afternoon, I am winning at life.

Manchester United versus Reading is on the big screen, United's 56th consecutive FA Cup tie to be televised, a 4-0 win that sees Wayne Rooney equal Sir Bobby Charlton's goal record. Pretending to ignore it is an unfamiliar Manchester City/Chester fan fresh from watching City progress with a 5-0 win at West Ham on the Friday night ahead of today's infinitely more important National League game.

Six Hours In The Car/Frank Sidebottom is also in, and is astonished that I am not with The Driver, assuming that we were joined at the hip. Telling him that we travelled separately due to my prior engagement in Coventry, he claims to be a fan of Half Man, particularly the song *Sweaty Betty*, which is of course by the vastly inferior Macc Lads. After pointing out his fundamental error, I turn the tables and ask him how long it took to get here. He seems genuinely horrified that anyone should care and rejoins Le Chat Noir and gang. They're all staying in St Albans, living the dream.

In the ground before kickoff, I have fulfilled my duty to The Card in trying circumstances. The Wetherspoons posse turn up, full of wild tales of cheap beer and cheap food, chastising me for being a miserable bastard. There is also a rare appearance from The Evertonian, here with his son, each resplendent in matching Everton hats. Confusingly, he was wearing a Tranmere shirt when I first met him in the halls of residence at Liverpool University shortly after Chester had dicked Rovers 2-1 at Prenton Park.

Spreading himself thin, his allegiance approximates to Everton, England, Tranmere, Chester, and even a bit of Northwich Victoria. As a show of primary support, he had the Everton motto tattooed on his arm, albeit so cheaply that Nil Satis Nisi Optimum eventually shrivelled into the word Nissan. As they say in Latin, nothing but the best is good enough. Something like that anyway, as The Driver should be able to confirm.

As well as being a fanzine co-conspirator, he was fundamental in instigating one of the stranger eras of Chester support when he got us both a gig stewarding at the freshly opened Deva Stadium. Not particularly compatible with the student lifestyle, our timekeeping was often an issue, although we were usually at the front of the queue when the tenners were handed out after each game: last in, first out. This didn't endear us to our fellow stewards, but that all changed one match day when a man with a cobweb tattoo on his face randomly invaded the pitch. Instantly off the blocks, The Evertonian gave chase, hunting him down like a dog and apprehending him with an impressive rugby tackle near the centre circle. Nobody criticised us again. Bizarrely, our exploits even appeared in a short-lived cartoon strip called *The Stewards* in a short-lived football comic called *The Red Card*. You couldn't make it up, except I did, as I wrote the script for it.

A large bulk of our time as stewards coincided with the tenure of hard-tackling midfielder Graham Barrow, who would later return as manager. An absolute gentleman, almost without fail he would pull out a pair of free tickets for us at away games. Allied to The Evertonian's foolproof Ladbrokes system, this paved the way for many a big day out, throughout the North West and beyond. Arguably the strongest trip was to Brighton for the last game of the 1992/93 season, the weekend beginning with a powerhouse performance by The Fall in Manchester on the Friday night. From there we got a midnight National Express coach direct to Brighton, where we enjoyed breakfast on the beach before attending the match sporting policeman's helmets and accompanied by an inflatable banana. Our deranged state was exacerbated further when an already relegated Chester side went 2-0 up in the opening minutes before eventually being pegged back to 3-2, also passing the landmark of 100 league goals conceded. Good times.

Here we all are then. 2017. Braintree in January, as grim a prospect as any on The Card. With no segregation in place, the Chester massive gather behind the goal that we are notionally attacking. It's a fruitless tactic, as almost all of the play is up the other end where despite their lowly status, The Iron are laying siege to our goal. Their pressure eventually pays off, and they score a bullet header for a deserved half-time lead.

The fans change ends, and Chester come out unrecognisable from their first-half torpor, going for the throat from the outset. With Sam Beasant — son of '88 FA Cup final hero Dave Beasant — in goal, Braintree hold on until the hour mark when Alabi gets behind him to equalise with a strong header. With no suggestion of taking a point, it's a thrilling game that sees us constantly on the attack, albeit with the jeopardy of possibly conceding on the break. With Alabi in Beast Mode, Braintree are run ragged, and with six minutes to go he unleashes a first-time shot that screams into the bottom corner. By way of celebration, he simply flexes his muscles in front of the away fans with steam pouring out of his head as a pile-on ensues. In the hometown of The Prodigy, he's a Firestarter, a twisted Firestarter.

We hold on for a memorable win, and on the way out manager Jon McCarthy shakes hands with every Chester fan and thanks them for coming. As The Evertonian says, "You don't get that in the Premier League".

The Junior Evertonian asks me if I'd rather have James Alabi or Romelu Lukaku up front. I concede that while Lukaku probably has a superior overall game, there's a question mark as to whether he could do it on a freezing January afternoon in Braintree. We may never find out.

Back in The Orange Tree, I buy The Driver a celebratory pint when my phone chirrups. It's a text message from the elusive Chris Iwelumo: the interview is on, right here, right now. Legging it back to the ground, The Driver leaves the pints with Le Chat Noir and comes along for the ride. We meet Iwelumo in the club car park, and what follows is the arguably most painstaking seven minutes of my career. For a former attacker, he's incredibly defensive, refusing to answer almost any question, simply replying, "I've said this already" or "This has all been in the press".

Instantly entering my top three worst interviewees alongside such exalted company as Alan Shearer and Kevin Pietersen, I am only grateful that I didn't mention his famous miss for Scotland. I need the money to fund The Card, but wish I hadn't bothered as the day has been sullied. As I joke to The Driver, "I hope we fucking go down".

Back in the pub, we sup up and fuck off. Riddled with rage and fatigue, I almost clip the pub sign, miss a turning, slew into the kerb and generally risk my life in pursuit of a pointless invented achievement acknowledged only by a handful of spotters. Good. Regaining my composure, I pull into a petrol station, only to find The Driver in there, plastic gloves on, topping up his car with a shit-eating grin.

   "Go away!"

   "Yeah, see you next week."

Attendance: 707 Position: 9th ↑

Forest Green Rovers (H)

Saturday
January 14th
2017

FA Trophy
Second
Round

3pm K.O.

Game 32 of 50 →

The Driver is working late, cannot guarantee kickoff, and suggests that I make my own way to The Deva. Sod that, I'll take my chances. The FA Trophy is a tournament in which we have historically had little success, the best run in recent history being an unsuccessful two-legged semi-final against Canvey Island in 2001. It is however a route to Wembley, an outcome that would require me to activate my historic pledge to climb over my back fence and walk unerringly towards the iconic arch. Sadly, bogey team Forest Green stand between me and that dream, having beaten us in each of the last eight meetings. What could possibly go wrong?

Leaving home at a more civilised hour than usual, The Boy waves me off in tears. I sometimes consider the prospect that it could be the last time I ever see them, given how The Driver drives. Switching cars at Ardley at the allotted time of 12:30pm, we are cutting it fine, but with a temperature of three degrees and a dusting of snow, the roads are at least free of people having 'a nice drive out'.

That said, we don't want it to get any colder, and the relatively local Port Vale has already fallen foul of the weather. Historically considered something of a derby, darts legend Phil "The Power" Taylor once rode from The Potteries to Sealand Road on his moped for a night game between Chester and Vale. What a story, as once told to me by the man himself at Crewe station.

As I get in his car, The Driver is on the phone — hands-free of course — to Boston James, who occasionally accompanies him to Bordeaux when he's not watching Boston United. Finishing his phone call, he gets through some basic admin then casually announces, "So, got married on Monday".

He's clearly looking for a reaction, and manifestly gets one. What the actual fuck? That's less than 48 hours after I saw him at Braintree, where not a word was mentioned, unless he made an official announcement in Wetherspoons and nobody thought to tell me. All business, it turns out that it's easier to emigrate if you make some nebulous reversible vows to a non-existent deity followed by a slap-up feed for people you'll never see again. He didn't even go that far, simply bunging 75 quid at a registry office and repairing to the pub. It is however a huge step in his commitment to go through with this emigration nonsense, and consequently another nail in the coffin of my future lifts. As such, it's even more important that I nail The Card this season.

Making time in perilous fashion, we leave a trail of dead on the A41 and get into the Blues Bar for an easy pint. We have a chat with an affable former England hooligan who used to post me his Wembley tickets so he didn't have to go, but could still qualify for away games. It's a week until Wrexham are due here, and talk turns to the bubble, with our friend expressing the perfectly feasible opinion that if the travel restriction is ever lifted then every lunatic on both sides of the border will be "sharpening their knives".

Unfortunately, and unfathomably, I have forgotten to wear the smock of invincibility. It doesn't hugely influence the betting markets, but does leave me feeling vulnerable. Although surely we have to beat these at some stage. We were decent in the second half at Braintree, and as Iwelumo assured me in one of his more verbose responses, the dismal double against Solihull was "a blip". Our assistant manager is again absent today due to media commitments, something that riles The Driver, who remains resolutely unmellowed by married life. As he says, the first question in his interview should have been "Can you work Saturdays?" followed by "Can you send in the next candidate?"

As for the game, there's good news and bad news. The good news is that I manage to snag the last Chester Pie, a mouth-wateringly arid combination of chicken and ham in a flaky pastry case. The bad news is that Forest Green bloodlessly dump us out of the Trophy 2-0. I didn't want to go to Wembley anyway — it's a shithouse.

Filling up with diesel at Morrisons, we spot the famous Chester Hippy, still sporting the same hairstyle and retro shirt, but sadly without the trademark scarf tied to each wrist. Hitting the road, we are now free to concentrate on the league, unencumbered by such fanciful notions as winning silverware or visiting the national stadium. Furthermore, a run to the play-offs notwithstanding, it is now looking like a 50-game Card. Bullseye.

Back at Ardley, the least I can do is buy The Driver a pint to celebrate his recent nuptials so we dive into The Fox and Hounds for a swift one, no sirloin. It's not as swift as hoped due to the utter incompetence of the barmaid, only on her second day having been released from Wetherspoons by mutual consent. Eventually offering my congratulations, we retrospectively classify Gateshead away as his stag-do.

The only other person in the bar is a thickset meathead who has just watched live television coverage of Chelsea's 3-0 win at Leicester City. As he succinctly informs us, "Leicester were shit".

As is his wont, The Driver cannot wait to let him know where we've been, as if he's somehow going to garner his respect. He can't help himself, and it's probably why he knows so many people. Instead of being impressed, the meathead simply looks at him as if he was boasting about driving 200 miles to wank off a dog.

Sending my commiserations to The Driver's wife, I set the controls for the heart of the moon and hit the M40. Accompanied by some banging house tunes, this seems to elevate my speed to above the recommended 100mph and I am soon turning onto my street. Spotting the outline of a woman and child, I gleefully recognise them as Her Indoors and The Boy. Almost tearful, I am actively pleased to see them, and generously give them a lift. The Boy has been to a birthday party, followed by an after-party, and promptly declares it the "worst day ever". Welcome to my world.

We get home in time to see Chris Iwelumo freely chatting on Channel 5, seemingly holding it together following the end of our cup run. Looking out the of the kitchen window, the Wembley arch is lit up in red and white, presumably in tribute to former England manager Graham Taylor, who sadly died in the week. It's a nice touch.

Attendance: 1,250

Wrexham (H)

Saturday
January 21st
2017

3pm K.O.

Game 33 of 50 →

We've got to stick it up these. Whatever else happens during the season, a certain amount of goodwill can be earned by tearing Wrexham a new arsehole, and a win on top of the draw secured at their place would give us so-called bragging rights until at least the next meeting. Of course this time round it's their fans' turn to spend a tortuous hour or so in the bubble, although they do have the added incentive of getting out of Wrexham for the afternoon.

Their journey is extremely straightforward compared to the convoluted machinations required to deliver we three pricks to The Deva, and much of the preceding week is spent coming up with the most elegant solution to a series of logistical quandaries. I deliver the final document with a day to spare, and it goes a little bit like this: I leave on the Friday night with The Boy and drive to Birmingham where Her Indoors has *Strictly* business, and crucially, a hotel room. On the Saturday morning The Hack drives from Sussex to Ardley where he can rendezvous with The Driver and Wife, fresh from Newbury. The Driver drives them all north, but the newlyweds plan to visit The Driver's dad before the match. The Hack wants no part of this, so they will eject him at the Newcott Chippy on the A41, where I will pick him up en route from Birmingham, having left The Boy and Her Indoors to get the train home. We will then all meet up in Chester, have a couple of easy pints, and stick it up The Goats. What could possibly go wrong?

Picking up The Boy directly from school, we briskly march to the car to avoid getting a parking ticket, thus maintaining our 100% record. They might catch us eventually, but the money saved over the years should cover the fine. Bidding the other parents a good weekend, I don't believe that any of them are planning to attend a non-league football match 200 miles away. In fact, they're more likely to be doing cosmic yoga, tantric tai chi, or even being injected with Colombian frog venom (I shit you not).

The M1 is relatively clear, but it's a gruesome January day, made infinitely more so by listening to live coverage of Donald Trump's inauguration. It's a vile oppressive occasion and as I glance back at The Boy's angelic sleeping face I genuinely despair at the kind of world that I have brought this child into. All a mere footnote in comparison to the cross-border derby of course, and indeed The Card, which is rapidly approaching its third act.

Following a decent start, traffic grinds to a standstill around Birmingham. While it's not Card-threatening, it is exceedingly dull, exacerbated by a banal local radio phone-in during which hapless callers posit whether a joint first XI selected from all of the Midlands' professional football clubs would be remotely competitive in the Premier League.

Progress is painstaking, but the satnav eventually informs us that we have arrived at our destination, despite the fact that we are in the car park of a deserted office building, and not apparently at a Malmaison. Annoyingly, this time it's down to human error — who knew there were two Wharfsides in Birmingham?

I piss on a tree, curse the day I was born, select the correct Wharf-side and start again, angry not disappointed. The rage bubbles to the surface when roadworks send me on three laps of the city centre, past the hotel a few times, before finally alighting in its car park. At which point our car alarm goes off, one of the doors refuses to lock, and The Boy bursts into tears.

Heading out for sustenance, we pause to watch through a pub window as Sheffield Wednesday miss a penalty at Brighton, then scoff pizza as I follow Lincoln v Dover on my phone. Sport never sleeps. First thing in the morning, I watch a bit of Melbourne Victory, notionally my Australian team on the basis that I've been to one game. Randomly, on the train to the ground I ended up chatting to a Wrexham fan, not something that will be happening today.

Following a family breakfast, full English of course, I step outside the hotel and am immediately confronted by hordes of paparazzi.

Admittedly, The Card has picked up some momentum through *The Non-League Paper* and word of mouth, but I certainly wasn't expecting this. Covering my face, I demand that they respect my privacy, something they are more than happy to do, instantly lowering their cameras and saving their flashbulbs for the stars of the *Strictly Come Dancing* live show, who are staying here as well. Also hovering outside the hotel is a handful of fans who have been standing in freezing temperatures since dawn in the hope of seeing someone off the telly and maybe getting them to write their name down. We all need a hobby.

After walking the family to nearby New Street station, I set the controls for Shropshire's premier fast-food outlet-cum-supermarket-cum-nitespot, and eventually extricate myself from Birmingham's clogged arteries. Hitting the A41, by a matter of seconds I find myself stuck behind a lorry carrying a digger. What would The Driver do? Absolutely anything to get past it. What do I do? Hold my nerve and get there eventually. It's a big match, but not worth dying for.

Bleak, deserted, and shrouded in winter mist, pulling up at the Newcott feels like a scene from a spy film. Scanning the area, I spot The Hack alone in the restaurant, casually reading a newspaper with a plate of bones in front of him. I could easily walk up behind him and perform a double-tap to the back of the head. He wouldn't see it coming. Or I could hilariously leave him there, stranded in the middle of nowhere. Top banter, as they say, they being pricks.

Instead, I make myself known and ask him how long he's been there and what he's had: about 20 minutes, chicken and chips. Not really a breakfast dish, I think to myself, although he has been up for about six hours. Resisting the urge for a Greedy Pig Box, we hit the road and cruise into Chester, finding a solitary parking space opposite The Chichester Arms, which back in the day used to make The Bouverie Arms look like Claridge's. Lured by its apparent facelift, we pop in and find it unrecognisable from the shit-pit of yore, with big screens showing both live matches. Chester's finest soon rock up, accompanied by an unnecessary police escort. As one lad says, "What do they think I'm going to do? Smash up my own pub?"

The Driver and Wife turn up, and we all repair to The Bouv for food, a sop to modernity that The Chi has yet to embrace. It's wall-to-wall Chester, and the postman known as Gandhi approaches The

Driver wielding some kind of Bouverie Blues business card, replete with a Latin logo that he wearily translates.

Mrs Driver heads into town for a look round the shops, while her husband drives us the final mile and doesn't even charge for diesel. The Blues Bar is heaving, and for once we can't sneak in via the smoking entrance, forced to begrudgingly pay the £1 entry fee, a dunderheaded slice of economics that engenders ill will and probably costs the club money. If you want to squeeze extra cash out of the fans, just add 50p to the price of a pint — don't charge them a quid for the privilege of buying one.

Most people are gathered round the TV, watching the final knockings of Swansea's unlikely Premier League win at Liverpool. As the game ends, they remember why they're here and burst into anti-Wrexham song. On cue, the convoy arrives from Wales, a series of identical and grammatically incorrect 'Pats Coaches'. Who pats coaches? Maybe he pats coaches?

On the McNally, we are surrounded by part-timers, or by regulars who have been displaced by part-timers. As such we are up close and personal with a ginger-bearded hipster who leans back to bellow his non-sequiturs with such gusto that he appears in danger of dislocating his neck. It's a sight to behold, and difficult to keep a straight face when he's in full flow.

As is often the case with these occasions, free flowing football is at a premium, but there's a decent atmosphere and Rooney gets the obligatory dog's abuse, to the extent that he bottles out of taking a corner down our end. Goalless at the break, the second half is barely ten minutes old when a sickening roar from the away end signals a goal, with the red-shirted scorer mounting the fence and climbing into the frenzied Wrexham hordes. It's John Rooney of course, who in the corresponding fixture last season scored a superb free kick in the same goal for us against them. What's the fucking point?

Mercifully we are soon thrown a lifeline when James Alabi performs some kind of high stepping dance routine in the penalty area and is brushed against by a Wrexham player. The ref awards a spot kick, Alabi steps up and sends the keeper the wrong way to restore parity, prompting the hipster to produce a hitherto unseen flag from his pocket and run behind the goal brandishing it.

This sets up a grandstand finish during which our captain is sent off and we are ultimately hanging on to the draw that would at least keep our self-respect intact, with the pain of failure arguably greater than the pleasure of success. Or arguably not. The defeats can feasibly be dispatched to the back burner of memory whereas the famous victories burn bright for years to come.

In the event, it finishes 1-1, honours even, prompting an almighty scuffle — on the pitch, between the players. Punches are thrown, there's something for grapple fans, and even a suggestion of racial abuse from a Wrexham player. Lovely stuff. The irony doesn't go unnoticed that while the supporters were kept apart, the players maintained the tradition of a derby-day dustup.

The Driver drops us back at my car and I warn The Hack that I have had three pints of cooking lager and cannot guarantee his safety. Some hours later I deliver him to Ardley without incident and we head our separate ways, a point in the bag. See you at Dover. Tired, so very tired.

Attendance: 3,961 Position: 9th →←

Game 34 of 50 →

A regular fixture in recent seasons, a trip to Dover always feels somewhat exotic, despite the fact that they play at a place called Crabble. The High Speed 1 train from St Pancras rips through the Kent countryside at blistering pace, and it's almost like being in Europe, as opposed to the 1970s theme park that much of the UK rail network resembles. Unfortunately, in a state of befuddlement I somehow manage to buy the wrong ticket, spending £40 instead of the requisite £30, an erratum that sullies the entire day before it's even begun.

Spotting a fan called Adam on the escalator, we are soon joined by Exiles royalty, Pauline, and at Stratford by a guy called Rich, who I briefly played with in a darts league for the Exiles. Like a portmanteau Hammer Horror film, we are four strangers on a train, thrown together by a nebulous concept, hurtling towards our doom. Maybe we're already dead, maybe the club never reformed, maybe we just get dicked by Dover. Perhaps I'm overthinking things.

Either way, I bury my head in yesterday's *Evening Standard* while Pauline and Adam spend the entire journey vociferously arguing about the club's finances. Apparently, despite constantly begging for money, Chester are sitting on a £100k rainy-day fund, which Pauline believes should remain just that, to be used only in case of emergency. Canvassed for my opinion, I say we should immediately spend every penny on strengthening the team. Every day's a rainy day and we have never been this close to the play-offs at this stage of the season. In *Bullseye* parlance: Gamble. We'll all be dead one day, that's an emergency — let's live a little.

Mercifully, Dover Priory soon looms large. Other than Chester itself, it's probably the longest schlep from station to ground in The National League. As such, we jump in a cab that takes us past the pound shops and knocking shops of this squalid seaside town on the easterly tip of this crumbling nation.

No pissing about, we head directly for the pub nearest the ground, The Cricketers, where we are soon joined by The Hack and Wife. Utterly freezing and wholly unwelcoming, it almost defies the concept of a public house. With décor straight out of *The Sweeney*, there's nothing to suggest it isn't 1974 apart from a vast TV with HD so crisp that it's almost too realistic. Providing an uncanny valley version of football, it's more like a game of *FIFA*, or the superior *Pro Evolution Soccer*, than the real thing. Liverpool are playing Wolves in the FA Cup and have fielded a weakened team, a despicable show of arrogance that disrespects both the competition and their supporters. We may have fallen at the first hurdle in Southport, but at least we gave ourselves a chance.

Rumours of food spread around The Cricketers, with reports reaching us that the Breville sandwich maker has been plugged in. Inquiring as to the bill of fare, the barman deadpanly informs me that there is "cheese, cheese and onion, cheese and ham, there's no ham". Cheese and onion it is then please, barkeep. The Hack even manages to liberate a frozen pizza. Quite the bon viveur.

Fresh from breaking the land speed record, The Driver swans in and immediately embarks on a lengthy conversation in French with a Marseille fan — sworn enemy of Bordeaux — who is embedded with the Chester Youth, and I don't know what's real any more.

Liverpool shamefully relinquish the FA Cup due to their loathsome conceit, which more importantly signals that it's time to go and watch some real football. Stepping out of the pub to the sound of distant drums, what's that coming over hill? It's some kind of urchin-led marching band who mystifyingly are chanting an anti-Wrexham song despite manifestly not being from Chester. If you want to defeat your enemy sing his song. As they stream past the pub, Four Cards casually asks, "Where you from lads? Are you game?"

They are indeed game, and a minor scuffle breaks out on the approach to the ground. Led by an angry little Dover Hobbit, despite his shortcomings elsewhere, he delivers one of the greatest insults of this or any season when he points to one of the Chester Youth and shrieks, "You're wearing your mum's coat!"

It's all over before it really begins, as the stewards move in. One of them simply picks up Bilbo Baggins by his collar, still spitting venom with his little legs kicking the air. Further investigation by The Driver reveals that Dover had some previous with Wrexham, hence the percussion-led ditty, a paean to a famous battle in a distant land. Or maybe just some pushing and shoving outside the ground.

Crabble, I am in you, comfortably in time to keep The Card intact. We are in deep, and it would be a real shame to balls it up at this late stage. The game is unsegregated so we take the traditional place behind the goal we are attacking, unlike the bulk of the Chester support who segregate themselves into the other end. As such, without safety in numbers, I feel slightly more self-conscious about opening proceedings by bellowing, "Come on Blues, these are garbage!"

They're actually one of the better teams in the league and we never get anything here. For reasons unknown, McCarthy has dropped our favourite floppy-haired keeper, Lynchy, and his deputy is soon picking the ball out of the net as Dover take the lead with a penalty. We may be few, but we are perfectly situated to see Alabi's spectacular long-range equaliser four minutes later, and head into the bar at half-time with some optimism. There's a lively atmosphere, and The Dover Youth are baiting Grandad, who offers one of them a clip round the ear, the archaic threat only making things worse.

Joining the throng for the second half, it is at this end where we once witnessed a dramatic last-minute winner against Margate — who were ground sharing — headed in by Big Dave Cameron, not to be confused with the pig-worrying failed Prime Minister. The goal prompted such wild celebrations that Cameron, The Driver and I all appeared on the front page of *The Non-League Paper*, locked in a joyous embrace. But the real story is that Parky, who was on the train with me, had to get off and turn back en route to the game because his wife rang up with gut rot. The Driver never fails to relate the tale, the aborted trip arguably giving him more pleasure than the goal.

Parky will no doubt be listening in today from Australia, headphones on in bed, frightened to move lest he disturb the wife, presumably celebrating the equaliser by clenching his spare fist. It's a world away from winter in Dover, although he may be pleased to know that The Curious Case Of Benjamin Button is in, off the crutches but still limping after his alien abduction.

A win today against play-off rivals will kick start the final push, but all hope is extinguished by two early Dover goals, and we spend the final half an hour simply going through the motions, full of piss and regret. They lock it down for a 3-1 win and Wembley is trickling through my fingers.

No hanging about, The Hack drops me off at the station, although I still have time for a quick one in the foul pub opposite. A full-scale Madchester party is in place, with The Chester Youth singing along to *I Am The Resurrection* by The Stone Roses followed by *Hallelujah* by Happy Mondays, replete with DJ Grandad cupping an invisible headphone and spinning an invisible turntable. There's some anti-Wrexham bile, and a rousing chorus of "We are the famous 125!" It's a tribute to the veteran Chester firm named after the high-speed train that used to come as close as Crewe. You then had to change to the North Wales Sprinter, which didn't have quite the same ring.

Back on High Speed 1, serendipitously I share a table with the train gang, who are locked into a deep conversation about the 175, gauge sizes, coupling mechanisms, the works. I am unqualified to contribute, although manage a bit of Biscuit chat with Howie. I offer him a lift to the Oxford gig after Eastleigh at home, but of course he's on the Biscuit Card and is doing a double-header with the Worthing gig on the Friday night. What a way to live.

Spat out at St Pancras far too soon, I still have time to kill. After drinking alone for hours, I go to see The Fall on my own. Bliss.

Attendance: 1,183 Position: 10th ↓

Dagenham
& Redbridge (A)

Saturday
February 4th
2017

3pm K.O.

Game 35 of 50 →

Thirty years to the day since four pricks in a car drove across the Pennines to see us play Sheffield Wednesday in front of more than 20,000 in the FA Cup, one prick on foot gets the Tube across London to see us play Dagenham & Redbridge in front of more than 1,000 in The National League.

Despite its relative proximity, it's not a trip to be relished and we genuinely never get anything there, shipping six goals on each of our last two visits, including an opening-day 6-0 drubbing in torrential rain.

Accompanied by my family early doors, we take the Jubilee Line to London Bridge to meet The Hack, who has got the Thameslink up from Brighton. Of all the carriages on all the Tubes, who should limp on to ours but The Curious Case Of Benjamin Button, growing younger by the day. Spotting me, he cheerfully asks if I'm going to the game. I appreciate that it's just something to say, but he could probably hazard an educated guess. I've been to every game, it's the day of the game, I'm heading in the direction of the game: yes I'm going to the game.

We're running late so The Hack has spent an hour touring Borough Market and helping himself to the numerous free food samples. We find him holed up in a fetid pub watching Chelsea beating Arsenal on two adjacent screens, which — spoiler alert — are out of sync by a couple of seconds. Her Indoors stays for a quick drink, thus increasing the female population by approximately 100%. The barman short-changes me by 50p, but I simply can't be arsed to argue. At half-time we go our separate ways, the men to Dagenham & Redbridge Football Club, and the woman and child to the Fashion and Textile Museum in Bermondsey, later described by The Boy as the most boring thing he's ever been to. And he's been to the best part of 20 Chester games.

It always takes longer than you think to get to Daggers as the District Line slowly trundles east into the badlands of Essex. The deeper you go, the bleaker it gets, and the more numerous the St George's Crosses become: tatty flags draped over fences and flapping out of windows. The grey scenery is enlivened by flashes of blue en route as away fans join the party, including one hapless berk seemingly under the impression that a replica shirt alone is ample protection against the February elements.

Finally alighting at Dagenham East, we dive into The Pipe Major, a new pub that has sprung up since our last visit. A huge modern family-friendly food-based affair, there's an all day carvery, accessible by paying for either a small, medium or large plate. What a time to be alive. Maybe not today, definitely not tomorrow, but one day, if we're still in the same division, I plan to eat that meat. Got your big plate, Alan?

There are a few Chester dotted about, including a rare sighting of a man known only as Belgrano. A West Ham fan by trade, he turns up to the odd game with his Chester mate, Carl, who is a ringer for a mid-period Olly Reed. The Driver and I first encountered them before a game at Wycombe Wanderers. Both falling down drunk, they were convinced that The Driver was in fact Jean Jacques Burnel, the bass player out of The Stranglers — no relation to The Strangler. Our new Cockney friend then earned his soubriquet by spending the entire match shouting "Oi, Belgrano!" at Wycombe's Argentine midfielder, Sergio Torres, a reference to the battleship sunk during the Falklands conflict with massive loss of life.

Not tempted by the carvery buffet, The Hack needs chippy, and chippy he shall have, courtesy of a chippy over the road, where he orders a small fish and chips for the bargain price of £3.50. I do the same, only to be told that The Hack has had the last small fish, and that the next price point is £6. Absolutely crestfallen, I am paralysed by this news, and don't know whether to stick or twist. The Hack comes up with a third way, suggesting that I offer £4. To my astonishment, it's accepted. Everything is negotiable. Minus the 50p swindled out of me in London Bridge, I am £1.50 up on the day before a ball has been kicked. I'll take it.

The day gets even better when The Driver strolls into the club bar, pulls out an envelope full of £20 notes and promptly gives us one each, no strings. Happily, it's that day of the season when the school he works at puts him in charge of a dozen or so foreign students for the weekend. Naturally he bundles them all into a minibus and drives them to wherever in the country Chester are playing, replete with a fairly liberal approach to expenses, hence the generous bung. The downside is that if he is seen drinking he will immediately lose his job. As such, he minimises the possibility of this by necking a pint of Nutty Slack in about eight seconds before disappearing to check on his young charges.

Mainly from Spain, they have been sent to England by wealthy parents to learn the language firsthand, although it might be advisable not to repeat much of what they hear today. They are at least getting a football education. Raised on the Nou Camp, Bernabeu and Mestalla, what they make of the Chigwell Construction Stadium is anyone's guess, although we are seated in the impressive new Traditional Builders' Stand.

It's not exactly *Sensible Soccer* but it gives us an elevated view of Dagenham's early penalty and subsequent SAVE! Get in — or not, in this instance, the diving stop prompting a celebration almost on a par with scoring a goal. Sadly, despite us playing surprisingly well, it's only a stay of execution as Dagenham score a long-range goal on the stroke of half-time for an undeserved 1-0 lead. Bemoaning what a shit sport football really is, I head for the bowels of the stand and drink a plastic pint of the most horrible fizzy Carling imaginable, a deeply unpleasant and wholly unnecessary experience. So why do I do it? Fuck knows — because it's there.

With the Spanish Armada seemingly shovelling the entire menu into their greedy maws, the second half begins and within five minutes we twat in an excellent equaliser. Actually get in. Scenes. Chips everywhere, limbs, barking, roaring, a proper bundle. Eight minutes later, it goes from the sublime to the ridiculous when we take the lead to near incredulity. It's on for young and old. What a sport.

Playing an almost unrecognisable brand of controlled expansive football, we are taking the piss out of Daggers, not for the first time this season, with a high-profile double drawing tantalisingly close. There's an argument that if things are going well, don't change it, but on 75 minutes McCarthy makes a substitution that seems to unbalance the team. With four minutes of normal time remaining, a Daggers header beats the keeper, but defender Johnny Hunt dives full length to claw it off the line — with his hand. It's a blatant penalty and a sending off, one of the rare occasions when it is actually deliberate handball. If we save the penalty, it's worth it. If not, we're hanging on to a point with ten men.

Obviously, it's the latter — the spot kick is dispatched and the onslaught begins. It's unbearable, and as the clock hits 90 minutes the ball thuds against our crossbar and bounces back into play. It could go anywhere, but as time freezes it falls to the feet of their striker who sticks it in the corner for the winner, right in front of us. Our players fall to the ground disconsolate, burying their faces in the turf. It's absolutely monstrous, and I cover my eyes so as not to witness the celebrations. Fuck it all. Trudging out in a daze, we walk straight into a bunch of jubilant Daggers. Invisible to them, our pain is their joy.

Back in The Pipe Major, The Hack and I join Pauline, Pauline's sister, and Pauline's sister's husband, all of us sat round a table in a state of shock. The only solution is to throw alcohol at it, and within the hour there's some minor thawing of mood. The Hack causes a further problem, however, when he reveals that every season he puts £50 on us to be relegated. He sees it as an insurance policy, but Pauline's sister takes genuine exception, branding him disloyal and a disgrace. He eventually has to leave, but I stay and drink, to kill time and numb the pain. I'm looking for positives: The Card is intact, we played well, and at least we didn't pay to get in. Although I would have gladly paid double to hold on to the win.

Finally heading west, they all get a train to Cambridge while I make my way to Camden for a prearranged meeting with Ipswich fan, Bealesy, fresh from reporting on Southend v Scunthorpe for Sky Sports News. As arranged, we go to see Julian Cope at The Roundhouse, but he's either shit or I'm too pissed to enjoy it. We have a quick pint in The Hawley Arms afterwards, which I believe to be my 11th of the day. A filthy doner kebab sees me to the last train, on which I briefly fall asleep. Stumbling home, muttering to myself, the unblinking red light of the Wembley arch greets me from the kitchen window. So near, yet so far away.

Attendance: 1,250 Position: 12th ↓

Gateshead (H)

Saturday
February 11th
2017

12:15pm K.O.

Game 36 of 50 →

If an algorithm existed to determine a match not to attend, it would struggle to come up with anything more appropriate than this. Where to start? It's 200 miles away. It's a home game. We're playing against a team that nobody cares about. The season has gone to shit. It's bitterly cold. It's an early kickoff. And it's live on television…

What bliss to sit at home with a warm brew and shout at the telly, essentially the default position of the overwhelming majority of so-called football supporters. In the fanzine that I was involved with in the early 1990s, *Is It Red?*, we had a cartoon strip about a character called Bostik Arse, a pastiche of the archetypal armchair fan. And this was before Sky bought football, effectively reducing it to a kind of sporting wallpaper as opposed to appointment-to-view television. One Sunday, I worked out that I could watch 18 live football matches. And by could, I mean did, or at least dipped in and out, watching the odd goal in the same way that one might listen to a song on the radio.

Nevertheless, whoever chose Chester versus Gateshead to be broadcast live to the nation has really shit the bed. BT Sport's coverage of The National League is exemplary, and they try to give everyone a fair crack of the whip, but this is an absolute dog's breakfast. Optimistically billed as the battle of the play-off contenders — which admittedly sounds better than 12th v 8th — it's unlikely to trouble Arsenal v Hull, which kicks off on Sky Sports quarter of an hour later, thus affording us a tenuous 15 minutes of fame.

In the normal scheme of things, I would be nowhere near it, instead spending the morning attempting to make BT Sport come on my television without it jerking like a two-dollar whore. But The Card is no respecter of algorithms, and this is my morning: 7:30am alarm.

Get up. Wash arse. Put on smock. Cut off top of thumb with bread knife. Get in car, openly bleeding from gaping wound.

It's not a great start, but all is not lost as I can spend the journey getting on with some important work. As self-appointed The Fall correspondent for a retro music magazine, I have been commissioned to review five reissued CD's, some of which are in the car. Possibly allied to the early start and minor blood loss, I become so immersed in the music that I start to lose all sense of self, having to pinch myself to bring me out of my reverie, at which point I realise that I am travelling at 120mph. Not wanting to spoil The Card by becoming one of the million plus people killed on the road each year, I ease off the accelerator and cruise into Ardley for 9am.

It's going to be tight, but The Driver is the man for the job. We once got pulled over for speeding on the way to Scarborough, but the officer said he couldn't book him as he was going too fast to register on their system. He maintains a similar velocity today, but it's still a nerve-wracking business, with the integrity of The Card hanging on the vagaries of the hopelessly outdated motorway system. The route north is OK so far, but observing miles of static southbound traffic, The Driver chillingly describes it as a Card killer.

And then we spot it, sat motionless in a sea of cars, a solitary 'Pats Coaches' full of Wrexham fans, going nowhere, or Dover as it's better known. It's pathetic, but it absolutely makes our day, the thought of them all, up since sparrow's fart, trapped on a grammatically incorrect coach. The frustration of strangers is an abstract thing to take pleasure from, and while I am morally obliged to hate Wrexham as a concept, the two Wrexham fans that I actually know are perfectly decent individuals, more or less. All the same, you have to laugh.

Leaving 'Pats Coaches' in our rear view mirror, The Driver performs his usual death-defying feat, and we are at The Deva in good time. The club has promised all manner of extra-curricular activities to create a bumper atmosphere for the cameras, and the car park resembles the *Phoenix Nights* family fun day, with some kind of caged activity as well as a demonstration of the self-explanatory FootGolf.

Swerving it all, we sneak into the Blues Bar for a swift one, where we join Le Chat Noir in front of the TV and enjoy the novelty of watching the build-up to the game that we are about to attend. I wonder if any tightwads will simply choose to watch it in the bar. It would certainly be warmer, the weather now half a world away from that scorching opening day when we flew to the North East and Gateshead brutally handed us our arse.

They're still a decent side, although the opening minutes are utterly turgid. It was a frame of snooker, there would be a re-rack. At one point, Tom Shaw has a shot, which allied to the lack of action leads to a conversation about a theoretical situation in which he'd score an own goal and then shank in an equaliser, thus spawning the headline 'SHAW SHANK REDEMPTION'. You're welcome.

Loads of squeaky-voiced kids have been press-ganged into the away end in order to avoid the embarrassment of showing empty seats on TV. As such, they get a close-up view of the opening goal just after the half-hour mark when to everybody's surprise we actually take the lead. It lasts all of four minutes, and we head into the break level, giving me the opportunity to enjoy a balanced diet of a pie and a tea.

In the second half, Gateshead take the lead. Despite a bit of huffing and puffing they manage to hold onto it, thus completing the double over us while propelling themselves towards the fringes of the play-offs and stranding us in mid-table obscurity. As the old song maintained: "We won't win the league/ We won't win the cup/We're not going down/We're not going up". We are, very much like 'Pats Coaches', going nowhere.

In a break with tradition — maybe to pick up a stash of mucky books — The Driver stops at Hilton Park services, where somebody appears to be selling puppies out of the back of a transit van. For once, the Services are notably free of angry/happy/indifferent fans in polyester replica shirts. Our early kickoff has put the entire day out of sync, with other matches starting as we're on our way home. We even drive past Villa Park while there's a game on, a glimpse of the blazing floodlights proving impossibly exciting. To think, it's only 42 years since we played a League Cup semi-final there in front of 48,000, coming within one goal of breaking our Wembley duck. More recently, I saw us play a second-round tie there in space year 1999, going 5-0 down and then scoring a late consolation penalty, only for the ref to order a retake for some perceived infringement, which was promptly missed. The rules are the rules, but if ever there was a case for turning a blind eye...

Nobody has set fire to my car at Ardley, where I wearily pay the ferryman and head home, studiously ignoring the advertised fact that the M40 is closed between junctions 6a and 8 due to an accident. Failing to act on the information, I somehow hope that perhaps they're lying, or that it will maybe sort itself out before I get there. I have time to reflect on these choices when I sit in static traffic for 40 minutes as emergency vehicles hurtle down the hard shoulder, my bladder rapidly exacerbating the inconvenience. At least 'Pats Coaches' probably had a bog on board.

At one point, people start to get out of their vehicles and pace around in consternation, as if that's somehow going to help. Some mobile phone research reveals that there have now been three accidents ahead, so there's nothing to do but stare into middle distance, try not to piss myself, and listen to non-stop sport. England beat Wales at rugby, Liverpool beat Spurs at football, and the world continues to turn. We finally get moving, and I arrive home scarcely any earlier than usual. I do at least have time to eat my tea before watching our assistant manager Chris Iwelumo provide televised tactical analysis of other teams. I bet he's never done The Card.

Attendance: 2,095   Position: 12th →←

Maidstone
United (A)

Saturday
February 18th
2017

3pm K.O.

Game 37 of 50 →

Her Indoors is in Liverpool doing something unspeakable with Gary Barlow and Danni Minogue. This means that I either have to take The Boy or dump The Boy. I love the bones of the little chap, but on match day the latter option is generally preferable. That said, if I take him on the train I can get arseholed, or as arseholed as you can get while in charge of a minor. If I dump him I have to drive, so can't get arseholed, so may as well take him. It's one of the great philosophical dilemmas of our time, a kind of Schrödinger's match.

In the event I drive to South East London and dump him with someone I met in a strip club in Bucharest. It's TV's Ellie Gibson, a Scummy Mummy whose jokes I write when she appears on video games-based panel show *Dara O'Briain's Go 8 Bit*. The showbiz connection doesn't end there. Much more interestingly, her dad is Jossy out of *Jossy's Giants*. Shown on BBC One in 1986 and 1987, the Sid Waddell-penned children's footballing comedy drama is fondly remembered largely for its jaunty theme tune: "Here go Jossy's Giants/Football's just a branch of science".

Despite this unique head start in life, Gibson hates football. She has little or no concept of what happens on the pitch, and I think that she thinks that every single person who goes to the match is in the National Front and that everybody has a fight and it's always cold and always raining and always miserable. There might be an element of truth to this, but it's a bit like saying that everyone who plays video games is a sexually inactive acne-ridden poop-socking high school shooter.

The truth, as ever, is somewhere in between. In 33 years of attending football, I have neither taken nor given a punch, although my younger brother and I were once actually chased out of Exeter by the National Front. As I have explained, supporting a football club involves travel, eating, drinking, laughing, singing, and occasionally dancing. Taken individually or collectively, these are all ostensibly good things. Saying that, The Evertonian was once thrown out of White Hart Lane during a League Cup tie for the specific crime of dancing, as clarified by the ejecting officer. He did actually last longer than another friend, who was thrown out for falling over upon entering the ground. Lost 4-0.

With respect, the opposition is more modest today, and this will represent my first visit to Maidstone United's Gallagher Stadium. To my knowledge, I have never even been to Maidstone, and why would I have? Why would anyone? They say that travel broadens the mind, but what they don't tell you is that football broadens the travel. We do occasionally talk about meeting up in random towns for a drink, but without the incentive of football it's never going to happen, despite the fact that the drinking is frequently better than the game. To quote myself: "As a football fan, the pre-match build-up is often all you've got. That blissful period of hope when the beer and conversation flows, before the match itself interrupts the day like a gash of despair".

Having abandoned The Boy in floods of tears — him, not me — I leave the capital and head down the M20 into deepest Kent, dazzled by the unfamiliar sight of sunshine as the orange ball of fire that gives us life unexpectedly emerges from hibernation. Spring has temporarily sprung in the Garden of England. Aside from another set of fixtures in The Shithouse League, it's FA Cup 5th Round day. Improbably, Lincoln City from our division are still in it and are playing at Premier League Burnley in the early kickoff.

Commentary of the goalless first half gets me to Maidstone where I am cordially greeted by a cheery steward who gives me a comprehensive rundown of my parking options, pausing only to guide in the official Chester supporters' coach. Having set off at 7:45am, The Gallagher Stadium must look like an oasis. Some might say they are glad to be here now, ready for cigarettes and alcohol.

Inquiring as to a pub in which to watch the second half, the steward suggests that I infiltrate the stadium bar. It's reserved for home supporters only, but he disagrees with the policy and actively zips up my big coat to hide the smock. The subterfuge fails when another steward spots a flash of blue and refuses me entry, despite my protestations that supporting a football club is not an official status and that I've changed my mind and now love The Stones, as us fans call them.

Hot, hungry and cross, after a fruitless search of nearby pubs I head into town and look into the vast Wetherspoons, where I spot an unlikely pairing of APJ and Gaz, who leaves The Deva after 25 minutes on Tuesday nights. Following our unscheduled tear-up at Borehamwood — game five, way back in August — he's glad to hear that The Card is still intact. APJ informs me that The Driver is in the house, pretending to forget his name as a wilful show of disrespect. He is indeed, tucking into a vast burger and chips with The Hack and Wife. They've cut me out of the loop, and seem to have been enjoying themselves in my absence, however implausible that may seem.

Even more ludicrously, they have no interest in watching the FA Cup, so I am about to leave them to it when The Wife buys me a pint. I eventually corral them into the nearby Duke Of Marlborough on the hour mark, where unfeasibly it is still goalless at Burnley. The Hack immediately declares it to be in his top ten worst pubs. Well lit, and with more television acreage than floor space, it's everything he hates. His misery is compounded when he learns that nutty options are restricted to the much-maligned Doom Bar, something of a bone of contention in the casketeer community. Despite a fanciful back story about it being distilled from the tears of smugglers by Cornish handmaidens, it was recently revealed to be made in a giant vat in Burton-On-Trent, just like practically every other pint of piss or swill ever poured. As for The Wife, she has a red wine miniature, which is a credit to the airline.

There are a few Chester faces in, including a man known as Statto due to his freak resemblance to the Skinner and Baddiel sidekick. An abject miserablist, he once chided The Driver and I for enthusiastically celebrating a goal at Histon. Also holding court is Baz, who has something of a chequered history on away days, yet can be found diligently forking the Deva pitch at home games in his alter ego as club groundsman. Apropos of nothing, a man at the bar starts doing Brian Clough impressions.

What happens next is one of the great stories in FA Cup history and you'd be a prick to miss it. Lincoln not only hold their own, but grab an 89th minute winner to become the first non-league team to reach the quarterfinals in over a century. It's arguably a measure of the contempt with which Premier League clubs treat the competition as opposed to a signifier of the strength of The National League, but one fuck of a story all the same. Even The Hack admits that he enjoyed it, which may be another first. The result does however come with a caveat. We are scheduled to play Lincoln on quarterfinal weekend, so our game will now be shifted to a Card-threatening Tuesday night. Wankers.

There's further bad news when we reach the ground to be greeted by a printed notice stating that no hot food is available, and advising a trip to the high street that we've just walked down. I'm absolutely starving, and a packet of crisps and a Snickers barely touches the sides. The away end is home to a handsome new stand, which unfortunately isn't open yet, forcing the entire Chester contingent to squeeze against a fence. Basically, if you haven't got your elbows on it or aren't seven foot tall, you can't see the game. My younger brother has managed to get a prime vantage point, but wastes it by spending the entire match on Facebook.

It's just as well I didn't bring The Boy, although Maidstone have generously reserved nine seats in a different stand for visiting supporters, giving them a decent view of the shiny plastic pitch. The 3G technology is far in advance of the glorified trampolines of the 1980s, but aesthetically it still seems wrong, giving the match more of a feel of a post-work kickabout. Football should be about mud, sweat and tears, not scientifically engineered Astroturf.

As it transpires, those who can see the action envy those who can't. We go 1-0 down after two minutes and then 2-0 down after five. We steady the ship for all of nine minutes, conceding the third goal with 14 on the clock. And to snuff out any remote hopes of a comeback, Maidstone score their fourth on the stroke of half-time.

People are shell-shocked. Some have already left. Fans start turning on each other. Baz reports news of a man in a red coat who claims we're playing okay. Chas, Club Historian and Statistician, declares it the worst half since reformation. The Hack counters this by claiming it to be the worst half of his life. I just get some more crisps, safe in the knowledge that The Card is intact.

We do actually score an early penalty in the second half, then a Sam Hughes header makes it 4-2. It's a minuscule glimmer of hope — if only we'd been slightly less fucking hopeless in the opening minutes we could have had a game on our hands. But it's not to be. The Stones lock it down and we trudge out on the back of four straight defeats.

If there's any consolation to be found, at least I'm not on the coach. Overtaking it on the approach to the M20, I consider some kind of gesture of solidarity, but I get caught in its blind spot and it slews across me, almost killing us all. The living would envy the dead.

Attendance: 2.120   Position: 12th →←

Game 38 of 50 →

Complications. Originally scheduled for the following Tuesday, the match has been brought forward to the Saturday when we were originally scheduled to be at home to Barrow. However, Barrow are still in the FA Trophy, which takes priority. Southport have also been left hanging, so rather than both teams enduring a dreaded blank Saturday, the game has neatly been rearranged. Ostensibly, this is a good thing, but it's a decision that has enormous repercussions on the world of football and beyond.

The bad news is that The Driver can't make it, the distance being just out of his range for a midday dash, meaning that he will finish the season without a visit to Haig Avenue, having also missed the FA Cup exit. As for The Hack, his radius of attendance is plummeting by the week, and this is simply a non-starter for our Sussex-dwelling pessimist.

I make a half-hearted attempt to sell the family into a bracing February weekend at the seaside, but the reality is that I am facing a solo venture to Merseyside. I'm still yet to do a solitary door-to-door trip, but my options are limited. The Watford Gap is at his Portuguese villa playing golf with himself, and the House of Doom in February is colder than a witch's tit. A lifeline is thrown my way when The Watford Gap's wife phones to quiz me about my liberal use of their Sky Go account, and ends up inviting me to stay. I decide that it would be too awkward on my own so invite Her Indoors and The Boy to join me.

It's a sequence of events that sees me shitting blood in Toddington Services on a Friday night while my family wait patiently in the car. Following on from my FA Cup fever, the curse of Southport has struck again, and illness has consigned me to the passenger seat. Rummaging in the door, I find a leaflet for the Lion Salt Works near Witton Albion, a relic from earlier in the season when Wembley was still a possibility and we didn't routinely lose every week.

It's an unwritten rule that whoever controls the wheel controls the radio. That means Absolute 80s all the way up the M1, with Her Indoors caterwauling along to some ghastly U2 abomination. If there's one thing worse than listening to U2, it's listening to U2 accompanied by someone who patently can't sing. This is the kind of hardship that I am prepared to endure in order to support this team and complete this Card.

In his absence, The Watford Gap's wife attempts to instigate some sporting chat by proxy, proffering a cursory mention of Claudio Ranieri, recently sacked by Premier League champions, Leicester City. That's about as far as it goes, and they resume their conversation about the correct potato sizing when making mash, a disastrous New Year effort by Her Indoors still casting a long shadow of recrimination.

Heading off early doors on Saturday morning, because I'm a maverick who plays by my own rules (and to minimise time spent on the M6) I head up the M1 past Leicester. As I drive past it, Ranieri is there saying his farewells, stabbed in the back in a Shakespearian football drama. Turning left at Derby (scene of an epic League Cup win at the old Baseball Ground) I head towards Stoke (scene of two epic league wins at the old Victoria Ground) where short-lived UKIP leader Paul Nuttall has also been run out of town. Apparently the country is full, but all I can see is mile after mile of empty scrubland.

Overtaking a couple of Nottingham Forest coaches, they don't know it yet but they're on their way to Wigan for a 0-0 draw, a shit day out in anyone's book. Once a regular fixture, the away end at Wigan's Springfield Park was little more than a grassy knoll, slippery when wet. It was from there that I once saw us go 3-0 down, pull it back to 3-3, and then lose 6-3. The man in goal that day? David Felgate, our current goalkeeping coach. Anyone can have a bad day.

We also leaked six (without reply) on my only visit to Forest, including a Nigel Clough hat trick in a hailstorm, all of which were offside. The midweek trip represents my only experience of a Football Special, the bespoke trains forever associated with the good old days.

True to form, Chester's finest smashed it up, thus inconveniencing their fellow supporters.

I'm basically driving round the motorway system on my own in a garish smock recalling epic victories and heavy defeats. It's a life, of sorts. This reverie is broken on the M6 when The Driver phones on his way to Lille v Bordeaux, picking up Boston James on the M20. He can't make a 3pm kickoff in England, but he can manage an 8pm start in France.

I went with him once, almost to see if it was real. After a bit of Biscuit in Southampton on the Friday night, we set off at noon for Caen, arriving about an hour before kickoff for cans of lager and *merguez frites*. Greeted warmly by the Bordeaux Ultras as soon as he got out of the car, The Driver slipped into fluent French for most of the match. The atmosphere in the away end differed wildly to The National League, not least due to fans casually smoking vast quantities of industrial strength weed through an impromptu bog roll bong. Lost 1-0. Got home at 6am. 14 hours in the car for that.

Prior to my only Bordeaux game, perversely there was a period when the husband of one of Her Indoors' school friends was their manager, and indeed The Driver got to know him by association. *En famille*, we stayed with them in Bordeaux once, and I sent The Driver interior photos of various bits of paraphernalia.

While there, we had a dads and lads kickabout in the back garden. Possibly intimidated by the presence of a World Cup finalist, much to my shame I ballooned the ball into next door's garden.

The Driver's Bordeaux trips will soon be marginally shorter, as while he's on the phone he casually mentions that they've had an offer accepted on a house in France. He's actually fucking doing it. Until now, it's been something lurking in the background, a bridge to be crossed if or when it arises. But he's triggered his own personal Article 50 and is intent on becoming an immigrant, a free transfer from Chester to Bordeaux. The selfish prick.

I've never been more alone, and consider this a dress rehearsal for the future. He'll miss this, I think, as I drive past Southport's rain-lashed Haig Avenue. In my handful of visits here I've never seen anything but the ground and the pub near the ground, Thatch & Thistle. Today this changes. Unshackled from The Driver, I am free to explore the more cultural aspects. If I want to go to the Lawnmower Museum, I'll go to the Lawnmower Museum. I don't want to go the Lawnmower Museum, not now, not ever, and am astonished to see a sign for it. What is wrong with people?

What I want is a nice bit of fish on the beach, so instinctively head for the sea, spotting a grand total of two Sandgrounders en route, one on a bike, and one in an electric wheelchair. Traditional home to golf-playing retired footballers, Southport seems moderately civilised, all twee shops and Victorian parks. The beach, however, is a disgrace, in so much as it doesn't appear to exist. There's a wall, the sea, and some kind of mulch in between, the grey bleakness interspersed by a perfunctory pier. Crucially, there's no chippy, shattering my dreams of crispy batter on golden sands.

Dying for a piss since about Uttoxeter, I neither pay nor display, but get out of the car, at which point Storm Doris whips its contents into a miniature tornado of litter. Skulking behind a sand dune, I hose one out, remembering the old adage about never pissing into the wind, a strategy that proves partially successful.

Mission aborted, I head for the pub near the ground and inhale a steak baguette while watching Sheffield Wednesday miss a penalty at Leeds. Familiar faces are thin on the ground, but I have a brief chat with Pauline's sister and Pauline's sister's husband, who asks me if I've ever considered motivational speaking. As I explained, I'm simply here to fulfil a fixture, the 38th of an idea that has spiralled out of control and still has me in its grip for the next two months.

Trudging into the ground, I immediately bump into Big Al, no arrangements required. We are joined by The Colonel and Howie, but crucially no Wainwright, one of the founding fathers of The Card not managing to make the short trip. The Maidstone recriminations continue, although Howie reveals that he missed our two consolation goals as by that time he was drinking in Strood on the basis that beer never lets him down.

The first half is wind-afflicted, and the ball bounces randomly around either area without ever quite managing to go into the net. The catering hasn't improved since our FA Cup visit, and I give up queuing for non-existent half-time refreshments. Taking my chances in the Portaloo, I splay my legs in front of the crapper, embracing the

margins for fear of falling through the floor, weakened by seasons
of spilt piss.

Back on the terrace, Le Chat Noir comes over and tells me to tell
him (The Driver) that we are both cordially invited to join him as
his guests in the Legends Lounge prior to the final match. Hugely
impressed by the whole project, he would like the pleasure of our
company to share in celebrating the completion of The Card. It's an
extremely generous offer, and I gratefully accept. At least I might get
some decent scoff for a change.

The wind cedes for the second half, and with Chester attacking the
500-strong throng of away support, a semblance of football breaks
out. In the 67th minute, Evan Horwood attempts an audacious lob
that goes so high that people start talking among themselves before
it even reaches its apex. However, as it starts to drop it appears that
the ball might still be in play. Dropping... dropping... DROPPING
INTO THE FUCKING NET. It's a hell of a goal, and I attempt to
enjoy the celebration, although stranded in mid-table it's hard to
commit more than half-heartedly. I do at least stay for the rest of the
match, unlike Grandad and his cohorts, who consider it a job done
and fuck off back to the pub.

With Steve Burr long gone, and fighting for their National League
lives, the goal belatedly spurs Southport into action and they twat
the crossbar twice in as many minutes. It's to no avail though, and
we run out 1-0 winners, our second victory of 2017.

Hitting the nearby Chinese chippy, the proprietor evidently didn't
get the memo about the fixture change and has only just opened —
possibly only just woken up — thus missing the lunchtime trade. He
keeps asking me if we're playing here again on Tuesday, and I keep
telling him that we're not.

Sitting in the car in a cul-de-sac, I tuck into the northern delicacy
of chips and curry sauce, or chips and a blob of yellow, as it was
known at university. It is said that the olfactory sense is the one most
associated with nostalgia and I am immediately transported back to
the streets of Liverpool, fresh from stewarding at The Deva, a football
pink in hand, the paper-based analogue results service long since lost
to progress. A simpler time, and considerably more shit. Flooring
it south, McCarthy appears on the radio, claiming that Southport

turned off the wind in the second half. As an orator, he makes a great manager, and this is his first win since signing a frankly staggering two-and-a-half-year contract. We may be stuck with his linguistic anomalies for some time.

Back at Watford Gap, the conversation has turned to a discussion about what colour room is best for aiding digestion. I almost yearn for The Watford Gap to return and explain the difference between rugby league and rugby union. Even in sleep, the hell continues, as I endure a stress dream about queering The Card by missing a 4-3 defeat at Aylesbury Town, who don't exist. I don't know what's real anymore.

Attendance: 1,496 Position: 11th ↑

Tranmere
Rovers (H)

Friday
March 3rd
2017

7:45pm K.O.

Game 39 of 50 →

We're back on the box, the blight of being a big club. After the shit sandwich that was Gateshead, BT Sport are undeterred and have selected what they erroneously describe as the cross-border derby, unless they're referring to the border between Cheshire and Wirral. It's a return to Friday Night Fever for Tranmere, once their traditional slot to avoid fixtures clashes with Everton and Liverpool. It's also the inspiration behind the Half Man Half Biscuit song, *Friday Night And The Gates Are Low*, with its baleful lament about all-seater stadia: "I can't stand any more/Because I can't stand anymore".

We have experimented with Friday night football ourselves in the distant past, the main effect being my school friend Mikey getting absolutely leathered prior to a 1-1 draw against Brentford. For all the initiatives that the club — or any club — has tried over the years, from mascots to cheerleaders to half-time entertainment, the overwhelming factor in attracting fans is, in pundit-speak, winning matches of football.

Despite this, and the live TV coverage, it's a full complement of southern pricks today, with a staggered start and elaborate three-car shuffle in place. It begins with me driving to Hillingdon station car park, where I have an argument with a ticket machine because it doesn't give me a ticket, instead acknowledging the presence of my vehicle through some higher power, or maybe a camera. Logic dictates that I would get a Tube to a Tube station, but due to the evening kickoff I won't be back until the last train has departed.

Having settled my differences with the sentient machine, I emerge as The Hack pulls in fresh from Sussex. He then delivers us to Ardley with the minimum of fuss, revealing that he has booked a holiday during the play-offs, a fairly low-risk gamble. Coming the other way, we spot the Doncaster Rovers team coach, en route to Crawley for an overnight stay and a goalless draw. The glamour.

The Driver is of course running late, so we repair to the pub for halves and crisps. Conservative with a small c, The Hack goes for plain, which is not a flavour. Tick follows tock, and The Driver reports an accident on the A34 that has delayed him further. We may as well have opted for pints and meals, and are about to order more beer when the landlady informs us that she's closing early to do the school run, thus directly contravening the sign outside the pub. Hungry and angry — hangry — this leaves us standing in the road for the best part of half an hour cursing The Driver, who eventually rolls up with a shit-eating grin and a tiresome back story.

With only a Scotch Egg Bar for sustenance, I attempt to sleep in the back, accompanied again by the harmonic melodies of Teenage Fanclub. The Driver and Wife were down the front of their gig at Shepherd's Bush Empire the previous Sunday, whereas I was down the back, eventually squeezing my way forward only to discover that the lead singer had morphed into Alan Bennett since I last saw them.

With steady rain throughout the afternoon, it's a seemingly endless journey, with the main event of note being the brutal death of a bird of prey on the M54, coming second best to a truck windscreen. There's even a 14-minute delay on the A41, as helpfully predicted by my phone seconds before we grind to a halt.

By the time we get to Chester, The Hack and I are in a state of hunger-induced rage, and demand that The Driver stops at the first chippy, the untested and fancifully named Sea Breeze. While The Driver carries on nibbling at his packed lunch, The Hack and I have the sweatiest, greasiest fish and chips of this or any season, requiring both an *Evening Standard* and a *Metro* underneath it to avoid soiling my jeans. Washed down with an ill-advised can of Diet Coke, I have gone from famine to feast in a matter of minutes, sending my metabolism into rebellion.

The Blues Bar is teeming, but with my guts in turmoil the lager proves a chore, and I only manage two and a half pints, the driver chiding me for the half, the first time he has ever seen me take such a desultory approach to my vocation. Despite numerous assurances that my Cestrian10 voucher is valid for the all-ticket game, as a precaution I avoid the turnstile where the ill-informed operator lives and go to the farther one, where to my relief the girl accepts it. To be honest, she looks as if she would have accepted a leaflet for the Salt Works, but at least I am in and The Card is safe.

The minor detour means that I have to walk back across the goal, noticing that a man is lying prostrate on the terrace behind it. It's a disturbing sight and seems more serious than a slip, with emergency services already congregating. Nevertheless, the game begins on time and we are awarded an early penalty that Alabi duly dispatches. It's hard to celebrate when a fellow supporter is receiving CPR, and he is eventually wheeled out on a trolley to heartfelt applause from all parts of the ground.

The Friday night fixture has taken its toll on a couple of likely lads, who are literally falling down drunk in the home end as well as openly smoking cigarettes. I inquire as to whether they know what year it is, and one of them asks me if I'm offended before losing his footing for a third time, eventually having to be treated for a head wound.

Astonishingly, we get to half-time still 1-0 up, at which point The Driver disappears. We presume that he's doing his rounds, but he's actually gone to the bar and convinced them to put Bordeaux v Lyon on the TV. Furthermore, having seen the replay he can confirm that our penalty should never have been given as the foul occurred at least a yard outside the box, which makes it all the sweeter. He still has time for a chat with his mate Tom, who is watching the match from the home end with the girlfriend of the Tranmere player, Mekki, who is Tom's nephew. Honourably, he has no split loyalties though, and indeed when we equalised at the away game he had to stifle his celebrations as he was sat with the Tranmere squad's families. We met Mekki's parents outside Prenton Park after the game, up from the south, a strange nomadic existence of supporting a different club every couple of seasons at the whim of the transfer system.

Riding high near the top of the league, Tranmere have turned out in their droves tonight, a mainly black-clad mass that somehow looks like the embodiment of evil. Indeed, there are reports of a pub in town being smashed up by 30 of Birkenhead's finest, including one sporting a Russian-style face mask.

They are soon celebrating as they grab an equaliser early in the second half, and the inevitable seems inevitable. But under constant pressure, we somehow manage to earn a corner. It's a rare close-up view of our players and I attempt to take a photo. What comes out is a blur as Big Ryan Astles gets there first and plants a header into the net to send the Harry Mac into bedlam. I am out of control and run to the front to hurl a tirade of foulmouthed abuse directly down the BT Sport pitch-side microphone. It's absolutely fucking brilliant, sticking it up the Tranmere again, a generation since we last beat them.

Which makes it all the more galling when they equalise with nine minutes to go. Fuck it, we'll take a point. That is unless they twat in a screamer in the 89th minute to send their fans feral and leave us standing in mute despair, followed by a cacophony of 'fuckits' and 'fucksakes'. All over, the misery is compounded by 1,300 Plastic Scousers marching up Bumper's Lane singing, "Chester's a shithole/I wanna go home". Home to Birkenhead, that celebrated beauty spot.

It's more than I can take and I impetuously vow to set fire to my Half Man Half Biscuit records as soon as I get home. Naturally, I have to retract this idle threat, as that would make it harder for me to blatantly steal their lyrics on an industrial scale, something that may irk the purists.

We have now lost more games than we have won, which seemed unthinkable going into Christmas. Fuck Christmas. Still shell-shocked, the mood in car is sombre, only enlivened when The Driver gets into a needless duel with an 18-wheeler on the M6.

Back home for 2am, the Wi-Fi kicks in and my phone chirrups with the tragic news that the stricken Chester fan has sadly died. I shed a tear. I didn't know him, but he was us and we are him. Rest in peace, fellow Blue.

Attendance: 3,696 Position: 11th → ←

Eastleigh (H)

Saturday
March 18th
2017

3pm K.O.

Game 40 of 50 →

Due to Lincoln's freak run in the FA Cup denying us a Saturday game, I have enjoyed a full two weeks off. A perfect opportunity to enjoy some warm weather training in Malaga ahead of the final push, I have instead pissed it up the wall, sitting around the house watching non-stop sport. Embarrassingly, once the postponement was announced I had to un-invite us from a previously arranged weekend at Her Indoors' brother's house in Northamptonshire, within striking distance of Lincoln. With the game removed from the equation, there was obviously no point in leaving London and facing the horrifying prospect of uninterrupted human interaction.

Mercifully, we managed to switch the visit to this weekend so I can at least spend the bulk of Saturday in the car on my own listening to football and music while muttering to myself. The Driver is lost in France so it's another solo venture, hence the helpful head start. In the event, it turns into something of a hybrid visit, as The Watford Gap pressgangs me into participating in his village quiz on the Friday night.

Fresh from a session of static backstroke at the nearby golf resort, he bundles me into a car and delivers me to a freezing village hall for an interminable quiz hosted by a deaf septuagenarian. Sucking on pissy cans, the questions are banal, and the only highlight is a break when everyone gets fish and chips. Everyone except The Watford Gap that is, who claims that he has never had fish and chips in his life and doesn't intend to start now, instead opting for a piece of rancid chicken, the remnants of which he later fishes out of the bin after someone mistakes a handful of gnawed bones for litter. A truly unique individual.

Also on the quiz team is a mysterious character known only as The General. With no interest in football, he has only ever been to two matches in his life. The first was Nottingham Forest versus Manchester City in 1990, featuring the historic incident when Forest's Gary Crosby controversially headed the ball out of the upturned palm of City keeper Andy Dibble and rolled it into the net for the only goal of the game. His second and last game was a 4-0 home win for Chelsea against Derby in 1997, including a Gianfranco Zola hat trick. What a record. Oddly, The General has no interest in completing his own hat trick by coming to Chester v Eastleigh in the morning.

The quiz finally ends in antipathy, and I get a rural taxi the short distance back, throwing a £20 note at the driver and politely telling him to shove the rest of it and fuck off back to wherever he came from (Daventry). Awaking on Saturday morning in the splendour of Staverton Hall — Northamptonshire's most luxurious bed and breakfast destination with stunning views and premium facilities, reasonable rates, call for details — I draw myself a deep bath and watch a bit of Melbourne City versus Newcastle Jets.

The car is gone. It's been sent to Daventry, famously the home of 2004 World Darts Championship runner-up Kevin 'The Artist' Painter. He doesn't know anything about it though. Her Indoors has taken it so that she can do yoga with The Watford Gap's wife. In a state of constant dread, I have issued express instructions not to hang about chatting and to return the car as soon as possible. A man's Card is at stake here.

Meanwhile, her brother has returned from a gruelling four days at the Cheltenham Festival. Having long since completed The Card of English racecourses, he boasts an encyclopaedic knowledge of every horse race ever run. Unsurprisingly he likes a bet, in much the same way as George Best liked a drink. He once came with us to nearby Nuneaton away, and was acting strangely in the pub beforehand, taking his jumper off, putting it back on, pouring a drink over himself and generally bucking and twitching like a mental patient. The Watford Gap, who had also invited himself, eventually asked him if he was all right, and he admitted to having had a cheeky bet on Chester to win.

"How much?" I inquired.

"Five hundred."

"You twat!" I said instinctively, recalling a vodka-fuelled conversation from the previous evening when I told him that we were in reasonable form. I thought he might stick on a tenner to make it interesting, but was not expecting him to wager half a thousand pounds on one of the least successful teams in the history of English football.

He was nowhere to be seen in the first half, and as Chester went 2-0 down we speculated that he was in the bogs, bleeding out. However, his absence behind the goal was explained by the fact that he was unsure of the etiquette of walking in front of people. He got a negligible run for his money when we pulled it back to 2-1, but we ultimately succumbed 3-2 as a bookie somewhere rubbed his hands in glee.

Largely nonplussed by the score, he was more upset by the vaguely homophobic treatment meted out by our lot to Nuneaton's goalkeeper — Andy Dibble's son — on the basis that he was sporting a salmon pink kit. It was probably best for everyone that Nuneaton were relegated that season, although he does occasionally take his boy to see Northampton Town, once mortifying him by handing out salmon sandwiches to fellow spectators. Crusts removed, of course.

The sound of tyres on gravel signals that it's time to hit the North, and I gratefully receive the car keys. It's all lambs and daffodils until I reach Birmingham, where I have a minor panic attack near Fort Dunlop when the realisation suddenly dawns that I am driving the car, not The Driver. Dutifully following his time-honoured route, I am surprised to see that they're queuing three deep for The Butty Man, who has adorned his mobile kitchen with a St George's Cross, presumably in an attempt to attract the more patriotic lay-by diners.

While it is certainly tempting, and boldly advertised as 'THE BEST THERE IS', I hold my fire until Telford's Warehouse, arriving minutes before The Hack and Wife, who have taken a four-hour detour on their way back from a holiday in Northumberland. Eating at the bar, we are tutted at by a Real Aler as it makes it harder for him to take a photograph of one of the pumps. Hung over from quiz piss, and clearly confused, I even drink a pint of swill myself, which makes me feel worse but earns the tacit approval of The Hack. His wife asks me if I'd ever consider moving back here — probably not, although it would certainly make things easier. Meanwhile, The Hack reveals that as a youth he never went out drinking in Chester as there were three pubs in his village. Three pubs.

Wainwright is in and checks on the progress of The Card, outwardly encouraging yet perhaps secretly tinged with envy that he may never again know such rarefied triumph. Immortality awaits, but until I am across the line I am merely standing on the shoulders of giants. Talking of which, Howie is notable by his absence as he's doing the second leg of the Worthing/Oxford Half Man double header, part of a shorter but no less noble Card. Sadly I have had to sacrifice Oxford, which would have been a bridge too far, even by my spectacularly impolite standards.

My Card is stamped, figuratively at least, and we are underway in front of a sparse turnout. As a football match, it makes a great somnambulant, unrecognisable from the thrilling 3-0 win at their building site in November. Almost nothing happens. It's a football vacuum, a kinetic art installation on the futility of existence. Still, a point is a point if we can just defend… this… stoppage… time… corner…

Guess the rest. It's almost comical, like it's been staged, but the ball is in the net and their 15 fans are going off their collective nuts as ours stream out bellowing recriminations.

"Worst game I've ever seen," yells one. Steady on now. Let's not get carried away…

On the drive home I repeatedly slap myself in the face. Not as a supplementary masochistic measure but simply to stay awake, and consequently alive. It's a strategy that successfully returns me to the sumptuous Staverton Hall — where guests can enjoy unlimited use of the swimming pool and snooker room — in one piece. Nobody really knows or cares what I've been through, and the response is similar to if I'd told them that I stubbed my toe or saw a dead badger. Nevertheless, my glass is full, literally, if not figuratively.

Ten more games.

Attendance: 1.643 Position: 15th ↓

Game 41 of 50 →

This is an abusive relationship. A mere three days after a slap in the face from Eastleigh, I'm heading back for Macc, a pitiful wretch throwing stones up at the window of a callous lover. This time it'll be different. People can change...

Apart from the psychological trauma and physical distance, a massive spanner has been thrown into the works. Her Indoors has announced that she needs the car to go to a meeting in Milton Keynes, and will not budge, Card or no Card. It would be a tepid way for the whole thing to collapse at this late stage, so an alternative is urgently required. The Driver is back in the country and is going to the match, albeit via a meal with his dad, and travelling from and back to Berkshire. I'm welcome to stay under his Chester double duvet, but have barely been home since the last match. There's also the perennial midweek predicament of childcare issues, and I have had to pull in yet another favour from the Yummy Mummies of NW10.

In a panic, I book a Virgin Train direct from Euston to Chester, something I'd happily do more often if it weren't prohibitively expensive. Who uses trains these days? Oligarchs? Minor Royals? The Chester Youth. And why does it cost three times as much to do an identical journey barely an hour later? Fuck knows. Ask Richard Branson. Perhaps as a pre-emptive response to the bearded entrepreneur stealing money from rail passengers — or perhaps because I was really pissed — I once nicked a wooden Buddha from Branson's house after a poker tournament in his back garden to celebrate the launch of Virgin Poker. Shamefully, I was found out and had to give it back.

With the alarm set for 11:30am, I pre-empt it by minutes and arrive at Euston in good time. Strolling down the slope towards the platform, a gruff yet vaguely familiar voice behind me says, "Bloody hell, these weird Chester fans you bump into".

It's a man who stands to our left on the Harry Mac, and to whom The Driver has cursorily spoken for as long as I've known him. All that I know is that he lives in Ipswich, and hence has had to come down to go up for today's game, with a seat booked a couple of rows ahead of me. Anyway, what weird Chester fans? Does he mean himself, or is he referring to me? In something approaching a moment of clarity, it crosses my mind that perhaps I'm the weirdo. I always thought I was the only normal one, walking a path of righteousness amidst a cast of oddballs.

Settling back in to the once-frequent routine of train travel, I stick my headphones in and turn the volume up. After a minute or so I am aware that people are staring at me disapprovingly. After about another minute I realise that I haven't plugged my headphones into my phone and have consequently been treating the entire carriage to the collected works of The Jesus & Mary Chain. Fuck 'em — it might liven these stiffs up.

Hotter and slower than I recall, the train also appears to be emitting an unusual smell. Far from a foolproof method of travel, I was once on a train to Chesterfield that broke down, requiring me to get a taxi from Kettering to Lutterworth, where The Driver came to my rescue. I was compensated for the taxi, but not for missing the opening minutes of the game, during which Chesterfield hit the bar — you can't put a price on that.

The train is now going so slow that it has stopped. Oh, we're off again. Oh no, we've stopped again. There's clearly something wrong, and eventually an announcement is made that this service will be terminating at Milton Keynes where a new train is being prepared. You couldn't make it up. Fuck you, Branson. Why is this happening to me? I am John Cleese in *Clockwise*, boiling with rage, constantly foiled by circumstances out of my control.

I keep telling myself that it's not a Card-threatening delay, although I am sorely tempted to phone the nearby Her Indoors and ask her to bring the car to the station. But it's still early afternoon, and it's in Virgin's interest to keep us moving. According to The Ipswich File, who knows about these things, any delay in excess of 30 minutes qualifies for compensation. As such, we are bundled onto the new train and fired up the track with a minimum of fuss.

The rearrangement now means that I am sat across the aisle from The Ipswich File. After at least a decade of nodding to him, it's the first time we've had anything approaching a conversation. It turns out that his family left Chester in the late 1960s, but he is primarily an Everton fan due to his dad, only going to watch Chester as a kid with a neighbour. He never wants the teams to meet, but if they did he concedes that he would have to support Everton.

Possibly more upsettingly, he reveals that he first met The Driver on a groundhoppers' day, something that he has singularly failed to mention in all the years that I've been sat in his car. That said, when I first started getting lifts from The Driver, he was working his way through the Ryman League, his membership of the exclusive 92 Club not enough to sate his craving for new experiences. In fact, when he ticked off his 92nd and final league ground, he admitted to feeling almost nothing. It reminds me of the Irvine Welsh short story, *Snuff*, about a loner who fastidiously watches every movie in *Halliwell's Film Guide*, finishing with *Three Men and a Little Lady* before promptly hanging himself. Hopefully, my reaction to completing The Card will be less extreme.

Following the train switch, I'm now sharing a double seat with a middle-aged woman from Chester. Perhaps emboldened by the communal inconvenience of the unscheduled change, or simply thrilled by the subject matter, she joins the conversation, revealing that she once saw Chester play Wolves in the FA Cup in the late 1970s. Less significantly, she also claims to have seen George Best play for Manchester United at Anfield.

She gets the full story of The Card, listening with a mixture of astonishment and horror before studiously asking, "Is this your Everest?" I hadn't really thought about it in those terms, but I suppose it is. If I am a latter day Edmund Hillary, then The Driver is the loyal Sherpa Tenzing, performing the bulk of the heavy lifting.

She also asks me if I play football. Of course I don't. Why on earth would I do that when I can shovel pies and pints into my gaping maw and loudly tell other people how to do it? I am a truly awful footballer, and wholly unqualified to instruct anyone, yet do so with a fervour bordering on frenzy. It's a funny old game.

The entertaining chat eases us into Chester painlessly, mere minutes before the compensation cut-off. We each go our separate ways: our new friend to her home to relate the tale of meeting two weirdoes on a train; The Ipswich File to a fleapit hotel near the station; and my good self to walk the earth like Caine out of *Kung Fu*. Actually, I stroll down the canal and get a nice bit of fish from Chip-O-Dee, traversing the Roman wall and wolfing it down in the shadow of the cathedral.

With hours to kill, I wander round town, near The Old Queens Head where four teenage pricks would congregate on a Saturday night to forensically analyse the afternoon's match in extreme detail, and where we were once starstruck by the appearance of jinking winger, Brian Croft. In Wainwright's legendary fanzine, *The Onion Bag*, there was a section on misspelled player names, with Croft memorably appearing in an away programme as Ryan Crass, something I'm not sure I'll ever get over.

Sadly, the excellent Penny Lane Records is long gone, but on the plus side I've probably got away with shoplifting that Sex Pistols 12-inch single. Also consigned to history is the short-lived Sports Bar, where late one night I watched Maradona cheat England out of the '86 World Cup. Heading back past the Tesco where I used to blow my Giro on food and essentials, I go to Oddfellows Arms, where as a 15-year-old I first bought a pint. Re-enacting that heady moment, I buy a pint from the same bar, and sit in the sparse tavern, comprising little more than some tables and a dartboard. Appropriately, I read a bit of Sid Waddell's book, *Bellies and Bullseyes: The Outrageous True Story Of Darts*, laughing out loud at the line "a man after my own throat", and making a mental note to steal it.

Next port of call is The Bull & Stirrup, another old haunt, and one of the first pubs in Chester to boast a video jukebox. It used to play Rick Astley and Mel & Kim on heavy rotation, the only respite coming when one of us put on *London Calling* by The Clash. It's now a Wetherspoons, of course, recently opened by the actor Ricky Tomlinson, who took the unusual step of using the occasion to make the outlandish claim that the late *Countdown* host Richard Whiteley was in fact an MI5 spy. There is a vague spy connection in so much as there's a picture on the wall of Daniel Craig, one of Chester's most famous sons, and naturally a Liverpool fan.

You drink quicker on your own, so by the time I get to Telford's I am more than usual pissed, yet there's still no sign of The Driver, despite assurances that he's on his way. It gets to the point of no return, whereby if he doesn't get here now I won't make kickoff, a ludicrous scenario given how long I've been in town. When he finally deigns to turn up, he still insists on having a pint, so by the time we reach the turnstile it is 7:43pm and there are at least ten people in front of me. I should really be issued with a physical card that allows me to jump the queue, but I hold my nerve and mercifully make it in before kickoff, which is slightly delayed by a moving tribute to the fan who sadly lost his life at the Tranmere game.

There are some hard men in tears, but life and football goes on, and we are soon celebrating an early goal. Naturally it doesn't last, and Macc go into the half-time break 2-1 up. We do manage to scramble in an equaliser with 15 minutes left, but we all know what's coming, it's just a question of when. The answer is 85 minutes, as another long-ranger flies in to give The Silkmen the points in the latest instalment of football's very own *Groundhog Day*.

It's tough to take, but at this stage my priority is getting home. There's no chance of getting a train from anywhere, so I have convinced The Driver to take me to the Oxford Tube, the misnamed coach service that for reasons unfathomable runs throughout the night between Oxford and London. Cue two very tired men sat in a deserted car park in the early hours of the morning, cursing the day they met.

The so-called Tube finally arrives, and I bid The Driver farewell. There are about four people on the coach, and I take a seat upstairs, logging into the excellent Wi-Fi. Hurtling down the M40 on an empty bus watching live baseball on my phone in the middle of the night, throughout the entire Card this is the closest I have felt to actually going insane. I'm not OK.

Jumping out at Kensington High Street, I could get a cab but I have come this far and masochistically wait out the night bus as a prick in a yellow Porsche performs a wheelspin. Finally walking through my front door at 3:30am, there's nothing to see here. I make a brew and watch a bit of *Bullseye*. Super. Smashing. Great.

Attendance: 1,802 Position: 15th →←

Bromley (A)

Saturday
March 25th
2017

3pm K.O.

Game 42 of 50 →

On this day in 1989 I witnessed possibly the best goal I have ever seen live, Graham Abel's long-range effort at home to Wolves. On this day in 2017, my phone wakes me up with a video of it, courtesy of the mind-boggling Twitter account, 'Chester FC OnThisDay'. What a time to be alive. It's the first time I've seen footage of it, and while not quite the halfway line screamer of memory, it's still one hell of a hit. I view it three or four times before getting out of bed, feeling slightly jaded after a night at Brixton Academy watching The Stranglers.

Unlike the good old days, there are no more heroes, but after three straight defeats, something better change.

Without hanging around, I jump on a bus to Victoria Station where The Driver is already waiting. An anti-Brexit demonstration at Hyde Park means that the bus grinds to a halt at Notting Hill Gate, against the will of the people on it. I take back control of my journey by disappearing into the bowels of the earth, re-emerging from the Tube at Victoria, from where The Driver and I get the train to Bromley South. It's a rare foray into the world of public transport for our eager road warrior, and released from his vehicle he's like a tortoise without its shell, or Darth Vader without his helmet.

Swerving the Wetherspoons opposite the station — scene of a minor post-match altercation last season — we head to The Bricklayers Arms en route to the ground. As gleefully confirmed by The Driver, it has everything you need — beer, food, and football on the telly, with BT Sport showing Lincoln's seemingly inexorable march to the title. That said, the TV wouldn't look amiss as Bully's Special Prize, and appears to be broadcasting from VHS.

Choosing my weapons, I raise an eyebrow at the lesser spotted Dutch lager, Oranjeboom. Hardwired by a memorable 1980s TV advert, I instinctively parrot the line, "Oranjeboom, Oranjeboom, it's a lager not a tune…" The barmaid at least feigns amusement, and then I grimly remember that I said exactly the same thing to her last season. I also order exactly the same meal: three sweaty sausages on a pillow of mashed potato in a lake of gravy. I'm in a rut; I've got to get out of it.

The power of advertising earns Oranjeboom a belated sale, but although the archaic ditty is technically correct — it is a lager as opposed to a tune — it's actually sub-Foster's filth. Vowing not to be fooled again, I chew down a pint of something called Whitstable Bay before settling on the Japanese fighting lager, Asahi. A potent brew, it was a staple of the 2002 World Cup, along with Sapporo, named after the city where England beat Argentina, the most expensive football match I have ever attended, coming in at just over £5 per minute. And that was just the ticket. Sapporo is also where The Driver and The Hack first met, their eyes meeting across a crowded post-match noodle bar with a glint of recognition.

It's a chance encounter that ultimately leads to The Hack and Wife joining us in a somewhat less exotic pub in Bromley 15 years later, having apparently endured a fractious journey of maps and arguments. Despite owning a perfectly serviceable satnav, he seemingly considers it to be an emergency item rather than the default method of navigation: get in car, enter address, drive to address, get out of car. Hopelessly out of touch with the modern world, it's a similar mindset to people who send a text then turn off their phone.

Either way, it has cost them valuable drinking time, as the game is almost afoot. There's still a further alcoholic hurdle to negotiate, however, as the away end is churning out San Miguel, prompting some last-minute speed-drinking. The Driver even breaks his self-imposed curfew, prematurely declaring it to be British Lager Time. Desperate for a piss, I take a wrong turn and am greeted by the unusual sight of a one-man tent that is providing temporary shelter to a young boy engrossed in a mobile device, presumably some kind of impromptu bring-your-kids-to-work scheme.

With absolutely nothing of interest happening on the pitch, the traditional game of Chester away bingo begins in earnest. APJ is providing a tactical master class, Adam is demanding full financial transparency, and Pauline thinks that we have simply been unlucky to lose every single week. There's also an appearance by the enigmatic Goby, a rotund man of many clubs, resplendent as ever in RAF issue bomber jacket and mustard yellow corduroys. And I am swiftly reacquainted with The Ipswich File, our midweek rail journey now upgrading our relationship from nodding to small talk.

Oddly though, there's an entirely unfamiliar bunch of young blokes bolstering the 152 fans in the away end. All with jarring southern accents, they intersperse shouts of "Cam on Chest-ah!" with a series of incongruous anti-Palace songs — Crystal, not Buckingham. I even take the bold step of asking Grandad if he knows where they're from. As he growls, "They're not from Blacon, they're not from Lache," citing the two urban hotbeds of Chester support, and crime.

As a spectacle, the game is absolute dog shit. Staring into direct sunlight, it's played in blustery wind on an arid pitch that emits a puff of dust with every bounce of the ball. I cannot wait for half-time, primarily because I'm about to piss myself, an unfortunate side effect of the pre-match rake of lager. When the fourth official indicates three agonising minutes of injury time, it's more than I can take and I make a bolt for it, ecstatically hosing one out, oblivious to the non-events on the pitch. Wainwright is also in there — the shame of missing Southport still hanging heavy — as is Four Cards, now of course closing in on his fifth consecutive Card. In total, that's virtually ten Cards gathered in one tiny urinal. Pro rata, it's surely unrivalled at any game in the country.

Following a token San Miguel, the second half continues in a similar manner. But about halfway through I am celebrating wildly, embarking on a fevered run after Evan Horwood sticks it into the... side netting. The anti-Palace Youth, whoever they are, take great pleasure in mocking my premature surge, with no respect afforded to my lofty status. Despite the mild humiliation, I attempt to regain my composure, ruling out the goal in the manner of a cricket umpire and dismissing the celebration as a dress rehearsal. Meanwhile, the Bromley contingent start chanting, "You fat bastard!" at someone near me, although strangely I can't see anyone who fits that description.

On the subject of humiliation, The Hack reminds me of the one and only appearance of a specific flag at the corresponding fixture last season. Wielded proudly by an elderly couple, it simply read CHESER. Not CHESTER, but CHESER, without a T. An otherwise professionally produced item, at some stage in the entire manufacturing process, which presumably took place in or around Chester, did nobody think to double-check the spelling?

Other results are already trickling in, but Bromley versus Chester cannot be stopped. With 88 minutes on the clock, Elliott Durrell picks up the ball outside the area, surrounded by defenders. Presumably knackered, he simply leathers it towards the goal. He's all of 25 yards out and it seems wasteful, but like the JFK magic bullet, the ball seems to deviate from its course, bouncing up off the surface like a skimming stone, over or through the keeper and INTO THE FUCKING NET.

Actual celebrations, a smoke pellet, the lot, as we do to Bromley what so many teams have done to us. And it feels so good. Absolute scenes, an abomination of a match instantly elevated from the mire by the swing of a boot. Astonishingly, we manage to hold on to the lead, thus securing our monthly away win.

Bowling back towards the station with The Driver, we walk on by The Bricklayers Arms. For about five seconds. I'm just going to have a quick look in — see you next Tuesday. I emerge five hours later, almost blind. I did at least solve the mystery of the random away fans, speaking to one of them who claimed an allegiance due to the fact that his Grandfather used to run a Punch and Judy show in Chester. You couldn't make it up.

Attendance: 1,237 Position: 13th ↑

Barrow (H)

Tuesday
March 28th
2017

7:45pm K.O.

Game 43 of 50 →

For the umpteenth time in my life I am sitting in a car driven by a madman heading to a city that neither of us has lived near for decades to watch a football team that nobody has ever heard of. We've all got to do something, and there are probably worse ways to spend a Tuesday afternoon. But not many.

One of the huge perks of my imaginary celebrity status is getting sent a free copy of *The Non-League Paper* every week. On the downside, it doesn't arrive until Tuesday. On the plus side, this gives me something to read while The Driver wages war with the motorway system. Flicking through it in the passenger seat, there's a cursory report of our smash-and-grab win at Bromley, as well as an engrossing and hugely amusing article about a hapless London-based Chester fan who is doing the entire Card, home and away, wearing an ill-fitting polyester smock.

The rag is also awash with league tables, and it's that time of the season when we start looking at the ups and downs in earnest, if only to find out which shitholes we might be visiting next season. Studying the National League South, I spot that Hungerford Town are in with a sniff of making the play-offs.

"Not bad for you, that one," I point out instinctively, due to its relative proximity to The Driver's house. Even as I say the words, they hang in the air, followed by an awkward silence as the mutual realisation dawns that he's not going to be here next season. He's actually going, leaving this all behind after 42 years of hurt. In fact, as it transpires, barring an improbable volte-face this is the last time we will ever make this particular pilgrimage together.

I won't miss his habitual air drumming, and I imagine he won't miss my chronic flatulence. To be fair, there's been little of either thus far today, and with Frankley Services on lockdown my traditional foray into Ginster's Paradise has been curtailed, which is probably for the best.

I manage to survive until The Sandstone, where The Driver's dad has brokered a half-price deal on steak and ale pies, so whatever happens tonight, the journey has been worthwhile. Under new management, the barman spots the Chester paraphernalia and reveals that he served five years working in the hospitality lounge at Wrexham's Racecourse Ground. Kicking over the table, we drag him into the car park and beat him to within an inch of his life. Back in the real world, we have a strange conversation about the history of Wrexham Lager, which he claims was served on board the Titanic. That could explain a lot.

Perusing the pub notice board, The Driver spots an advert for a circus, which is apparently taking place at the Deva Stadium tonight. I had vaguely read something about it, but presumed it to be a generic reference to the club, not an actual circus.

Bidding his auld fella a heartfelt farewell, we sup up our beer and hit the road. As we pass the B&M store that stands on the site of the old home end, The Driver asks me if I have farted. For once, I haven't, and the acrid smell appears to be an unwelcome return of the notorious Sealand Stench. When fans of a certain vintage talk fondly of the old stadium they generally fail to mention that matches were often played against a backdrop of the most acrid eye-watering stink known to man. Due to a faulty sewer, season after season was spent breathing in particles of human faeces, the experience exacerbated by the shit being served up on the pitch. And for one night only, it appears to be back, the vile pong instantly transporting us back to an earlier age.

At the other end of Bumper's Lane, as advertised, the circus really has come to town. Bowling towards the stadium, we are greeted by the unlikely sight of a big top surrounded by various bits of periphery, the whole operation taking up the bulk of the car park. As Gandhi the Postman points out, tonight's match has been rescheduled from last month, hence the unfortunate double booking. It does give amateur comedians something of an open goal however, and I opt for, "Clowns to the left of me, jokers to the right".

Stuck in the middle is the referee, who comes in for absolute dog's abuse from the off for the unforgivable crime of giving a throw-in the wrong way. Worse is to follow when a Barrow player appears to be clearly offside, but is allowed to race clear and calmly slot the ball into the net for the opening goal, with two minutes on the clock. After all the late goals, it's something of a novelty.

The referee's performance goes from bad to worse, and it's more than Big Al can take. Reaching deep into his arsenal of verbal volleys, he brings out the big guns, unleashing a guttural, "Fucking die, you horrible cunt!"

Strong words, but the ref is having a stinker, constantly falling for Barrow's time-wasting tactics. Game management, they call it, otherwise known as cheating, which occurs at all levels of the game. As do refereeing mistakes, the reason being that football is unrefereeable by humans. Throughout the history of the sport, there have been countless recorded incidents of referee error, and indeed much of modern punditry involves the forensic analysis of these mistakes. Either introduce video evidence (itself often inconclusive) for the entire match, or simply accept that there will always be human error and embrace it as a random element of football, in the same way that the best starting hand doesn't always win in poker.

Just please stop talking about it. But they can't, an endless stream of opinion and counter-opinion filling the airwaves every day forever. It is largely for this reason that when I watch televised football I switch it on ten seconds before kickoff and switch it off immediately afterwards. I have no interest in hearing one manager say that he disagreed with the decisions that went against his team, and then the other manager saying that he agreed with those decisions, but disagreed with those that went against his team, with which the other manager agreed.

It's one of the great things about darts. You never hear Raymond van Barneveld complaining about the ref in his post-match interview. In the entire history of televised darts there has only been one refereeing error of note, when Taylor was inadvertently awarded a treble 20 when he had in fact hit a single 20. To his ultimate dishonour, he scampered up the oche and removed the offending dart before the error could be rectified. I lost a lot of respect for him that day.

Conversely, in football there has almost certainly never been an error-free match played. Definitely not tonight, where the man in black is in danger of losing control, and Big Al is in danger of exploding. Some refs are better than others, some ref's mothers are better than other ref's mothers.

For all the incompetence displayed by the officials, the crucial goal is due to a goalkeeping error, as Lynchy lets a long-range shot under his body for 2-0. We do actually pull one back, scoring in the 88th minute for the second consecutive game, this time to a somewhat less euphoric response. But it's a false hope, and Barrow take the points to continue our appalling home run.

My run home is arguably even more appalling. With petrol low, the car sets me a tortuous run chase, at one point claiming that I have enough fuel to get home, but then constantly reassessing this evaluation, not in my favour. I panic on the M40, and pull into Beaconsfield Services despite the worrying cluster of traffic cones. Infuriatingly, the entrance is open but the exit is closed, meaning that I can't simply rejoin the motorway and instead face a rural diversion. Attempting to second guess the hieroglyphics, I embark on a 20-minute tour of country lanes and re-emerge exactly where I started. It's as close as I've come to crying since Dagenham away. I finally find a lorry to follow and get home at 2:30am, an hour earlier than the previous Tuesday. I can't live like this.

> **Attendance: 1,501   Position: 13th   →←**

Torquay
United (A)

Saturday
April 1st
2017

3pm K.O.

Game 44 of 50 →

One of the first fixtures you look for on the calendar, a trip to the self-styled English Riviera is almost impossibly exotic. I first went in '85 on the official supporters' coach, which oddly dropped us off in the town centre, meaning that we had to get a local bus to the ground. The overriding memory of that short journey is of a home end regular, for reasons that still escape me, leading the top deck in a rousing chorus of *Chanson D'Amour* — "Ra da da da da!"

As teenage drinkers, we were thrilled one night to recognise that impromptu bandleader celebrating his 25th birthday in Cinderellas Rockerfellas in Chester, one of those rare occasions when you see a fan out of his natural environment, like spotting a teacher in the supermarket. Astonished that someone so old could still be going to the match and to nightclubs, we showered him with respect, and possibly lager. There has been no communication since, apart from an incident at Kidderminster a couple of seasons ago when he told me to "FUCK OFF" for making an optimistic penalty appeal.

As I recently discovered, also on the solitary supporters' coach that day in '85 was a fresh-faced The Driver, years before chance threw us into this symbiotic state of despair. And where is he now? He's in deepest Devon, whale watching with his wife. As he explains to me on the phone, he thinks they may have seen a couple of porpoises and a seal. Up the Seals.

And this April Fool? I am barrelling through an area of outstanding natural beauty, intermittently blinded by glorious sunshine then doused by violent showers as the weather puts in a ludicrously clichéd performance. Oh to be in England in the springtime, under the April skies.

It's a solo drive, having left the family at my mum's in Bournemouth following a tactical Friday night stopover. As usual, it's a strategy that's tinged with resentment, in so much as we're clearly only visiting because of the football. Alternatively, the fixture list has thrown up a joyous opportunity to spend precious time with her delightful grandson. As of next season, he's in the car with me.

Catching the first tantalising glimpse of the Plainmoor floodlights at high noon, I park next to the ground, safe in the knowledge that only severe trauma can threaten The Card. Heading straight to Boots & Laces, I chew down a pint while watching the Merseyside Derby. Liverpool take an early lead, but when Everton equalise I instinctively celebrate, the remnants of a brief dalliance still pervading my psyche. In the mid-80s, at the very nascent stages of my Chester support, a school friend dragged me to Goodison Park a few times. Intoxicating though it was, I found myself more concerned with events elsewhere, and the die had already been cast.

Which is ultimately why I am sat in a smock on my own in the Torquay United club bar, watching a packed Anfield on the TV, while keeping one eye on Wrexham v Tranmere on my phone. Begrudgingly lured into town, every person I ask for directions is a Scouser. I eventually find The Driver, The Hack and respective wives in The Dog & Duck, an absolutely foul hostelry that goes straight in at number one in the worst pubs of The Card. At one point, The Driver's wife returns ashen-faced from the bogs, astonished to witness a living tribute to *Trainspotting* in this quaint seaside town.

It is at least near a chippy, and I wolf down a nice bit of fish while watching Liverpool eventually swat Everton aside. This signals that the main event is almost upon us, and as we trudge back to Plainmoor we pick up various stragglers en route. History will record that 180 Chester fans made the trip, but that does not tell the full story. Subjected to a token search at the turnstile, the legendary Richie from Flint indulges in some minor joshing with the steward, who then ludicrously deems him too drunk to enter. It's a despicable decision and an affront to his human rights. If you're going to sell people drink, you have to expect them to get drunk — that is the entire point of the exercise. As long as they're not a danger to others, or operating heavy machinery, what does it matter? In an absurd twist, a full seven hours later the same steward — now turned bouncer — will admit him into a Torquay drinking establishment.

As for those who are allowed to attend the match, it's mainly the usual faces, including Cinderella Rockerfella, now a bitter middle-aged man in a pair of ill-fitting shorts. But as ever, there are a handful of people that I have never seen before, including a sinister looking bloke wearing a Children Of Odin T-shirt. It's one of the great mysteries how after so many years you can still spot new faces in a small away turnout – once seen, never unseen. Presumably there's some kind of crowd theory to explain the phenomenon. Maybe it's his first match. Or maybe he's always been there and is wondering who this prick in the smock is.

Little of note happens in the first half, although right at the end Torquay have a man sent off for bringing down James Alabi on the edge of the area. We are subsequently awarded a free kick that appears to be on the Torquay 18-yard line. No such verdict exists — if the foul occurred on the line then it should be a penalty. In refereeing terminology, this is an Error In Law, one of the greatest dishonours that can befall an official. The free kick comes to nothing and we hit the break goalless. I have a mooch around at half-time and bump into Gaz, one of the Shearings Six who have infiltrated a pensioners' coach trip in order to secure a cheap weekend in Torquay, presumably an orgy of bingo and cream teas.

Attacking the away end in the second half, playing against ten men should theoretically be an advantage, but frequently isn't, as many a pundit will attest. After all, only one player can have the ball. Nevertheless, we give a reasonable account of ourselves and appear to be taking the novel approach of actually attempting to win the game. That becomes a distinct possibility with ten minutes to go when highly fancied teenager Sam Hughes has a dip from distance that takes a cruel deflection and majestically arcs into the net to spark wild scenes on the terrace. No matter how many goals you've seen, it's still an absolute surge that cannot be replicated in any other walk of life. I'm so dope-brained with adrenalin that as Hughes performs a classic knee-slide on the rain-sodden pitch, I somehow manage to run the wrong way, thus missing the opportunity to star in the local press, unlike The Driver, of course, whose gurning visage appears front and centre.

We hold on for our monthly away win, and I walk The Driver to his car so that I can ponce his season ticket for next week. As he's rummaging in the glove compartment, we become aware of a distant female voice.

"Cooie!"

"Yoo-hoo!"

Finally attracting our attention, the source is a mad old bat on a nearby balcony surrounded by plants — Sybil Fawlty versus *The Day of the Triffids*. Wanting to know the score, I relay the bad news and she flaps her hands disdainfully before disappearing into the foliage.

After a glimpse of the sea, I floor it from coast to coast, once again drifting into the petrol *Twilight Zone*.

With only five miles left in the tank, I mercifully find a garage outside Honiton and celebrate with a Scotch egg and a Diet Coke. Overhead, a rainbow appears. I chase it back to Bournemouth, where I immediately go to see The Jesus & Mary Chain.

Tomorrow, I fly to the French Riviera. It's a shithouse.

Attendance: 1.181 Position: 13th →←

York City (H)

Saturday
April 8th
2017

3pm K.O.

Game 45 of 50 →

We go again. Can't stop now. With six games left, I'm pretty much on tour for the rest of the season. Name: Stephen M Hill. Occupation: doing The Card. Specialist subject: Chester FC 2016/2017.

Friday night. M1. Bound for Watford Gap. QPR v Brighton in the Championship on the car radio. Come on The Hoops. Despite driving directly away from the match, I am notionally supporting my local team. This is partly due to spurious geographical reasons, but primarily due to my irrational hatred of Brighton & Hove Albion. This all stems from an incident in February 2000 when Brighton came to the Deva Stadium and beat Chester City 7-1 in League Two.

Cataclysmic though it was, that wasn't the incident. The incident occurred some weeks later when I finally came face-to-face with a Brighton fan of my acquaintance at an office that I occasionally frequented. Spotting my presence, he sprinted off as fast as his legs could carry him and returned bursting with glee wielding a homemade banner that read 'CHESTER 1 BRIGHTON 7 (SEVEN).'

Made with considerable effort, the 'SEVEN' in brackets was a nice touch, a nod to the vidiprinter custom of spelling out any goal tally over six lest casual viewers consider it a mistake. All the same, classic early banter. A few months later, after a stay of 69 years Chester City were relegated from the Football League on goal difference. Fuck him, and fuck Brighton. What a twat (TWAT).

As usual, I lose reception around the black hole that is Billing Aquadrome, with the radio retuning itself to a discussion that begins with the burning question, "How big is your wardrobe?" Fuck me, I thought my life was tragic.

Arriving in time for a few scoops with The Watford Gap in the village pub, tonight's snippets of football trivia include the fact that he once played for a team that has won the FA Cup, albeit over a century ago. And there's a man who lives in the village whose son hasn't missed a Crystal Palace match in seven years. What is wrong with these people?

Following a nightcap of golf, baseball, rugby league and ice hockey, I'm up early on Saturday morning, all business. I almost never watch it, but flick on *Soccer AM*, still presented by Torquay fan Helen Chamberlain, who once shook her arse in my face after winning $80,000 in an online poker tournament.

The relentless showbiz connections continue in the car, with talkSPORT's Chester-born Evertonian Mike 'Porky' Parry relating the tale of a man who is dragging a canal barge to London over the course of 20 years. An enthusiastic drinker, Parry once inadvertently barged into me at a press event for the World Darts Championship, before profusely apologising.

Heady days, but this is my life now, over eight months of it lost to The Card. But as I begin the final heroic push to the summit, it's the kind of day that almost makes you glad to be alive. Almost. Sun's out, buns out. Shorts and shades on, it's a big day in the North, and even the A41 radiates a kind of faded glamour. A beautiful day for eating fast food next to a road, The Butty Man's patch is threatened by a brace of fair-weather rival traders in nearby lay-bys. And astonishingly, a few miles further along, people are actually camping at the roadside in tents, presumably voluntarily.

Hitting the top of Bumper's Lane with 90 minutes to spare, I splash out on a Tesco meal deal and park within sight of the ground. Unless I fall asleep or drop dead, The Card is safe. Unlike York City, who are fighting for their National League lives. As the red-shirted fans trickle past, I feel their pain, having flashbacks to the giddy nausea of a relegation battle. When we went down in 2000, I got the train up from Euston with The Evertonian, the tension ratcheted to fever pitch by an article in *The Times* that chillingly declared that one of three teams would be left "twisting in the breeze". Following a tumultuous afternoon of rumour and counter-rumour, sadly it was us, an utterly numbing experience. Big Al was inconsolable, trudging silently to his car at funeral pace, his head in his hands the entire time.

The Blues Bar is offering free entry, and is consequently packed with paying customers. Gandhi the Postman gives me a spare Guinness and reaches into his wallet, producing a small photo of The Driver celebrating at Torquay, snipped from *The Standard*. Showbiz wanker.

There's a flurry of mobile phone betting activity and I even get sucked in, having a modest wager on a Chester victory allied to a Wrexham defeat: "I never felt more like singing The Blues/When Chester win/And Wrexham lose/Oh City/You got me singing The Blues/[trumpet]".

It is of course an idiotic notion. Despite being below us, York are the bookmakers' favourites, and the bookmakers are rarely wrong. But the home hoodoo has to end some time. Now into its fourth month, it's been half a Card since me and The Boy watched that dark, freezing, fogbound victory over The Shots a week before Christmas. But with the sun shining and a bumper crowd in attendance, this is our moment, this is our time...

1-0 to York. You could make it up. Returning from a half-time slash, as usual an exit gate is open to enable smokers to kill themselves. Absent-mindedly strolling towards it to stretch my legs, mercifully an invisible force prevents me from crossing the threshold, like a vampire unable to enter a house unless invited. One foot outside the ground and the entire Card would have been invalidated.

It's a sobering moment, and I regain my composure by reading the Harry McNally plaque for the umpteenth time. I once mumbled a few appreciative words to the great man prior to the final game of the season at Scunthorpe in '86, only retrospectively presuming that he had just stepped out of a pub, albeit with promotion already secured. At the same game, a few Chester fans had an impromptu pre-match kickabout on the pitch, during which I famously struck the bar from the edge of the area.

Less than two decades later, I would write McNally's obituary in *FourFourTwo*, which ended like this: "His uncompromising approach saw him physically throw an injured player back on to the pitch during a cup tie at local rivals Wrexham, later stating that he should be prepared to die for the cause. And bizarrely picking himself in a pre-season friendly, McNally went into a challenge knowing that he would break his leg, claiming that he had to set the right example.

An intelligent and articulate man, his off-the-pitch teambuilding antics were nevertheless the stuff of legend, receiving mainstream publicity when both he and striker Keith Bertschin had their stomachs pumped following a Christmas party. An avid connoisseur of red wine, McNally was latterly spotted quaffing a Rioja from a shoe."

Whatever his flaws, he remains one of our greatest ever managers, playing a key role in my burgeoning support of the club. He certainly wouldn't have stood for this shit, which we watch standing on the terrace that bears his name. When York go 2-0 up with quarter of an hour to go, it's more than Big Al can take and he vows not to return. Of course he will. I don't even have his phone number on the basis that I know where he'll be at all times. If everybody's attendance was based on results, there'd be nobody here. Even so, this current home sequence is a test, and York celebrate their victory with jubilant chants of, "We are staying up!" Presumably, so are we, but nobody is celebrating that.

Back in the car, it's a sweltering 21 degrees on Bumper's Lane. I can't face the M6 roadworks and make the rebellious decision to go off-piste, taking the lesser-used A51. The Driver wouldn't approve, but The Driver is in France buying a house.

We're at Lincoln on Tuesday so it's a hardly worth going home. Instead I decide to squat in the House of Doom, maintaining a holding pattern until the next match. Negotiating the overgrown garden, I push open the door to oppressive silence. Where once I would be greeted by a hot meal, a can of Stella and some mild baiting, there is now only stillness, the creak of an unwound clock.

In need of emotional nourishment, I speak to The Boy on the phone. He claims that we lost because he forgot to kiss the badge when I left, now a regular ritual. In an attempt to cheer me up, he reminds me of the time we put eight past The Shots.

Facing a second night away from my family in return for 95 minutes of horse shit, I crack open a Pot Noodle in front of Channel 5. That's living all right.

Attendance: 2,235 Position: 14th ↓

Lincoln City (A)

Tuesday
April 11th
2017

7:45pm K.O.

Game 46 of 50 →

I have been holed up in the House of Doom since the York defeat, basically keeping myself alive until the next match. Presumably concerned for my physical and mental well being, my family get the train up — at considerable expense — to join me on the Sunday. Despite my Card-based malaise, I manage to wolf down an entire roast dinner outside a pub in some backward village. It's an unfeasibly sweltering day, and I have to cool down by drinking pints of cold lager. We have a look at some pigs. That's as good as it gets.

Match day finally ticks over, a day like no other. There are two types of day: match days and non-match days, the latter considerably less interesting. Raring to go, I am already in the smock by 10am. Despite the rearranged Tuesday night fixture, three grown men have no other pressing engagements and are mustering here: Bucks before Lincs.

The Driver is stuck in traffic on the A34, his default state, ringing me with regular updates. The Hack is en route from Sussex, where one of his neighbours was astounded to learn that he was going to Lincoln, and equally surprised that it would only take him four hours. He may as well have told him that he was going to John o'Groats or Land's End or Timbuk-fucking-tu. Not a clue. If you don't follow football, or perhaps drive a lorry, you have absolutely no concept of the country that that you live in.

The Hack rocks up first and indulges The Boy in a back garden kickabout. They're soon joined by The Driver — a qualified FA coach — and by the time I limber up it's a four-way session of keepy-uppy in the long grass. Attempting an audacious high back heel, I catch The Boy full in the face, splitting his lip open and unleashing a torrent of blood and tears. It brings the game to an immediate and shocking end, and is not a great way to leave things. But kickoff is only around six hours away and The Driver is worried about traffic, his default state.

Ripping up the A46 — Expressway to the East — it flies by in a blur of truck stops and porn shops, soundtracked throughout by indie doyens, British Sea Power, who The Driver and I have tickets for the following night. The Hack hates them. He hates all modern music. The only live entertainment he ever goes to see is the German comedian Henning Wehn, with whom he and his wife have an unhealthy obsession. I tell him that I briefly spoke to Wehn at a Fall gig, but he's not interested.

We're soon cruising through the suburbs, and are pleased to see the Lincoln Bra Lady, a shop offering "Impeccable lingerie, perfectly fitted". You can't ask for much more than that. Parking near the ground, we stroll through the city centre towards the vast cathedral that dominates the skyline. The Driver ducks into HMV to buy the new British Sea Power CD, while The Hack and I press on to what claims to be Lincoln's lost pub, despite a prominent position on the high street. He begins to lecture me on Real Ale, but I cut him short, advising that, "I can't listen to this shit any more".

The détente is broken by the arrival of The Driver — CD in hand — and we sup up and head up the perfunctorily named Steep Hill (no relation) where Her Indoors and I once saw our then manager Keith Curle having a pre-match stroll. Lost 3-1. Diving into some other mock Tudor atrocity, we take a seat in the window and spot Deva groundsman Baz sauntering past, hand-in-hand with his on/off girlfriend, love's young dream on a romantic away day.

Deciding to eat here, we order pies all round and convene to the restaurant upstairs, where we are the only diners. It's not surprising, as what we are served is an absolute disgrace to the pie industry. Perched on an elongated ashtray with a meagre selection of vegetables, I've had more substantial canapés. There's a door leading directly onto a backstreet, and with nobody around I jokingly suggest simply walking out without paying. The notion is rightly shouted down as it would be a tragedy to sully The Card by being nicked for stealing the world's smallest pie.

The Driver has been banging on about a fucking cheese shop all day, and is determined to find it, convinced that it's where he thought it was. As I point out, he's moving to France in a couple of months, he can have all the cheese he wants. He finally tracks it down in its new location, ten minutes after it closes, which will almost certainly prove to be the highpoint of the entire day.

Repairing to the Wetherspoons near the ground, it's called The Ritz, albeit a very different proposition to where Thatcher spent her final years. An old cinema ripped out in order to sell cheap beer to poor people, it's rammed full of Imps, with practically every other person sporting a suspiciously new replica shirt. Managed by non-league's poster boys, The Cowley Brothers, Danny and Nicky, Lincoln are having the season of their lives. Riding high at the top of the league, the coffers are groaning with the spoils of an astonishing FA Cup run that finally ended at Arsenal at the quarterfinal stage.

Despite still reeling from his fromage faux pas, The Driver announces that he is prepared to make a sacrifice for the good of The Card. As such, he heads to the ground to pick up the pre-ordered tickets lest we are stymied by any kickoff-threatening queues later on. It's a noble thing that he does. Meanwhile, still starving after Piegate, The Hack orders cheesy chips, finding a tiny table wedged between two fruit machines and a pillar. No table, no order.

Pints are sunk, The Driver returns brandishing billets, and we have a chat with an Imp who was at the Arsenal game. We also talk to a bouncer who confides that he has been informed of a threat of non-specific trouble. Yet still no cheesy chips. The Hack finally addresses the matter, and it transpires that at some stage of the transaction table 64 became table 84 and his chips have been touring the pub for the last half hour, now topped by a congealed mass of cold molten cheese. Incandescent with rage, he gets his money back and we head to Sincil Bank.

It's teeming with Imps, and The Driver brazenly asks them, "Where were you when you were shit?" He's effectively begging to be punched, but against my advice will not let up, openly baiting them all the way to our turnstile. Getting the tickets was absolutely the right thing to do, and we squeeze in before kickoff to be greeted by an extraordinary atmosphere, the entire city seemingly galvanised by their success.

A proper ground, in the city, packed to the rafters, under lights, it's almost like a European night. While the quirkiness and inherent crapness of traditional non-league grounds is not without its charms, this is really what it's all about. Stuck in a makeshift stand, the 97 Chester fans are outnumbered by about 75-to-1, drowned out by waves of raucous singing from the Lincoln masses. If we could somehow fuck this up for them it would go down as one of the great away victories.

We survive for 35 minutes before a minor balls-up sees Lincoln grab a scrappy opener, which is greeted by an impressive roar. Attacking our end in the second half, we attempt to engender some kind of atmosphere but it's a thankless task. The Chester Youth are in disarray, the lifers are virtually comatose, and Baz has simply gone feral, his girlfriend looking on with a combination of shock and awe.

We are thrown a lifeline when they have a man sent off, but fail to capitalise on the numerical advantage. In fact we level things up by picking up a red card ourselves, sparking a lengthy altercation between the respective managers. The rancour is mirrored in the stands, and I manage to call Danny Cowley a "P.E. prick," a hilarious reference to his previous job as a P.E. teacher. He doesn't hear me. In the near future I will meet him at an awards ceremony and apologise for my behaviour. He will be absolutely charming.

There are no further goals, and the reality is that we have been hammered 1-0. Back in the car, with The Hack sulking in the backseat, we have the new Sea Power album on heavy rotation. A spellbinding addition to their canon, under a full moon on the A46, hell, it's almost romantic. Less than 24 hours after the game ends, The Driver and Wife, and The Evertonian and I watch them at Shepherd's Bush Empire. Void of animosity, it is utterly euphoric. Nobody hurls obscenities at each other, and everyone goes home happy. Funny old game…

Attendance: 7,401 Position: 14th →←

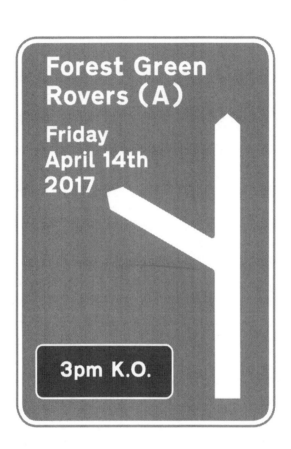

Forest Green
Rovers (A)

Friday
April 14th
2017

3pm K.O.

Game 47 of 50 →

Good Friday. Probably not. I have at least had two nights in my own bed, something of a novelty in the midst of this intensive end-of-season mini-tour. Today we go west for our third meeting of the season with the accursed Forest Green Rovers. And we all know how that ends. Nothing good ever happens there.

Indeed, it was that fateful night when nothing happened there that altered the course of history and ultimately led to the predicament that we currently find ourselves in. On Tuesday 9th February 2010, Forest Green were scheduled to play Chester City in the top division of non-league. I had already got as far as my older brother's place in Cheltenham when news broke that the match had been called off, three hours before it was due to start. It later transpired that the coach company responsible for transporting the Chester team had refused to depart unless they received payment up front. After months of financial turmoil, points deductions and supporter boycotts, this was the final straw. Chester City would never play another match. The punishment was swift and brutal. Less than a month later they were formally expelled from the Blue Square Premier and their results expunged from the league. On March 10th 2010 at a court hearing in London lasting under a minute, and with no club officials present, after 125 years of history Chester City were formally wound up. Gone.

It's one thing following a shit team, another thing altogether having no team to follow. But that was the desperate situation for me and the thousands of other Chester fans on the day the music died. Effectively a minister without portfolio, I was left bereft, facing a lifetime of meaningless Saturdays at home staring into the abyss.

However, the writing had been on the wall for some time, and behind the scenes the fan base was rallying. A new Chester FC arose like a phoenix from the flames, run by the fans for the fans. No more despotic owners or shady businessmen, this was to be a true democracy, albeit one beginning three divisions lower, in the Evo-Stik Division One North, and even that was after an appeal.

Mercifully, the reformed Chester FC were allowed to play at the Deva Stadium, and the fans turned up in their droves to watch them roll over glorified pub teams. Shrewdly managed by Merseyrail employee Neil Young, a travelling army got to visit such footballing hotbeds as Prescot Cables and Harrogate Railway Athletic, swamping these tiny grounds, with the home clubs relishing the big payday. For once a big fish in a small pond, Chester stormed the league and went into the final game at Garforth Town needing only a point to secure the championship and solitary automatic promotion place. Millions tuned in to the Royal Wedding. But on a nerve-shredding afternoon in Yorkshire, backed by more than 2,000 away fans, we went 1-0 up and then 2-1 down while closest rivals Skelmersdale embarked on a scoring spree, sparking gut-churning fears that they might overhaul us on goal difference. They eventually beat Ossett Albion 7-2, and Chester were promoted by a margin of two goals. The scorer of those two Ossett goals was later given the freedom of the city.

The next championship was secured in more straightforward fashion, as was a third consecutive title, on each occasion Chester breaching 100 points and 100 goals. This put us back in the big time, which is where we are now, our fourth straight season in The National League, on the way to Forest Green again, equilibrium restored. Whatever happens today, at least there will be a match to attend.

Serendipitously, the game falls a day before my older brother's birthday party in Cheltenham. As such, it's a family affair on Friday morning, with Her Indoors and The Boy bundled into the car to take our chances on the M4. Shortly after spotting a tandem, the first port of call is the village of Hermitage, home of Mr and Mrs Driver, at least for the next couple of months. They cannot fucking wait to get the laptop out and show off pictures of the ramshackle property they have bought in France, within striking distance of Girondins de Bordeaux, the team for whom The Driver is shamefully deserting the Mighty Blues. I offer little more than a cursory glance at the pics, largely because I find looking at photographs of empty rooms to be incredibly boring, but also because I'm still in denial and don't really want it shoved in my face. Eventually corralling The Driver into his car, we head towards Nailsworth whereas Her Indoors and The Boy go straight to Cheltenham, where I will later join them in either a good, indifferent or foul mood. All bets off.

There are an estimated 20 million cars on the road this weekend, and I have to be stuck in this one. After passing several more tandems, we hit the motorway and immediately grind to a halt. It's a potential Card killer and The Driver starts reaching for the atlas. Convincing him to hold his nerve, it swiftly clears and we are soon cruising through sun-dappled Cotswolds countryside on what will be our last ever trip together.

Embarking on a rural pub crawl, we stop at The Bell at Avening, a classic country pub that The Hack would absolutely love. He's boycotting today as last season he had an argument with a steward who correctly refused to let him leave the away end to go to the bar. To spite him further, albeit remotely, I even try the Real Ale, necking a couple of pints of Stunner. Void of the chemical buzz of lager, it just makes me feel tired and marginally more depressed. Next up is The Weighbridge Inn, a preposterous place with hundreds of ancient keys hanging from the ceiling. I have a pint of Gorilla, which tastes like a kind of smoky dishwater. The Driver inquires as to the details of the allegedly famous 2 in 1 Pie, and vows to buy one on the way home. Mug.

Forest Green's club bar offers more swill, with a variety of rancid vegan ales available. I have a quick chat with Chas, Club Historian and Statistician, quoting him some random stats before he reminds me that he wrote them. As The Driver frequently ponders, how the fuck are these a bigger team than us? Money, of course. Literally a village, the entire population of Nailsworth could comfortably fit inside the Deva Stadium. They're so backward, they haven't even put their clock forward. That would have been a tragic way for The Card to end, stranded in the twilight zone at the end of Another Way.

Safely in the ground, the gang's all here, including a parent, a brace of brothers, even an indifferent nephew. Visiting the renowned vegan food stand for a pre-match meal, I resist the urge to become the 10,000th arsehole to ask for a steak and kidney pie. Instead I go for a wildly expensive chips and curry sauce, which is passable but not a patch on the Merseyside equivalent of a bag of spuds and a blob of yellow. In the queue, an auld fella asks me if I'm the lad who is doing every game. Indeed I am, as is he. He's been going since '59, and having recently retired immediately made doing The Card his priority. A better man than I, he has even done every pre-season friendly and the Cheshire Senior Cup. Proud to meet a fellow traveller on this extraordinary journey, I shake his hand and sincerely wish him the best of luck in achieving membership of that exclusive club. Now so tantalisingly close, immortality awaits for we chosen few.

Forest Green almost score in the opening minutes, leathering post and crossbar in quick succession. Laying siege to our goal, miraculously we get to half-time goalless. Again I hit the food shop, or as it's officially called, Devil's Kitchen, somewhat ironically given that my Q pie is on the tepid side of lukewarm. I don't mind the Quorn, just give it 30 seconds in the wind-powered microwave. I shouldn't joke — preventing the self-inflicted extinction of the human race is a noble cause.

A friend of my older brother had intended to leave at half-time to pick up his daughter, but his car has been boxed in and he has to watch another 45 minutes of this shit. Also present — voluntarily — is Jilly Cooper, author of racy horse-based novels. Perhaps her next masterpiece will feature Big Ryan Astles dropping his voluminous shorts to service a callow stable girl.

Oh, they've scored. Oh, they've scored again. Oh, we haven't scored. Oh, it's finished. It's got to the point where people are talking about a 2-0 defeat as a reasonable result in terms of damage limitation to our goal difference. Hilariously, we're only four points off the relegation zone.

Attendance: 1,936 Position: 16th ↓

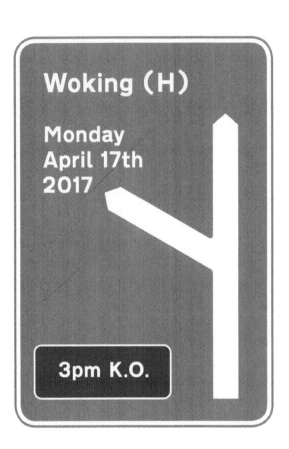

Woking (H)

Monday
April 17th
2017

3pm K.O.

Game 48 of 50 →

Bank Holiday Monday. Good for them. We're still on tour, having been holed up in a luxury hotel room in Cheltenham for three nights following the obligatory Forest Green defeat. As England fans sing when there's a vague possibility of getting past the group stage: "We're not going home/We're not going home/[pause]/We're not going home…"

We are going to a home game. The original plan was for Her Indoors and The Boy to get a train to London while I headed north for a solo Card-marking exercise. But in a last-minute change of heart she declares that we should keep the family unit intact — stronger together — a decision that has enormous ramifications on what is to follow.

Although she doesn't admit as much, I can only presume that she is lured by the incomparable thrill of a visit to The Deva, despite it currently being more of a Cathedral of Despair than Theatre of Dreams. She is also swayed by the prospect of a scenic route offering a "nice drive" with some "nice views". In the event, visibility is barely a metre as the rain sets in and we wend our way through some unfamiliar backwaters, the kind of places you'd move to if you ever gave up.

Perversely, at one point we find ourselves driving directly through Kidderminster, where The Driver has been spending quality time with his in-laws before heading to the match. There is probably a more ergonomic solution available, but this is our future, a Driverless existence.

It's not a great start to this brave new world as in an attempt to avoid Bank Holiday traffic on the usual route we find ourselves drifting perilously close to Wales. Fortuitously, a man comes on the radio advising that there is a total gridlock on the A5 either side of

Oswestry, stretching as far as Ruabon, no less. Without this warning, we would have been absolutely Card-endingly screwed. It's still by no means safe, and Her Indoors leaps into action, plotting a cross-country course that takes us down single-track roads with grass in the middle, presumably designed for horse and cart. With panic rising, I verbally hope that we don't get a puncture. This sets The Boy into a tailspin of dread, wailing out loud, convinced that it's going to happen.

In full *Colin McRae Rally* mode — "easy left into hard right, don't cut" — we tear up the countryside and eventually emerge onto something resembling a road. Having successfully circumnavigated the obstacle, the satnav takes over and leads us inexorably into the belly of the beast... 'Wrecsam'.

You couldn't make it up (you probably could) but we have drifted so far west that this is our only escape route, trapped in the one-way system and cruising through Wrexham town centre. I haven't been into the town for decades. Even pre-bubble it was always a smash-and-grab affair. It actually looks fairly normal, just another shit town, a world away from the horrors of my imagination.

And there they are, the massive floodlights of The Racecourse looming through the rain. Stuck at a red light, it suddenly dawns that I am yards away from our enemy's base, bedecked in a lurid blue smock with a Chester FC foam hand in the back of the car, surrounded by Wrexham fans. The first one shows a flicker of recognition, some half-remembered animosity. Then another appears, and another, as they slowly encircle the car. They are not few, they are legion, now pawing the windscreen and rattling the already loosened wing mirror. Eventually overcome by sheer weight of numbers, perhaps this is how it ends.

Not really. Nobody gives the tiniest shit. Apparently there's a world outside football where people spend their leisure time shuffling around an identikit town buying crap that they don't need. Or even standing frozen in time in the bus station, ripped on new designer drug, Spice, rapidly becoming the non-activity of choice for the non-busy North Walian.

As the lights change, I hit the accelerator and head for the safety of the border. Within 15 minutes we are in Chester's fair city, making a mockery of the preposterous bubble arrangement. Unprompted, Her Indoors correctly declares it to be considerably nicer than Wrexham.

Despite the traffic scare, we still have time on our side. Following an aborted Pizza Hut visit — no buffet — we raid the Tesco bargain shelves and head for the Blues Bar, again free, again full. Barely ten minutes before kickoff, The Driver phones and asks me to get him a pint of Spitting Feathers. Fuck sake. I begrudgingly comply, and spot him in the distance, running into the car park. Always late, always running. Sullenly pointing at his pint, I leave him to it and head for the turnstile, which has a queue of no people.

The big news is that Big Al is on holiday, surprising timing given that we are fighting for our lives here. Apart from generally being a waste of time, one of the dilemmas of holidays is that unless you're prepared to miss games you can only really take them in the summer. And the summer is the only time when this country is habitable, so you don't need to take a holiday. Particularly if it's in a static caravan in Aberystwyth.

Three points here will finally put this accursed season to bed, and there's a reasonable atmosphere, with Chester seemingly up for it. Ten minutes in, Her Indoors asks me which goal we are attacking. What does she see? Colours and shapes?

Despite our best efforts, we go into the break goalless. As per agreement, The Boy gets a family pack of Haribo and is just peaking when Woking take an undeserved lead. A minute later, a diving header from new boy Liam Davies flies majestically into the net to restore parity and send the McNally into bedlam.

Uncharacteristically trying to win, it's all Chester, and it's actually a decent game. Sometimes they say how can you watch that shit? But I have slept through enough so-called *Super Sundays* on Sky to know that the quality of the teams is not necessarily reflected in the quality of the match. Football is such an imprecise sport (you can't use your hands!) that two evenly matched sides of almost any standard can muster an entertaining game. Conversely, two shit darts players or two shit snooker players will almost always produce a shit match, as I discover when attempting to play every New Year's Eve. This is perhaps one of the reasons why football is the best sport, the margin of error dictating that the best side will not always win.

There can only be one winner here, with Elliott Durrell running the show and rapidly becoming The Boy's favourite player. With eight minutes to go, he absolutely smashes in a rebound to get the party started. The Boy is tossed into the air with aplomb and the celebrations begin in earnest, the home hoodoo surely finally put to rest. Seven points clear with six to play for, say we are staying up!

With her back to the game, Her Indoors is still taking photos of us when Woking equalise. There's a kind of numb confusion at the thought of settling for a point when three seemed so close. Fuck sake. Take a point, move on. But who's this, needlessly handling in the box in the last minute? It's our captain, Luke George, mindlessly gifting Woking a penalty that sneaks in for a criminal 3-2 win.

It's genuinely beyond belief, and fans start turning on each other, on McCarthy, on themselves. Thank fuck Big Al isn't here, I think he would actually explode. The Driver is furious, The Boy is despondent, and even Her Indoors describes it as heartbreaking. Win, lose or draw, she's generally oblivious, but the horror seems to resonate, the manner of the defeat finally giving her an insight into this cruel existence.

Outside, the Young Woody Allen aka Steve Wright In The Afternoon spills out of the main stand and starts shouting in my face about Neil Young, our former manager not the Canadian songsmith. All around is impotent rage, almost a state of unrest. I can't even numb the pain with alcohol, and get back in the car still in shock.

Unable to face the grim prospect of the M6 on Bank Holiday, I take the unprecedented decision to go down the A41, perhaps in an attempt to reverse time and hence the result. McCarthy eventually comes on Dee 106.3, participating in a surreal interview with respected broadcaster and journalist Neil Turner, who inexplicably makes a tortured Elton John analogy. As far as I can tell, the implication is that having a season ticket at Chester is somehow like watching Elton John but he's stopped playing *Rocket Man* or *Goodbye Yellow Brick Road*. It's frankly nonsensical, and McCarthy is rightly perturbed amidst his usual stream of consciousness. It descends into farce, and I'm embarrassed that everyone has to hear it. No analogy required, the real question should be, "You haven't won a home game since before Christmas, why are you still here?"

I just about manage to get to the cheapest petrol station on the

A41 without running out. It's a victory of sorts. While there, The Watford Gap phones to invite me, and hence us, to join him for his birthday celebration and inevitable overnight stay. After the trauma of the day, it's a lifeline. Hitting the boosters on the M54, Her Indoors feeds me a Chicken & Mushroom Pot Noodle using a pair of plastic tea stirrers as impromptu chopsticks. This is life on The Card. Two nights out of 11 in my own bed, and nary a point to show for it.

Attendance: 1.770 Position: 16th →←

Game 49 of 50 →

It's the last away match of a season that promised the earth, and delivered earth. The best part of eight months since we rolled over Sutton 4-0 at home, it feels longer, particularly for those of us who have attended every minute of every match. Still, it's a nice easy one to round off the away Card, at least in travel terms. That said, despite being considered a local game, from door-to-door still takes virtually the length of a football match.

I let the train take the strain, the Thameslink from West Hampstead snaking through London en route to Surrey. Facing backwards, yesterday's *Evening Standard* for company, smock on, headphones in. A bit of Joy Division kicks in at Elephant & Castle, and it's almost a shame the journey has to end. There's a decent view of Gander Green Lane as the train pulls into West Sutton, something that must have horrified Arsenal fans when they turned up here in the FA Cup. Following a monumental cup run almost on a par with Lincoln's, that's where it finally ended for the U's. And a man ate a pie.

Erring on the side of caution, I'm the first away fan in the social club and am cordially greeted by the Chester CEO, out of respect. I fight my way past the suits at the bar and perch on a stool to watch Lincoln v Macc on the box, with The Imps on the verge of sealing the title. A couple of likely lads bowl in and I eventually recognise them as Shane Pinnington from Dee 106.3 and Dave Powell from *The Chester Chronicle*. Powell, football's hardest working journalist, is due to meet The Chester Exiles to pen a story about this remarkable group of fans who live outside the city but occasionally try to get to a game. Chairperson Pauline is first to show for The Exiles, followed by the usual suspects, as well as The Hack and Wife. As the latter points out, she's been to more Chester games than some of The Exiles, and she's a Southampton fan who lives in Sussex.

As the interview is ensuing, we're joined by financial director, Laurence, the man who on that chilly evening at The Deva convinced me lash out a fiver on the smock that has seen me through this most stressful of seasons. While trying to rubberneck on the chat, I become aware of a creaking then a crashing sound behind me. Turning round, I am surprised to see Laurence on his back like a turtle, surrounded by chair legs and splintered timber. With guffaws all round, I help him to his feet, and he takes it remarkably well. Whatever Sutton made from their cup run, they are apparently yet to invest it in fixtures and fittings.

Having missed it all, The Driver sashays in and is simultaneously thrilled and horrified to learn that the Chester squad is rumoured to have stayed overnight at Chieveley Services. Effectively his local shopping centre, had he been better informed he could have feasibly spotted Big Ryan having a late night smoothie.

Lincoln win the league to spark joyous scenes at Sincil Bank and signal that it's time for us to take our punishment at Gander Green Lane. An untidy, disjointed stadium with no segregation, the whole thing has more of a feel of a village fête than a competitive sporting contest, with some kids even having a kickabout on the terraces.

It's another plastic pitch, which didn't work out well at Maidstone where we conceded in the second and fifth minutes. Lessons have obviously been learned and this is a huge improvement as we concede in the fifth and eighth minutes. Fuck off. What is the fucking point? With fans turning on each other, we manage to stem the bleeding until almost half-time. En route to berate McCarthy, a furious Four Cards stops by to vent some spleen as Sutton set up a free kick.

"This is in," I predict.

"It is as well," he confirms as it's floated into the top corner for a 3-0 deficit at the break. Technically, it's an improvement on Maidstone, which was 4-0 at half-time.

Whatever McCarthy says to them during the interval, it makes absolutely no fucking difference as Sutton score immediately after the restart. It's a full half hour until their next goal, a 30-yard rocket for 5-0. This is not good, as in really not good, with our goal difference taking a hammering and the relegation trapdoor still ajar. People are nervously studying mobile phones when James Alabi takes matters into his own hands by leathering in an angry brace in the space of three minutes. It's some kind of consolation, both emotional and mathematical, and the moronically optimistic point out that over the two league games we're 6-5 up on aggregate. Meaningless.

There's still a long ten-minute twitch-up to endure, and Adam reports that York have hit the post, an effort that had it gone in would have seen us going into the last game needing to get something. Our game finishes 5-2, and when the dust settles it transpires that a nine-goal swing on the final day will relegate us. Unlikely, but not impossible.

Some of our players come over and apologetically touch hands with the fans, but there's nothing much to be said other than let's get in the fucking pub. Despite bizarrely being unable to find a pie anywhere in the ground, I have already had three hot meals and a raft of lager, but this one really has to be put to bed. Besides, the FA Cup semi-final between Chelsea and Spurs is about to start, and they're showing it in The Plough nearby. The Driver has always got somewhere to go, but The Hack and Wife are up for it. Hilariously, there's no Real Ale. As the landlord explains, nobody buys it and he ends up chucking it way. Forced to drink pissy lager, The Hack seriously considers making this a late entrant for the worst pub of the entire season. I urge him not to be hasty, and to think carefully about what he's saying.

The Chester Youth appear to have been bedded in for some time and have evidently been making their own entertainment. Returning from the bogs, Adam declares that it's like *Scarface* in there. Meanwhile, Grandad, after a long day and a long season, is practically asleep at a table.

There is a roughly equal number of locals at the bar, and rarely has the North/South divide been more evident. Somewhere between Stone Island and Spike Island, our boys resemble Oasis roadies on a day off. As for the Sutton bunch, they're more Love Island, all ridiculously skinny jeans, tight T-shirts, immaculately groomed beards, and scarcely a pair of socks between them. One of them looks like the front end of a centaur.

They also have an extraordinary way of watching football, in so much as they don't really watch it. Largely standing with their backs to the screen, whenever Chelsea score they all celebrate and buff each other then immediately resume their positions to continue the posturing. It happens four times in what is a thrilling match, with Chelsea eventually winning 4-2. Against my better judgement, I have to miss the final minute to run for my train, bidding The Hack and Wife a swift farewell as I won't see them for months.

Catching up with Pauline, we are joined on the train by a mate of Gaz, who I previously met after Bromley away. Sadly, Gaz isn't here as he's gone on a Shearings trip to Ilfracombe, having presumably been enamoured by the Torquay experience. His mate phones his mum from the train to tell her that he's 75% certain that he recently made her a grandmother. It's complicated.

He gets off and heads for a hostel in Limehouse where he is apparently sharing a room with Poles and Lithuanians, so afeared that he sleeps naked with all his possessions in a locker. More straightforwardly, and with an end-of-term vibe, Pauline gets off at St Pancras and heads home to Cambridge, wishing me a good summer. I pile off at West Hampstead, which is swarming with Chelsea, so much so that I hide the blue smock lest I be mistaken for one of them. Legally drunk and desperate for a piss, I am forced to hose one out on Billy Fury Way. Halfway To Paradise. So near, yet so far away. One more game...

Attendance: 2,082 Position: 17th ↓

Game 50 of 50 →

It was always going to come down to this. Boreham Wood at home, a fix-ture etched in stone since this entire venture began. Ideally we'd be turning them over to clinch the title or a play-off place. As it stands, following our appalling run of results in 2017 — during which we are yet to win at home — we need to not get thrashed in order to maintain our place in the division.

Assuming that even we can't cock this up, none of that matters now. What matters is getting The Card over the line and taking my place in the hall of fame alongside the other titans of the game. Destiny awaits. As does a slap-up pre-match feed in the Legends Lounge, courtesy of our generous benefactor, Le Chat Noir, a fan I had never even met until he memorably recommended a Stockholm nightclub of the same name back in November. Having followed the progress of The Card with interest, he has generously invited The Driver and I to join him at the top table to celebrate its conclusion.

Typically, a spanner has been thrown into the works. Every match on the final day of The National League has to kick off at 12:15pm as one of them is being televised, specifically the game at York, who need to score a hatful in order to save themselves and possibly relegate us, assuming we get dicked. Given that we need to be at The Deva for a three-course meal beforehand, the timings are brutal, although I do spare a thought for the Dover fans heading to Barrow on a 3am coach.

The Driver is of course driving up on the day, and will inevitably get there on time, but I simply can't risk it. To fall at the final furlong would be devastating, like twisting your ankle on the last mile of a marathon. Taking a safety-first approach, I book a hotel for the Friday night within walking distance of the ground. Besides, it would be nice to have the family with me on this special day to see me get my Card. In Mafioso terms, it's like being made.

Once again bundling The Boy into the car straight from school, we kidnap Her Indoors from work and now the screaming starts, with a bottled u-turn sabotaging the journey and initiating the traffic hell. Stopping at Cherwell Valley Services for old time's sake, we enjoy a delicious evening meal in the car park.

The Card almost comes crashing to a halt when I slew across three lanes of M6 traffic so that The Boy can wave a Chester FC foam hand at the driver of a pick-up truck bedecked in Lincoln City paraphernalia, presumably en route to Southport. It's a mistake, and the gesture of non-league solidarity is only reciprocated by a feral stare from the wild-bearded Imp.

It's a full six hours until we check in at the hotel, nestled against The Roodee, the oldest English racecourse still in use, and makeshift training ground for various incarnations of Chester Football Club. The bloke checking us in warns us that there are a number of stag and hen parties staying, and that should we be disturbed we should contact him immediately whereby he will terminate them with extreme prejudice. Thanking him for his potential acts of violence, I pick up a local paper, the back page of which has an advert for 'Chester v Boreham'. Perhaps they charge by the word.

Given the late hour, there is no time for anything more than a quick nightcap, which is probably for the best. Effectively under self-imposed house arrest until The Card is completed, I can't even be on the streets at this point. Anything could happen. Holed up in the room with the door securely locked, I simultaneously watch two World Championship snooker matches until unconsciousness takes over.

Awaking as nervous as a kitten, it feels like the morning of a wedding. I can barely eat my full English breakfast, opting for a moderate portion with one eye on the early lunch an hour or so hence. Back in the room, Parky appears on the iPad, live from Australia. The man who introduced me to The Driver, and also assured me that I would barely see another game once The Boy was born, he doffs his cap to my 100% effort and wishes me all the best, seemingly genuinely impressed.

Having driven or been driven in excess of 15,000 miles, I decide to walk the final one, while the family take the car. I need to be alone with my thoughts on this historic day. For sheer perversity, I briefly consider wandering off to walk the earth, jilting myself at the altar. I'm bucked back to my senses when Her Indoors has to slam on the brakes to let me cross the road, something that confuses The Boy no end. Nevertheless, I press on with the hardest walk, glancing right at Bela Lugosi's chip shop — closed for lunch — historic scene of many a post-match meal and cursory score inquiry. The lesser-frequented Sealand Chippy is next, where Parky claims to have seen striker Gary 'Psycho' Bennett ordering sausage and chips, immediately adding it to his roster of stories.

Stadium Way retains the name, if not the stadium. It is at the other end where we stood for an age surveying the iconic Sealand Road floodlights after the last ever game in 1990. An emotional day, everybody piled on the pitch at the final whistle, collecting souvenirs and sods of turf, many in tears at the passing of The Old Lady, scene of so many life-affirming memories and friendships forged. One lad was so moved that he hauled his mate off the ground with the immortal line, "Ee-ar, I've got to get home for *Baywatch*".

Always a *Brookside Omnibus* man myself, but on this momentous occasion even that could wait. Unable to say goodbye, eventually there were four of us left in the ground: three Hill brothers and my mate Nick, a Watford fan by rights who got sucked in while at college nearby. With everybody wanting the honour of being the last fan to ever leave the stadium, a copper even allowed us to line up and simultaneously step across the threshold on his cue. At which point nobody moved. History does not record who officially had the last touch, but for argument's sake let's say it was me. It doesn't matter now, it's all gone, replaced by a low-cost furniture store and a Poundland.

Shanking left down Bumper's Lane, I head through the industrial estate towards the blue plastic box we now call home. I am barely into my stride when with cinematic timing, The Driver pulls up alongside me. Despite my pledge to walk, I instantly jump in and he drives me down the aisle for the last ever time. He doesn't even charge for diesel. With free parking secured, he announces that he's got something for me. Reaching round to the immaculately vacuumed back seat, he presents me with a framed certificate of The Card, witnessed and signed by himself, replete with some of the highs and lows of the season. Say what you like about him, and Christ knows I have, it's a very nice touch and I am deeply moved, proffering a firm handshake and sincere thanks.

Bounding into the Legends Lounge — above the Blues Bar — we're the last guests to arrive, and also the only ones clad in polyester, with everyone else in formal attire. We're immediately kicked out, if only to go back downstairs to get our tickets so we can be readmitted. The gang's all here, and we are greeted like heroes, with pints and congratulations swiftly forthcoming. And in a remarkable act of generosity, a table has been set aside with two bottles of Moét & Chandon and a bespoke cake marking the 46 league games, plus FA Cup and FA Trophy. There's even a copy of *The Non-League Paper*, folded open on my latest column, a bilious rant about Barrow. Imbuing a genuine sense of occasion, it's utterly surreal, and I am almost overwhelmed by the kindness of strangers, who I now consider friends.

There's more, as starters are interrupted by a tour of the home dressing room, the first time I've been in there since witnessing an astonishingly foulmouthed half-time team talk by Keith Curle. Space is at a premium, but we pose for photos with Big Ryan — thankfully already squeezed into his shorts — and congratulate him on the moment of the season, his exquisite left-foot finish to silence The Plastic Scousers at Tranmere.

It's all very relaxed, but suddenly I notice that lesser spotted assistant manager Chris Iwelumo is making a rare Saturday appearance. We didn't exactly part on good terms following the abysmal interview outside Braintree, and I'm suddenly paranoid that he'll recognise me and have me removed from the ground, thus killing The Card in the most improbable fashion. Hiding behind The Driver, I sneak out and we pose for more pics on the pitch, in the dugout, and even with genuine Chester royalty in the shape of former record scorer Gary Talbot, who once netted an FA Cup hat trick in three and a half minutes.

Back to the meal, the master of ceremonies has been briefed: "Today with us, two gentlemen who I am going to seriously embarrass now. They've been to every single first team league and cup and trophy this season."

Appreciative applause.

"Which is staggering when one of them lives in Newbury and one of them lives in London."

Stunned applause.

"And first game of the season up at Gateshead they flew from London up to Newcastle to go and watch us get beat 3-0. So today is a big, big thank you and celebration for anybody who can watch us play 46 games plus all the cup matches. You've got strong constitutions guys, I'll tell you. The cake and the bubbly is from their friend John, all their friends, for this fantastic achievement."

More applause.

It would be churlish to point out that The Driver didn't actually do the full Card, but Alun (aka Six Hours In The Car/Frank Sidebottom) pipes up: "And he follows Bordeaux as well."

"You haven't got a home life then, mate?" asks the MC.

"Day release," I confirm.

Ploughing through the roast beef and red wine, it's not over yet. None other than manager Jon McCarthy appears, taking time out from his meticulous pre-match preparations. He's only got half the story, but he means well.

"A couple of lads from London have been to every game this season, home and away," he begins to yet more applause.

"Enjoyed the good times," he continues. "And some of the disappointments..."

"YES," I confirm loudly to the latter, to gales of laughter all round the room.

"You've forgotten the good times?" he says, on the defensive and visibly squirming.

"No," I confirm apologetically, although I don't point out that most of them were in the previous calendar year.

"That's good," he says. "That's massive to us, and it is everything the club's about. So we might be joking about a little bit but we really recognise that and we really appreciate that downstairs so thanks very much. Enjoy the game."

"Thank you," I say in an attempt to make him feel better as he skulks out, crestfallen. He's not a bad man, just a bad manager. Or as he would no doubt insist, simply extremely unlucky over an extended period of time. Astonishingly, we have not won a home game since

The Boy and I saw us beat The Shots on that foggy day a week before Christmas Eve. When The Driver did The Card years ago he went six months between away wins, but this seems worse.

Talking of which, for the sake of The Card I should get my snout out of the trough and watch the kickoff. Taking my corporate seat directly behind McCarthy, architect of my woes, his instruction to enjoy the game proves impossible as it's an absolutely desultory performance with almost nothing to commend. Meanwhile, The Driver has vanished and reappeared on the home end, next to Big Al. He texts me the news that York are losing, meaning the relegation trapdoor is almost closed.

"Fucking hell," says McCarthy as Boreham Wood scuff one in from a deflection in first-half stoppage time. It sullies my half-time pint, but in the second half I am at least reunited with my family, who have clambered over to our section.

"I wish Boreham Wood didn't exist," says The Boy, speaking for all of us.

Their second goal seals the match, and condemns us to a club record eighth straight home defeat. What a season to do The Card. While it's hard to feel too elated in the circumstances, I am now a fully paid up Card carrier — 50 not out —something that may take a while to sink in.

Back in the Legends Lounge, a crowd is gathered round the TV. York have drawn, but a last-minute equaliser by Gizlee has seen them leapfrog and hence relegate The Minstermen. It's a chilling fate that could have been ours for the sake of one win. Indeed, the late equaliser at York that Parky missed has effectively sent them down. Or if the ref hadn't incorrectly given Gizlee a penalty against us, they could now be down. It's a reminder that every minute of every match is absolutely crucial, and players should always give 100% (whatever they say, it's mathematically impossible to give any more).

I of course have seen every minute of every match, give or take a piss break, and now the celebrations begin in earnest. Her Indoors and The Boy are snuck into the Legends Lounge for the cutting of the cake, and I am also presented with a football signed by the entire team. While The Driver and I take a bottle of Moét away, promising youngster Sam Hughes receives a bottle of Prosecco for his Man of the Match performance. It proves to be his last in a Chester shirt, as he will later be transferred to Leicester in a big money move.

The end of the season is a time for reflection, and Gandhi the Postman shows The Driver a picture of himself flanked by former Chester players Ricky Greenough and Gary 'Psycho' Bennett, back when they all had hair and before the latter appeared on Channel 4's *Couples Come Dine With Me*, showing off the Golden Boot he earned while playing for Wrexham.

A chap called Howard glances at a black-and-white print of the Villa game from the mid-70s and tells me that he was there, coming tantalisingly close to securing the Wembley appearance he still yearns for. He can't remember his first game, but I tell him that mine was a Division Four 2-1 home win over Darlington on 17th March '84, secured by a brace of Peter Zelem penalties in front of around a thousand at Sealand Road – a genuinely life-changing experience. Instantly seduced by the stench of cheap tobacco, the liberal use of foul and abusive language, and the sheer desperation, I saw out the season as we finished bottom of the Football League, mercifully before automatic relegation. Perversely proud of being rock bottom, the only way is up, I thought, somewhat naively.

Despite the ups and downs, I've never looked back, and it has remained an absolute constant throughout my wretched existence. Maybe it's the reassurance of always having somewhere to go, to be who you are, and to remember who you were. Players, managers, even stadiums come and go. But the supporters remain throughout, regenerating over time. The lizard sheds its skin. I'd like to think that in 50 years time a group will be sat here bemoaning another shit performance in this never-ending story.

The feast of friends continues, all thrown together by the shared memories of following this unremarkable yet wholly remarkable football club that we have come so close to losing. But eventually it's time to go. The Card: done. Stick it in the books, they can never take it away from me. I gather my trinkets, thank my generous hosts and prepare to say au revoir to The Driver.

"Give Chris a hug," says Her Indoors in the car park. His name's Chris. We've never embraced outside the feral blur of a goal celebration, and it's a hugely awkward mistake.

"See you, mate."

"Yeah, see you, mate."

So long and thanks for all the lifts. One era ends, the next begins. With apologies to Rutger Hauer in *Blade Runner,* please indulge me: "I've seen things you people wouldn't believe. Roadworks on fire off the hard shoulder of the M40. I watched floodlights glitter in the dark near the Exit Gate. All those moments will be lost in time, like tears in rain. Time to drive."

Attendance: 2,013 Position: 19th ↓

Living the Dream Tours is proud to present

THE CARD

to

Stephen M Hill

For services above and beyond the call of duty:

Putting up with the rantings of Adam and AP 'the problem is' J

Tolerating the virtues of various real ales being extolled (more often than not as 'hoppy')

Trying to comprehend the logic of people saying 'Not bad for you, this' in relation to travelling distances to Torquay and Forest Green

Pub of the Card: La Fontaine, Aldershot

Worst Pub of the Card: The Dog and Duck, Torquay

Off field highlight of the Card: Parky leaving early at York, missing Kane's equaliser

Off field low point of the Card: Breaking down at Witton

On field highlight of the Card: Big Ryan sticking it up the plastic scousers in the last minute at Tranmere

On field low point: anything that happened on a 3G pitch

'You couldn't make it up!'

'What a time to be alive!'

'These are garbage!'

Witness to the Card: ...Abraham... (The Driver)

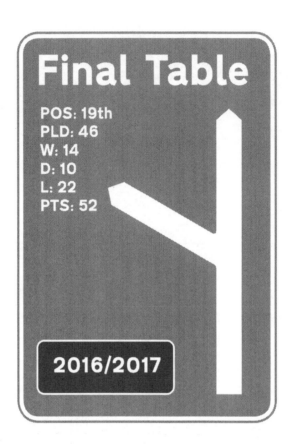

Final Table

POS: 19th
PLD: 46
W: 14
D: 10
L: 22
PTS: 52

2016/2017

Vanarama National League 2016/2017

		PLD	W	D	L	PTS	
1	Lincoln City	46	30	9	7	99	↑
2	Tranmere	46	29	8	9	95	
3	Forest Green Rovers	46	25	11	10	86	↑ Play-offs
4	Dagenham & Red.	46	26	6	14	84	
5	Aldershot	46	23	13	10	82	
6	Dover	46	24	7	15	79	
7	Barrow	46	20	15	11	75	
8	Gateshead	46	19	13	14	70	
9	Macclesfield	46	20	8	18	68	
10	Bromley	46	18	8	20	62	
11	Boreham Wood	46	15	13	18	58	
12	Sutton	46	15	13	18	58	
13	Wrexham	46	15	13	18	58	
14	Maidstone	46	16	10	20	58	
15	Eastleigh	46	14	15	17	57	
16	Solihull	46	15	10	21	55	
17	Torquay	46	14	11	21	53	
18	Woking	46	14	11	21	53	
19	Chester F.C.	46	14	10	22	52	←
20	Guiseley	46	13	12	21	51	
21	York	46	11	17	18	50	
22	Braintree	46	13	9	24	48	
23	Southport	46	10	9	27	39	
24	North Ferriby	46	12	3	31	39	

Epilogue

The Hero
The Driver
The Hack
Big Al

Parky
The Watford Gap
Jon McCarthy
Brothers
Her Indoors
The Boy

The Hero

Eventually missed a game, a 0-0 draw at home to Halifax the following season, feeling part sadness, part relief. Can still frequently be found on a crumbling terrace in a polyester smock bellowing, "Come on Blues! These are garbage!"

The Driver

The roads of England are a safer place as he and his wife finally moved to France in the closed season. At the time of writing he is yet to miss a Bordeaux game, including a Europa League tie in Hungary. Says it's "still not the same as Chester though". He'll be back.

The Hack

Didn't even put £50 on us to go down the next season as the odds were too derisory. Mindlessly misses games in order to go on holiday, and is still labouring under the misapprehension that one pint of slop differs from another.

Big Al

Stood on The Harry McNally Terrace loudly swearing at the referee. For all eternity.

Parky

Confined to Australia, but still knows more about the club than anyone in this country. Presumably regrets leaving early at York.

The Watford Gap

Continues to shout at televised sport on a daily basis. Yet to successfully explain the difference between rugby league and rugby union.

Jon McCarthy

Finally relieved of his duties eight matches into the next season, having failed to win a home game in 2017. Replaced by Marcus Bignot, who won his first game, at home.

Brothers

Older: will do Cheltenham, or Forest Green if he can get a lift. Younger: South, South East or South West, possibly Midlands. Youngest: once went to a Freight Rover Trophy tie and has never been back.

Her Indoors

Still gets dragged to the occasional game, and is yet to work out which goal we are attacking.

The Boy

Ticked off another couple of grounds, but still wonders why he's the only Chester fan at his school. Faces a future of unparalleled misery and joy...

YEAH, THANKS

Thanks to Dave Hartrick at Ockley Books
for having the vision to publish the book,
and to his team for putting it together.

Thanks to Richard Foster for being a non-meddling editor,
and for the motivational meetings at Maggie's Bar.

Thanks to Harriet and George for heroically
coping without me every Saturday.

Thanks to the Yummy Mummies of NW10
for Tuesday afternoon childcare.

Thanks to Shane and Bry for generously letting
me use their home as a glorified doss house.

Thanks to Chris for always getting
me to the match on time.

Thanks to Adrian for managing expectations
with his ceaseless pessimism, and to Jane for
putting up with him.

Thanks to John and the Blues Bar boys
for their overwhelming generosity.

Thanks to my Dad for taking me
to my first ever match.

And thanks to every Chester fan who
wished me luck along the journey.

UP THE FUCKING SEALS!